Lessons  from the Journey

Following Christ in a Hostile World

Rob Sugg

Cover art and interior graphics
by Nan Sugg

Special thanks to Harriet Sugg Fuller for her editing skills

Table of Contents

FOREWORD

Foreword

A braham and Jacob, two of the first patriarchs, met God on their life journey. Abraham first encountered God when God revealed Himself and told him to leave his father's house and country to go to a country that "He would show him." After he left his home on the way to an undisclosed location, he encountered God a second time at Shechem (Genesis 12:6-8). There he built an altar to commemorate the meeting. He continued his journey and at Bethel (Genesis 13:3) he met God again and built another altar. These altars were points of contact, places where God revealed Himself to Abraham. This continued revelation confirmed to him that God had indeed spoken and was leading him where He wanted Abraham to be. We know from the Genesis record that there were other recorded times when they communicated and I assume there were times in their relationship that are not recorded for us.

Years later after Abraham died, his grandson, Jacob, also was on a journey, but with a very different beginning. He was running away from his father's house because he had tricked his brother Esau out of his birthright and wanted to escape his wrath. During Jacob's escape from Esau's threatened violence, God appeared to him in a dream at Bethel, and he built an altar there (Genesis 28:10-22). This was a pivotal moment in Jacob's life: one of eight recorded times that God appeared to him. For both Abraham and Jacob, and their families, these altars were symbols of times when God met them for fellowship and instruction. The men were able to point out the monuments to their families and tell them the story of the supernatural encounter.

These are not the only altars mentioned in the Bible. For example, in Joshua 4 when the Israelites crossed over the Jordan into the Promised Land, Joshua directed one man from each of the twelve tribes to collect a stone from the bottom of the river. These were then stacked into a pile to form an altar. The purpose was to mark the point where they crossed the Jordan River on dry land into the Promised Land. It was also a reminder to Israel of how God had led them, protected them on their journey, and fulfilled His promise to give them a land of their own.

Another example comes later in Israel's life as a new nation. First Samuel gives a part of Israel's history, and in chapter seven we see how the Philistines were making life difficult for Israel. Samuel called them together for the purpose of facing their adversary, but the Israelites were very troubled and frightened. Samuel promised them that God would help and He did. The Philistines were defeated and at that spot Samuel selected a stone and named it Ebenezer, "The Stone of Help." He said it was because "God helped us here." Again, it was a permanent reminder of how God entered their lives and provided for them.

Today we do not build altars, at least not that kind of altar. Nevertheless, there are events in our lives that are equally as significant to us as were those events in the lives of Abraham and Jacob. Often we do our best to mark these events in our own memories. Later in life, we can look back at them – think of them as spiritual markers – and see where we have been or understand why we are where we are. Unfortunately, they are seldom recorded, and in time, the memory of how God worked becomes less well remembered; there is nothing permanent to mark those times. Consequently the incidents with their stories are seldom passed on; they remain private. That is unfortunate, since children and grandchildren never get to learn first-hand how God led us on our journey.

For example, my maternal great-grandfather, John Thomas Carroll, was a circuit-riding Baptist preacher in Webster and Calhoun counties, Mississippi. I once preached in a county church in which an elderly member told me that he recalled a time in his youth when there was a drought in the area. The church had prayed for rain, but none fell. Then one day, Brother Carroll announced that the following Sunday there would be a special prayer meeting for rain. The gentleman told me that when Brother Carroll arrived at the church on the designated morning for prayer, he was carrying an umbrella. When asked about the umbrella, his response was, "Brothers, we have met to pray for rain, and I don't intend to get wet on the way home." The story-teller said that when church was over and everyone headed home, the rain started, and Brother Carroll was the only man who stayed dry.

The family liked to tell another story about him, but this one had a different twist. Like many other pastors in that day, my grandfather was bi-vocational: he was both a farmer and a pastor. At that time, farmers would usually have to borrow money in the winter to provide for their families and when spring came, they would plant their new crop. They always hoped that when they sold the harvest, they would make enough money to pay off the debt. But they seldom did. Consequently, they lived most of their lives under debt.

One year, Pappy Carroll decided that when winter came, the family would eat only what they had grown and stored during the previous summer. The family story was that when they gathered at the table for a meal, they would always pray and express thanks for what God had given them. This particular year, as winter moved on and spring was approaching, the only food left in the house was dried black eyed peas and corn meal. That meant that every meal was cornbread and black eyed peas.

One day when the family gathered for dinner and everyone bowed their heads expecting Pappy to say the blessing, there was only silence. After a period of time, Pappy finally said, "I'm sorry. I just am not very grateful for this. Everyone go ahead and eat!"

When Nan and I started dating, I met her family. I was told that her grandfather, Lewis Franklin Gregory, had been a Baptist preacher in the Mississippi Delta. He had already gone to glory when I met Nan, so I never met him.

When Nan and I married, one of the gifts we received was a small purple vase from one of her aunts. I was told that this aunt had been a missionary in China and Nan's family supposed the vase was one she got while serving there. I was never told when or where she served, and I have no recollection of her name.

Those are the only stories I know of the faith of my family. I don't even know how or when my parents met Jesus and how they decided to accept Him. I don't know of their faith walk. Surely, there were times when they cried out to God for guidance or provision or strength. But I don't know the circumstances of those times or what happened. I know Mom kept a prayer journal, but I can only guess when she started it or guess about the stories for the entries she made.

However, I do have one vivid memory of a time when I saw Mom and Dad expressing their concern and sorrow over a developing tragedy. I must have been about nine or ten at the time. Our next door neighbors, good friends, had adopted a son. I recall he was always sickly and could not run and play with the rest of us. This particular night, I was headed upstairs where my brother and I slept. As I passed the door to their bedroom, I could see them sitting in chairs by the space heater. Dad had a cat in his lap and Mom was crying. I heard her tell him that Lady and Elks were going to lose their son. I assume they prayed together after I went on to bed. I do know that shortly after that, the son was gone. I never knew if he died or if he was sent back to the orphanage. That is the only glimpse I can recall of them sharing that kind of spiritual moment together.

For Abraham and Jacob, the altars they erected were so significant that they showed them to their children and told the story of why they were erected. Their children heard the stories and this became a part of their spiritual understanding of who they were and where they came from. Those backward looks provided a sense of direction as they contemplated where they should go. Their past shaped their future.

Like Abraham and Jacob, we have these spiritual markers in our lives. But unlike Abraham and Jacob, we often fail to discuss them with our children. If they are to understand the most important elements of our lives, there should be times when these stories are shared and explained. Those experiences with God not only defined who we are, they also guided us along our way and had an impact on the lives of our children and grandchildren. Our personal experiences with God should be a part of the spiritual heritage and faith walk of our children.

Life is a journey we make without clear signposts ahead of us. We have a map that gives us general directions – the Bible. But along the way, we face situations and must make decisions when even our map is not as clear as we would like. To be sure, in many ways, it is very specific and very clear. But in other ways, there are times when it is hazy and undefined, leaving us to make decisions according to the light we have. When we are in that situation, sometimes it is helpful to take a backwards look and see the markers that we erected along the way. While the way ahead may appear dim and foggy, sometimes by looking back we can determine that previous markers line up to point a direction for us. Hindsight helps us check past experiences which we couple with prayers for guidance. These two things work together to give us the direction we need in order to make a choice consistent with our journey so far.

Perhaps there will come a time when those who follow me will possibly say something like "I remember my grandmother and grandfather were missionaries in Taiwan. But I don't know why they chose that life or how they chose Taiwan or what they did there or anything about that part of their lives." I don't want that to happen; I want them to know more of my faith walk than I know about those in my family who preceded me.

I think of Psalm 71:17-18: *"Since my youth, O God, you have taught me, and to this day I declare your marvelous deeds. Even when I am old and gray, do not forsake me, O God, **till I declare your power to the next generation, your might to all who are to come.**"* That is why I want to mention some of my journey and the things God has shown me.

I must confess I have not always been as diligent a disciple or as eager a servant as I could have been. But the general direction of my life has always pointed towards the calling God placed on me at an early age. I will be quick to admit that there were even times when I wondered about what that call meant and how I would fulfill it. Likewise, I am sure there were times when I missed some of the tasks God intended me to do. But always there was one goal – to honor my heavenly Father and obey His leading as best as I could.

For Abraham and Jacob, the points of contact with God came through dreams or visions. For me, they came primarily through His written word, the Bible. Usually some verse or passage would stand out to me and as I meditated on it, the personal application would become clear. Of course, there were times when I would have an experience and later discover a relevant passage that seemed applicable to the situation. The Bible has been my guide through life, so as I recount some events, I will include relevant Bible verses and hopefully you will be able to see how they impacted me.

My journey has been long and led me to places I never thought I would see. For a young boy from rural Mississippi, my geographical knowledge really expanded. I traveled and lived around the world and back again, ministering in about fifteen different countries and seven different states.

Spiritually, I experienced God working in such wonderful and mysterious ways that were literally more than I had ever dreamed possible. The methods God used to reveal himself to me and the ways he used me are clear evidence that our God is a personal God who has an intense interest in every detail of our individual lives. The goal is for us to make the right choices along the path so we can successfully journey towards spiritual maturity and understanding. Often it is indeed the road less traveled. But it always leads to wonderful blessings.

In hindsight, I can identify four foundational truths on which I built my life. First, I am God's child. The Bible says in John 1:12 that *"… to all who received him, to those who believed in his name, he gave the right to become children of God."* I knew I believed in Jesus so I took the word recorded in God's word as fact: I am God's child.

Second, God has a plan for me. The Bible says in Jeremiah 29:11 *"For I know the plans I have for you, declares the LORD, plans to prosper you and not to harm you, plans to give you hope and a future."* Early in my life, I believed God had a plan for me and I determined to know what that plan was and then to follow it.

Third, I learned that submission to God and obedience to His will is expected in order to fulfill that plan. I looked to Jesus as my example. Often in John's gospel He spoke of only doing what His Father showed or told Him to do. In John 5:30 He said *". . . for I seek not to please myself but him who sent me."* The full extent to which Jesus went to please His Father is found in John 10:17-18: *"The reason my Father loves me is that I lay down my life – only to take it up again. No one takes it from me, but I lay it down of my own accord. I have authority to lay it down and authority to take it up again. This command I received from my Father."* That commitment to fulfill his Father's purpose was His goal in His life. In a far lesser way, that was the goal in my life as well – to please and honor my heavenly Father.

Finally, I came to believe that God communicates with His children. In John 10:27 Jesus said, *"My sheep listen to my voice; I know them, and they follow me."* I had to learn how to identify His voice when He communicated with me, but I did. His voice brought me comfort, guidance, and strength at times when I needed it the most.

Looking back over my life, I can honestly say I believe that every positive or beneficial act in my life and ministry flowed from understanding and following these four truths. I pray that you also will come to know these or similar truths about your walk with God and will wholeheartedly follow them.

As I share my experiences with you, I encourage you to examine your own life. Look back and identify the sign posts that exist in your experience. Once they are identified, find a way to clearly mark them so that they will guide you in the future. Be sure to share them with those closest to you. You will benefit from the remembrance, and their faith will be strengthened by learning how God worked in your life.

I also request that you be patient with me. There will likely be times when I ramble a bit, but that is what old people do. Come with me as I remember.

FOUNDATION

New Birth Produces Change

"For God so loved the world that he gave his one and only son, that whoever believes in him will have eternal life." John 3:16

Growing up in a Christian home, I was frequently reminded that the Bible is real and that there is a God who loves every person. As early as I can remember, our family was regular in church attendance and in those days, that was three times a week. Additionally, most mornings we followed breakfast with Bible reading and a short devotional thought from Open Windows. There were also times when Biblical truth was discussed or questions about Bible stories were asked and answered.

For most of my life, my dad's aunt and my mother's father lived with us. Both of them were Christians and had a good knowledge of the Bible. I especially remember my grandfather, Charles Edward Carroll, or Papaw, reading the Bible a lot and reading poetry. He was a self-educated man who read much and spent significant time thinking about weighty matters. I respected his understanding and perspective on life. He was a reformed alcoholic who tried to help others struggling with that addiction, and those experiences gave him a different perspective on life and God's love for us.

In addition to the regular weekly church meetings, we also had week-long revivals, which were morning and evening meetings at the church when a guest preacher would come to speak. I recall these meetings were twice a year, one in the summer and the second one in the winter. It was during the summer revival when I was nine that God became real to me. To this day I can remember standing during the invitation time, feeling compelled to "walk the aisle" and speak to the pastor. Admittedly, after almost seventy years, I can no longer recall what I said to him or what he said to me. But a week later I was baptized, and was now a Christian. I remember my parents and grandparents were very happy.

Immediately, I noticed four effects of that decision. First, for several months I had been worried to the point of having nightmares about hell. I knew enough about the gospel to know that those who did not become Christians would spend all eternity burning in hell. I was terrified that I would die before I could become a Christian. So, in all honesty, one part of my decision had to be to escape that awful punishment (fire insurance). But after I decided to accept Christ, the worry and concern about my soul's final state was forever changed. The nightmares disappeared and where there had been fear, now there was peace. I knew my future was secure.

Second, I now had a sense of wellbeing and joy. In a way I had not previously experienced, now I was at peace without realizing that I had been in turmoil. Of course, for a nine year old boy, how much turmoil could there have been? But the change was significant enough that I noticed it.

The third effect was that somehow I instinctively knew that now I was subject to a higher, more important set of commands. I knew what the Ten Commandments were and knew that I had to be sure to obey them. Later on in my life, I discovered that there were other commandments, other precepts to acknowledge and obey. Some of those were the most challenging to follow. It was not difficult to forsake worshipping idols or murder or adultery. However, offering unconditional love and forgiveness were two of the ones I struggled with a lot. But at the top of the list was unconditional surrender to my heavenly Father. That was a hard, long battle.

The fourth effect was that I had a compelling urge to share my experience with my two best friends. The joy I now had demanded to be shared with those closest to me. I recall both of them professed faith in Christ following my urging and our praying together. I don't know why that passion for evangelism seemed to dissipate as I grew older, but it did. The yearning I had for evangelism seemed to take a different path. In time I learned spiritual gifts can take many forms, if that is indeed what I experienced. At any rate, even though my passion was for a different expression of faithfulness, I never ignored the need to be prepared to share my faith if and when the situation demanded.

Of course, there were other commandments that were a part of living in my house with my parents. But those were the more common variety and I could sometimes let them slide provided I was willing to accept the consequences for disobedience. Since the penalty was often severe (this was well before the days when it was politically incorrect to spank a child), I seldom disobeyed.

The conviction to obey God's word remained an inescapable force in my life and influenced most of my life decisions from that point forward. I can honestly say that my inclination was always towards obedience. But that is not to say that I always immediately, totally obeyed what I knew to be God's commands or perceived to be His leading; I did not. I did have a fallen nature with a strong rebellious attitude. Following that rebellious nature sometimes led to unwanted and undesirable consequences.

Later in my Christian walk, I discovered Romans 7 where Paul wrote about his own struggle beginning in verse 21. In part, it is a discussion of the conflict between God's law and God's grace. In another part it is a clear presentation of the struggle in each person's life as they endure the battle of their sinful flesh with their redeemed heart. He summed it up quite well in verse 25b: *"So then, I myself in my mind am a slave to God's law, but in the sinful nature a slave to the law of sin."* He defined quite well the struggle I was facing. I easily identified with his cry in v. 24: *"Who will rescue me from this body of death?"* I could identify with him. I found comfort and strength in his answer in the next verse, 25a: *"Thanks be to God – through Jesus Christ our Lord!"*

Later in life I discovered John 1:12 – *"Yet to all that received him, to those who believed in his name, he gave the right to become children of God."* In a wonderful, mysterious way I knew I was God's child. I could not understand all that meant, but it was reassuring to think of myself in that way.

I also learned that as a physical child grows and matures, in the same way a spiritual child should grow and mature. There are parallels to the process: if a physical child exercises, eats right, and obeys the laws of science, he will grow into a robust, strong individual. In the spiritual world, it is the same. However, here the right thing to eat is spiritual truth found in God's word and the exercise is obedience. For one with a rebellious heart, that was not always easy.

Of course, those levels of understanding came later. Initially, it was enough to know I was God's child. I know that the initial step is necessary. The Chinese have a saying: "A journey of a thousand miles begins with a single step." In the same way one starts a journey towards a geographical destination with one step, the journey towards understanding what it means to be God's child begins with an expression of belief in Jesus. Without that first step of faith, all that follows is a continuation of life apart from God. In that state it is impossible to live any semblance of a spiritual life, for the heart will always produce its fruit. I pray that all of you who read this will be certain of making this first decision.

God Has a Purpose for His Children

"For I know the plans I have for you," declares the LORD, "plans to prosper you and not to harm you, plans to give you hope and a future." Jeremiah 29:11

A few years after accepting Christ as my Lord and Savior, I entered the teen years and was obsessed with one question: How do I know what God wants me to do with my life? I don't even know where that question came from. Logically, I could assume it stemmed from the Bible stories about Abraham, Moses, Samuel, David and many others. Those men obviously had a specific purpose and mission from God and perhaps I wondered if every child of God also had some kind of special purpose. Looked at in another way perhaps God placed the question there as a way to prepare me to receive His word on what He wanted to communicate to me about my future.

I had multiple discussions about this question with my parents and my grandfather, who was living with us at the time. I even approached my pastor a time or two seeking his answers assuming he would have some more concrete explanation. They all had basically the same answer and it had two parts. First, they assured me that, "God has a purpose for every life." Second, they were consistent in saying, "God will let you know when the time is right." Somehow that seemed too general and undefined for me at that time. It was frustrating.

Their response prompted a second question: "How was God going to let me know what his plan was?" I must have been a pest by asking the same question over and over. In time, I came to realize they were right because God did confirm that He had a plan for me. Until that confirmation came, I constantly switched my life goal from planning a career in the Air Force to being a soldier of fortune to being a spy in some foreign country or pretty much anything else a young boy would dream of doing. I must have been around twelve or thirteen when a new thought entered; it seemed that God might want me in missions somewhere and that was not something I had previously considered. Thinking along those lines conflicted with earlier dreams for my adult life and that brought more inner questions.

I found the sermons and other teachings in church to be of little help in making a firm decision about my future. There were plenty of stories of Biblical characters knowing and doing God's will and those were reinforced with stories of more modern strong men and women of faith who seemed to have certainty that God was leading them in one particular direction. But no one could explain how these people knew what God wanted them to do. So how could I know?? I muddled along as best as I could while continuing to read my Bible, attend church and Sunday School and trying to do the things I thought a Christian boy should do. When I was about fifteen or sixteen during a church service God impressed me that I should follow His leading in my life so I told our pastor I wanted to dedicate my life to full time Christian service. That is what we did back then when we were not sure exactly how we would follow God as He continued to led us. I think I knew He

4

wanted me to be a missionary, but it seemed quite presumptuous of me to make such a statement at that time. That did not completely end the inner struggles, but it helped a lot and provided some direction for the future.

When the confirmation did come, it was as my parents had said: I knew. Even now I am not sure how I knew; it was a kind of inner belief that I knew what God wanted me to do.

After I graduated from college and seminary, I accepted a position as Baptist Student Union Director at Blue Mountain College in northern Mississippi. Working with the students there, I was often in the position of having to help those young people answer the very same question I had dealt with so long. I hope I was able to provide them more help than I received in my early years.

Years later I read a quote I wished I had been given back when I was in high school; it would have helped a lot even if I had not known how to apply it at the time. It is this: "How to find the will of God for one's life is a question all young Christians have to face. Experience has taught that prayer, the leadership of the Holy Spirit, the dedication of one's talents to the service of God, and entrance into the open doors which God provides are ways to find the will of God. God's will cannot be known by foresight, like railroad tracks are seen before the engine's headlight; God's will is like the wake of a ship, seen clearly only in retrospect. The voyage must be made by faith." (Roland Q. Leavell, *The Apostle Paul*)

We must not miss the four elements Dr. Leavell lists for these are the very principles of a good strong Christian life. They are the principles I had been following even though I could not have listed them. When our lives are committed to God in this way, then our Heavenly Father has access to our hearts and can lead us according to His will for us.

We humans all want to see the road ahead, to be able to know where we are going. At the same time I must say that it would be impossible to count the number of people I have heard say something to the effect that "looking back on my life, I can see how God was at work leading me when I was not aware of it." That is the reality of the faith journey we live.

It should be obvious that this second step of knowing God's purpose is impossible unless the first step of believing in Jesus has been taken. I pray that you will earnestly seek to develop your relationship with your heavenly Father so that you will be able to clearly discern His leading in your life. I believe He has a purpose for you.

I had an interesting conversation that illustrated this reality. We had resigned from the International Mission Board and were working at First Baptist Church in Jackson on their mission staff. Our assignment was to plan mission trips for volunteers and then to train them as they prepared to go serve in various locations. One of the teams we trained was headed for China. We had not recruited the team and there were several members we did not know. One of them was a man named Vic Holsapple, who was an older gentlemen that had retired from the Army after twenty-some years and then taught school in Jackson until he retired again. In the training we emphasized that God had a purpose in calling the members for this particular mission journey. After the training, they went to China and had a good experience.

When they returned, I had the opportunity to talk with Vic several times and we became good friends. In our conversations, he revealed that he had gotten really interested in personal evangelism and wanted to receive additional training in Evangelism Explosion, the evangelism tool the church was using at that time. As we discussed the reason he felt so compelled to enter this activity at this particular stage in life, he said something that caught me by surprise. He said the training for the journey and the experience of actually putting it into practice on the mission field made him realize for the first time in his life that God did indeed have a purpose for him. What a revelation! And to me, it was sad that it took him 67 years to come to that realization. It should be a part of our lives as believers; God has a purpose for each of us. That was the core principle in Dr. Leavell's presentation and a point we emphasized in our training: God has a purpose for every believer. If we do not believe that truth, we will never look for God's purpose for our life. I pray that you find His purpose for you and that you follow it wholeheartedly.

Vision for Life

"Therefore go and make disciples of all nations, baptizing them in the name of the Father and of the Son and of the Holy Spirit, and teaching them to obey everything I have commanded you." Matthew 28:19-20

We lived in a small town that had very limited lodging facilities. When a church had a revival or some special meeting, many town residents would open their homes to the guest speakers even if they were not part of that particular church or organization. Mom and Dad were always quick to sign up to host someone for overnight or for a meal, especially if our church was involved. The guests were usually interesting, but when we hosted missionaries it was especially captivating for me. This small-town boy from North Mississippi was able to meet people who had been to exotic places and seen things I could not even imagine.

Perhaps those meal times cultivated the seed bed into which the idea of mission involvement was planted. If that is true, then I must say that the seed was cultured and nurtured once I joined Royal Ambassadors, a mission organization for boys. In RA's we memorized many scripture verses related to missions while learning a lot about missionaries and mission activities. Matthew 28:19-20 became my primary life verse. (It seemed others would become significant at different times in my life depending on what I was facing at the time, but I found this verse more than any other provided direction and focus for me.)

One part of our study in RA's was reading missionary biographies. I was deeply impacted by the story of David Livingstone, a doctor from England who served as a missionary to Africa. He spent his life ministering to the Africans and spreading the gospel there. Soon after I read that story (at about age 12), I told mother that I had decided I would be a missionary doctor. She asked if God had called me to that task. My response was, "No, I just figured if I wanted to be a missionary doctor, He would be glad to have me." Even though my initial inclination towards missions may not have been laid on the proper foundation, through the following years God confirmed numerous times that I rightly interpreted the desire He planted in my heart at that early age. The journey towards that goal was long and filled with doubts, distractions, and detours.

For example, when I was in the later years of high school, I decided I didn't want to be a missionary; I desired another line of work. As a result, when I graduated from high school I decided to follow my classmates and pursue a career in something other than religious work. The first semester was a typical "first time away from home" period in which my performance was far less than good. Over the Christmas break, I prayed a lot about my situation and admitted to myself and to God that I was really unsettled in my spirit. I figured out that was probably because I was not where He wanted me. As a result, when the second semester began, I changed my major from electrical engineering to music. I had been in the school and church choir at home and always enjoyed church music. So I thought I could make a bargain with God: I would do something in the church if He would leave me alone about being a missionary. That decision gave me some peace for that semester, but over the summer, I realized the issue was not really settled. That realization brought on more conversations with God which led to my decision to transfer to Mississippi College, which is a Baptist college, and major in Bible. I told God that I would be a preacher if He would let me alone about being a missionary. Through that process I discovered God really doesn't bargain.

For a year things were okay. I had peace and even sought out involvement in the local Baptist Student Union, specifically in their choir. I enjoyed the singing and fellowship a lot.

The following year, my junior year, a lot of us in BSU attended the annual BSU convention. One of the speakers was a missionary kid, or MK, who had been a counselor at a church camp I attended one summer. (He had grown up in Brazil and I thought that was very exotic; I had visions of him fishing in the Amazon and walking through the jungle.) I was really drawn to him and enjoyed talking with him. Now he was one of the primary speakers at the convention and his messages really touched my heart. Or, to be more truthful, God spoke through him to reach my heart. The conviction was so strong that by the time the convention was over, I knew I had to finally and completely answer the question about missionary service. That decision was a true act of the will: to totally submit to what I perceived to be God's plan for my life. In that one decision, the conflicted feelings of the previous three or four years were put to rest.

Once the commitment was made, it gave me a clear sense of direction of what my next steps would be. I knew for sure I faced more education: graduate from college and complete three years in some seminary. This would be followed by at least two years in my chosen field in order to gain some practical experience prior to being appointed as a missionary to go overseas.

The commitment solidified my belief that God did indeed have a purpose for me. I didn't know where this choice would lead me or what I would face along the way. However, I did have a strong sense that God would be with me in whatever I would meet on the journey.

That decision also produced a strength and sense of purpose I had not previously known. To be sure, I faced many difficulties, both as an individual, and later with my future family. But always the strong sense that God had selected me for this high calling gave me the strength and perseverance to endure them all.

I had always heard and read about God's saving grace. But now for the first time, I began to experience and understand God's empowering grace. There can be no other explanation for how I as an individual and we as a family came through all the trials and tribulations we faced. I don't recall hearing many sermons on this subject, which is sad since all of us struggle on this journey and need some reminder that help is available. This spiritual truth is very important.

After Nan and I were appointed as missionaries, one sentence we heard often was "God does not call the powerful; He empowers those He calls." Sometimes it was stated "God does not call the prepared; He equips those He calls." Either way the point is clear – God's sustaining grace is sufficient for whatever circumstance life throws at us to help us do whatever he calls us to do.

God has a purpose for you. As you explore that purpose, God will give you a vision of how He wants to use you in His Kingdom work. Through the discovery process and as you serve where He places you, you will experience the joy of His sustaining grace. I pray you will learn to depend on that grace. It will surely build your faith.

The Call

"It was he who gave some to be apostles, some to be prophets, some to be evangelists, and some to be pastors and teachers, to prepare God's people for works of service, so that the body of Christ may be built up until we all reach unity in the faith and in the knowledge of the Son of God and become mature, attaining to the whole measure of the fullness of Christ." Ephesians 4:11--13

At the time God was working in my heart to lead me to understand and accept his purpose for my life, he was doing the same thing in Nan's heart. Of course we didn't know each other at the time: she lived in Jackson and I lived in Eupora. However, like me, her mother was active in Women's Missionary Union and she was a member of Girl's Auxiliary (now called Girls in Action.) This was the organization for girls that emphasized missionary education. God worked in her heart and revealed His desire that she follow Him to the foreign mission field. And like me, during her last couple of years in high school, she also decided to follow a different path. It was not until she graduated from college that she renewed her commitment to God to follow wherever He led.

Through the years that followed, we both came to understand two things that were a vital part of our Christian walk. First, there is a sense of "call" or purpose for each individual believer. The New Testament is full of references to this expectation, which affects every area of life. For example, Jesus told His followers to forgive one another (Matthew 6:14-15), take up their cross daily and follow Him (Luke 9:23), and love one another in the same way that He loved us (John 13:34-35).

Then the apostles added to these directives by stressing that we need to die to ourselves and experience the new life in Jesus (Romans 6:5-14). Once done, there is the call to conform our lives to His word (Romans 12:3), to think on things that are above this earthly life (Philippians 4:8), do what the word says (James 1:22), and to purify ourselves just as our Father commands us to do (1 Peter 1:14-15). These are just a very few examples from their writings that emphasize the demands of living the Christian life. Some refer to this set of expectations as the general call to all believers. It is a call to live a life that "conforms to the image of Christ" (Romans 8:29): to be distinctly different from those who have yet to experience God's call. In other words, we are to live in such a way that our lives resemble as closely as possible the life of Jesus.

Additionally, in the same way that Jesus called twelve men to follow him thus becoming his disciples, and just as the Holy Spirit said to the church in Antioch *"Set apart for me Barnabas and Saul for the work to which I have called them."* (Acts 13:2), there is also a specific call to a special way of life and ministry. In the modern church, this specific call is often presented as a call to enter "full time Christian service." From time to time, it will be narrowed to specify a call to a specific type of service or ministry. That is what Nan and I both experienced. We knew God had a special purpose for us that would be in some foreign country.

We also learned that there is another, and equally important, aspect of the Christian call. We gradually came to understand that a person needs a strong commitment to follow the initial call. That is true whether one is experiencing the "general" call or a "specific" call. Early on, I only began to sense this truth, but the reality of it grew as I matured. Nan and I both discovered that there are times when only the strong-hearted person can persevere through the distractions, temptations, and negative life events to remain focused on maintaining a commitment to the call. It is true that sometimes only the strong can hold on to their faith in God as they deal with the hard issues of life. We witnessed this several times during our ministry. We learned firsthand that often the sense of call and the commitment to follow that call were the only things that would keep us on task (and on the mission field!).

Those who found the courage and determination to hold on to their call witnessed wonderful blessings, both personally and to others. They experienced the mysterious strengthening power of God's grace.

I must also say that when one has committed his or her life to follow Jesus, it's important to keep one's eyes on him and be flexible in following wherever He leads. Over and over again, I've seen Him call a person to a particular task or ministry, and then later redirect the call to something different. When this happens, it can create some inner turmoil as one seeks to continue on the life journey of faith. It is vital to always maintain the focus and openness to the leadership of the Holy Spirit, and the willingness to obey his leading.

One day Jesus said, *"No one who puts his hand to the plow and looks back is fit for service in the kingdom of God."* (Luke 9:62) As we matured in our faith, and especially once we were actively involved in ministry, we noticed that there were some who would start on the road of Christian service, but look back. It was obvious that some of those met actual physical difficulties that prevented them from continuing on their chosen path especially on the mission field. But there were others who, due to distractions, temptations, and life situations chose not to continue as they had begun. When those in the latter category turned aside from their original path they missed wonderful, exciting opportunities to see God at work and learn more intimately about the strengthening nature of His grace.

We also learned firsthand that often the sense of call and the commitment to stick to it were all that would keep us on task. Nan and I found this to be true in our own lives and ministry. There were a few times when this sense of call was the only thing that kept us on the field. It would have been easy to just pack it in and return to the States. In fact, there were at least two times when one of us was ready to leave, but the other held out and convinced the discouraged one to hang on a little longer. As a result, we got to see God do some wonderful things.

I mention this aspect of the Christian life here just to help you understand that there will be tough times and when they come, the reward is worth the effort to hold on to your commitment to follow Christ. Paul said (Romans 8:17-18) *"Now if we are children, then we are heirs – heirs of God and co-heirs with Christ, if indeed we share in his sufferings in order that we may also share in his glory. I consider that our present sufferings are not worth comparing with the glory that will be revealed in us."* We know we will never suffer in the same way that Christ suffered when He bore the sins of the world. But there is suffering involved in living the Christian life and in sharing His gospel. Our goal is to keep the faith and share in His glory.

I pray that when trouble and suffering for Christ enters your life, you will remember the glory that follows, and you will depend on God to strengthen you.

Just in Case You Wondered

"And we know that in all things God works for the good of those who love him, who have been called according to his purpose." Romans 8:28

As I mentioned previously, I grew up in Eupora, Mississippi. When I graduated from high school, I attended Mississippi State University for my freshman year. But in prayer, I felt led to transfer to Mississippi College for the beginning of my sophomore year.

Nan grew up in Jackson, Mississippi and when she graduated from high school, she attended Mississippi College. She was the third generation of her family to attend there: her grandfather, as well as her mother and father, all graduated from MC. She is one year younger than me, so we both arrived on campus at the same time, and I noticed her soon after school started.

My roommate that year was Jim Davis from Pensacola, Florida. He had a friend from Mobile, Alabama who was a black belt in judo and karate, which was unusual in that day. This fellow, Hugh Kelley, had a big tournament coming up and had no one to practice with. He told my roommate that he would give us lessons if we would work out with him. During the work outs, he taught us several things about the sport. Of course, the first thing he taught us was how to make a proper fall after being thrown so we would not get hurt. (We fell a lot: Hugh was really good.) That lesson came in real handy.

Soon other boys heard about the "class" and asked if they could join. By mid-semester there was a judo class of around 8 guys. And as it usually happens, soon word spread among the girls that there was a judo class. They approached Hugh and asked if he would offer a self-defense class for them. After obtaining permission from the Dean of Women, a class was offered when the second semester started. Hugh asked Jim and me to be his "dummies" and take the falls for the girls as they practiced their throws. (Hugh said he did not have time to teach them how to take a fall properly and was worried someone would get hurt. He did not have the same concern for Jim and me.) After having watched Nan off and on for a few months, I finally met her in the class. She often liked to say that the first time I saw her, she threw me. And that was not far wrong.

We would talk some after class and shared a Coke a time or two. I was painfully shy in those days and had a hard time talking to females I did not know. If they were beautiful like Nan, it was even more difficult. I think she saw me as a challenge; she was determined to get me to talk and she did.

When my junior year (her sophomore year) started, we did have a few dates. During the summer, Jim left to return to Pensacola and my new roommate was a friend from Eupora, Charles Bagwell. Those dates were mostly on the campus for ball games or walking to church on Sunday. During my senior year we dated a lot more.

She told me later that when her girlfriends in the dorm would ask about me, she'd say the only thing wrong with me was that I was a mission volunteer. At that time she was dead set against being a missionary.

Following graduation from MC, I had a talk with Nan and tried to communicate that I knew after I left school, there would be parties and activities and I wanted her to have the freedom to attend with a date. But she did not hear my intent. Instead, she heard me say

11

we were finished and would not be seeing each other again. I didn't find that out until much later - after we were married. That was the first time the demon of unclear communication entered our relationship, but that little booger would plague us for years to come.

That fall I started attending Southern Seminary in Louisville, Kentucky, but I was not content there. During summer vacation, I had a long discussion with my good friend, Charles Bagwell. Like me, he was a preacher and he attended New Orleans Seminary. What he told me about the school there sounded good, so I transferred that summer.

After I left MC for seminary, Nan continued her studies and graduated the following spring. She then got a job teaching at a school in Jackson and also worked with the young women of her church. It was during the Lottie Moon Christmas Offering season, (our church's convention's national focus on foreign missions) that God used the theme of the emphasis, "Here am I. Send me!" to speak to Nan's heart to renew her call to foreign missions.

During the fall semester after I transferred to New Orleans, I visited Jackson for a football game and met Nan again. One thing led to another and we started dating seriously. We were married August 19, 1966 in Jackson. We stayed in New Orleans for two more years until I graduated and then we moved to Blue Mountain, Mississippi where I was the Baptist Student Union Director for five and a half years.

During seminary and following, I realized that I really did not have to transfer to Mississippi College and graduate from a Baptist College in order to attend seminary or be a preacher. I had lots of classmates that followed different paths, but we all wound up at the same place. However, after a little more reflection, I realized that if I had not transferred to MC, I would never have met Nan. Even when neither of us was actively asking God about our life mate, He was bringing us together. I found out after we married that Nan's mother had been praying for her husband since her birth. She was a tremendous prayer warrior. God moves in mysterious ways to accomplish his purpose and work it for the good of those who love Him and are called according to His purpose.

I pray that you will develop such a close relationship with God that you will be able to see Him work in your lives. Often He works "behind the scenes" and we discover His handiwork only when we look back at our life. Hindsight allows us to see all the wonderful things He has done to direct circumstances around us to help us get to the place where He wants us to be. We just need to do our best to maintain a good, open relationship with Him so He can gently nudge us in the direction He wants us to go.

Children are a Blessing from the Lord

"Sons are a heritage from the LORD, children a reward from him." Psalm 127:3

Not every significant event that shapes our future is positive or even one in which we personally participate. While enrolled in seminary and prior to my marriage, I witnessed the almost daily encounter between a father and his son, approximately aged six. (I mean the son was aged six, not the father, although his behavior did seem rather immature.) This event played out the same way almost every afternoon in the cafeteria. The son apparently did something wrong and the father would drag him kicking and screaming into the bathroom, where a whipping occurred, accompanied by loud weeping and wailing. Everyone in the room was treated to this encounter on a regular basis. It did not aid digestion.

The second part of this encounter happened in class one day when I heard this same father state, "I believe that if I take care of God's business, then He will take care of my children." Even though single at the time, I became convinced that perhaps the father should pay more attention to his son. The result of that encounter was that I developed the philosophy that perhaps the most important thing I could ever do would be to rear any children God chose to give me in such a way so that when they matured chronologically, they would also be spiritually and emotionally mature.

My dear sweet wife helped me tremendously with this. I didn't know how to relate to children but she never allowed me to escape into doing "the man thing" and not participate in their young lives. She expected my involvement in every aspect of their upbringing and I benefitted tremendously from her expectations. Some of my most pleasant memories of our early marriage come from those years in Blue Mountain when the children were young. When I came home from school, she would have supper ready, and after supper she would wash dishes and I would wash the children and get them ready for bed. This always involved reading a bedtime story or two. Those were precious times indeed.

We did our best to rear the children in a home environment that was characterized by unconditional love, consistency in expectations, and daily conversations about whatever was going on. Most of the time those conversations revolved about what the children were doing, but as they grew older, there were frequent conversations about what was going on in our life and ministry. We hoped those talks helped them understand why we were where we were and why we were doing what we did.

There were also many family activities that were facilitated by living in a city in which there were few American children with whom our children could play. Could any of us ever forget Super Summer and the infamous "bike hike?"

This was intended to be a pleasant outing to a park Nan had found to have a picnic. We would all ride our bikes and have a leisurely, fun day. We took some back roads from our house to get to the park and I am sure the children, even with all their exploring, had never seen that part of Tainan. We finally arrived at the park and it was lovely with lots of

13

good trees for shade. Then we started home by some other back roads. I had never seen part of that route and suspected that Nan was "flying by the seat of her pants" and just following her nose to get home. In all, the trip lasted about seven or eight hours. We had a young friend of the children's with us who had just moved to Tainan. Her father was a teacher in the new medical school and this was her first time in Taiwan, even though her mother and father had grown up here. I thought she would never speak to us again.

Out of curiosity, when we got home and were a little rested, I got on my motorcycle and retraced the route. Nan had estimated it was about five miles. By the odometer it was 15.4 miles! None of us wanted to ride a bicycle for quite some time after that.

Due to God's grace and Nan's creative mind our family time was always rich and full. Except for some brief periods during the children's teenage years, we had really good communication in the family and grew to be very supportive of each other. I pray that as you establish your families, you will make the effort to establish and maintain good communication with whatever children God gives you.

One thing we found out was that it is important to talk to the children as soon as they can interact. That pattern, established early and maintained through the years, creates an environment in which they feel free to discuss the situations they face in their own lives as they grow up.

Pray for them and cover them with unconditional love.

PREPARATION

Marriage

"So they are no longer two, but one. Therefore what God has joined together, let man not separate."
Matthew 19:6

An experience can be a positive spiritual event even if one is unaware of the implications at the time. My marriage was that. Certainly there was never a doubt in my mind or in Nan's mind that God put us together. It was only as we journeyed together that God's intent and purpose became clear.

It would be accurate to say that we struggled with the whole "one flesh" concept. Whose flesh would it be? Mine or hers? At the time period in which we married, many pastors and teachers had a lot to say about the importance of becoming one flesh. One thing they neglected to talk much about was how to do that. One little topic in particular I never heard anyone address was that in order for the two to become one, a part of both individuals had to die. The desired goal of "two becoming one" does not just mystically emerge when two people of different backgrounds and temperaments start living together.

In those days very few pastors offered pre-marital counseling. The only preparation we had was what we observed growing up at home and then, after marriage, through observing other young couples. On rare occasions when guys were together one might complain about something his wife did. When that happened the other fellows would usually express surprise that any woman would do such a thing, all the while thinking, "My situation is not that bad." I have no idea what the women said to each other.

The first two years in New Orleans were really good. We enjoyed being together and getting to know each other in ways we had never before experienced. There were a couple of times when unexpressed expectations or miscommunication interrupted our feelings for each other, but we didn't think anything about them. Nor did we discuss them, partly because we didn't know what to say and partly because we thought it was normal. At that time we had no idea what caused them. That all changed after Harriet was born. The tension increased and things were not good.

Of course, while Nan was adjusting to a new role of being a "stay at home mom," I was adjusting to my new role as a campus minister. Both of us were under a lot of pressure. Nan wanted to stay at home and be a mom, but she missed interacting with people, especially in group projects. I was having to find a way to come out of my introvert shell and interact with young female students at the college I did not know. There was a lot of adjusting going on in our lives and it was not easy. Plus we had lost something we both enjoyed a lot. We could no longer hop in the car, drive to the French Market, sit in Café du Monde over coffee and beignets, and watch the Mississippi River flow stately by. That was a regular "get away" in New Orleans and was a great stress reliever. Those happy experiences were gone forever with nothing to replace them. Adjustments are hard.

The first couple of years in Blue Mountain were hard, but we did adjust and make progress. You will see all we faced and how we dealt with it in later chapters. But for now, just remember that we were committed to each other and committed to doing whatever was necessary to arrive on the mission field. Our joint vision of how God wanted to use us helped keep us on track. I pray for you all that when you marry, you will have the same commitment to God and to each other. That will carry you through a lot of deep water

Prayer is Real

"Jesus Christ is the same yesterday and today and forever." Hebrews 13:8

Nan and I moved from New Orleans to Blue Mountain, Mississippi in late December, 1968. I began working there as Baptist Student Union Director in January, 1969. Harriet was born in Ripley about six weeks after we moved. This was my first job out of seminary and I was both excited and terrified. I knew very little about BSU work and now I was the leader. Dr. Harold Fisher, president of Blue Mountain hired me and generally outlined my duties. One aspect of my employment was made clear; I was expected to have regular office hours and interact with the students as much as possible. That was kind of tough because here I was, an introvert who had never been comfortable talking to girls, coming to work in a girls' college. In addition, my office was up on a hill separated from everything else by about three hundred yards.

I did have a BSU council made up of about twelve students and a faculty advisor. We met often during that first year, and the BSU president, Charlotte Bryant, took charge and explained to me all that we were doing and what I needed to do. She was an angel sent by God to help me get a handle on things.

Every day I would arrive at the office around 8:15 and sit there alone until chapel time at 10:00. Then I would walk down to the main building where the classes, offices, and auditorium were located. I would sometimes hang out in the book store until chapel and then try and mingle with the students after chapel until they started class again. Then it was back to the office until I went home for lunch. The BSU held Noonday, a daily devotional period for the students that met in Broach Hall, where my office was. It was usually a song followed by a devotional thought by one of the students or sometimes one of the faculty. From time to time we had a special speaker who was speaking either in the chapel service or in one of the special church meetings. Following that, I was usually alone until time to go home around five. I had a lot of time to read and make plans for upcoming events.

In the summer, I was often asked to preach in one of the county churches when the pastor wanted to take a vacation. I enjoyed that and got to know some of the local churches that way.

It was spring of 1971 and I had been serving at Blue Mountain College for about two years. With all the time I had to read, somehow God drew me into a deep desire for more communication with him. I spent a lot of that alone time in the office reading the Bible, not necessarily for study, but just to try and understand God's character and nature. At the same time, I also spent more time in prayer asking for a deeper understanding of spiritual truth.

This was a growing time when I found confirmation for some spiritual realities I believed, but had struggled with pretty much all my life, because no one would affirm my belief. The basic issue was whether or not God still did the things I read about in the Bible – specifically healing the sick. I asked numerous questions about it at home during my growing up years and got no satisfactory answer. I was told that God did still do those things – sometimes. But I could not get a clear sense of whether or not one could count on seeing God act in the same way today. Those questions were answered while I was in college and seminary, not always directly, but through the lessons and commentaries I studied. In a polite way, the answer always came that we had the Bible now and God didn't need to perform those miracles anymore. That answer did not really satisfy me nor did it explain the infrequent reports heard in churches about people being healed or otherwise seeing God do miraculous things. The answers I got always made me sad. I gradually perceived that my theology was viewed as very simple and unsophisticated, and it was implied this type of thinking was common among less well-educated church members. The implication was that when you were well-educated and understood things, you would no longer need or look for this type of action from God. While in seminary, I learned to keep my questions and opinions to myself and just do the work necessary to obtain my degree. So perhaps this time at Blue Mountain was God working in my heart to call me back to those early beliefs.

Now with plenty of time just to read the Bible and pray, I was coming back to my original thought that God could still work the way the Bible recorded, and perhaps we should expect to see Him work that way today. While this opinion was still taking shape in my mind and heart, I received an invitation to preach a revival in Corinth, which was about a two-hour drive from Blue Mountain. I accepted the invitation, but about a week prior to the agreed-upon date, Nan came down with the flu. It was not the kind of flu we have today that seems to pass in two days; this kind took anywhere from a week to two weeks for recovery. She was really sick. She could do nothing but lie in bed and be miserable. (On a side note, that is when I learned to cook. I had a choice of skipping meals for me and our two young children or learning to put a meal on the table. We ate a lot of scrambled eggs, but I did manage some other things as well.)

When it was time to go to Corinth, Nan was feeling a little better, but still had not eaten very much, was still very weak, and actually had a hard time sitting up for very long at a time. Even then, she stated her desire to be involved in whatever was going on and wanted to go. I had been praying for several days about whether or not to call the pastor and cancel due to her illness. But every time I prayed, I felt that we should go, so I did not cancel my preaching in the revival although according to conventional wisdom, I probably should have.

The afternoon we were scheduled to leave, I went to her convinced that I should pray for her. While we'd had some devotional time together, I had never prayed for her as I would at this time. And I had never actually prayed for anything as specific as I was about to. But I was convinced I should pray and ask God to raise her up and give her the strength to go with me to this meeting. I prayed. Probably against sound advice, she went. Of course there was no one to tell us we were stupid. On the way I continued to be concerned about her ability to withstand the evening.

When we arrived, we went to the pastor's home and had supper with him. Nan actually ate something, her first real meal in several days. Then we went to church and she was able to remain upright for the entire service. (We all remember her determination to do what was expected and not make a spectacle of herself, but even so, I remain convinced that God was the one who gave her the strength to endure.) Naturally, she was worn out when the service was over and slept a lot on the way home. But she was able to return for the next two meetings and seemed to gain strength each day.

For me, it was a pivotal point in my spiritual walk. I think that was the first time in my life that I could honestly say I prayed a specific prayer and God answered. Needless to say, I was greatly encouraged in my faith through this experience and continued my personal study and prayer times with renewed enthusiasm.

Piety or Obedience

"If anyone loves me, he will obey my teaching." John 14:23

When Nan and I went to Blue Mountain College to begin our ministry, we made no secret of our dream to be appointed as missionaries at some time in the immediate future. I am not sure we actually broadcast this dream, but we never shied away from talking about it. The community was quite small so it was not surprising that many, if not all, the residents there knew of our plans. This was true whether they knew us well or not.

One day I was coming out of the local grocery store and met a woman that I recognized, but barely knew. She stopped me and said, "I have heard that you have plans for the future. You are planning on being a missionary." I responded that she had heard correctly. Then she said, "I had no idea you were that pious." With that statement, she turned and walked away. She obviously did not expect any reply, which was good since I was struck dumb by her comment.

As I reflected on her words over the next few days and weeks, I realized that I did not view myself as pious at all. I was responding in obedience to the last command Jesus gave those gathered on the hillside just before he ascended into heaven. Added to that, I had the deep inner conviction that God had communicated to me that His desire was that I serve Him on a mission field somewhere. Armed with those two truths, I realized that my long term goals were based on obedience to God's command and nothing else.

Through the years, when we returned to America for our time away from the mission field, I frequently heard comments from church members repeating her theme: we were something special, somehow more "holy" and "pious" than they viewed themselves. But in our minds we were only doing what God had asked us to do: we were simply being obedient. However, we often found that people - even good friends - seemed to be uncomfortable around us. It was as if they didn't know how to relate to us anymore.

In 2010 David Platt wrote the book *Radical*. The premise of this little volume is that today, the church in America has drifted far from the obedience that characterized the early church. When one does take the step of committing to a lifetime of mission involvement, his or her actions are considered to be radical. When looking back at the first century church, I suppose many of those believer's families considered them radical as well. After all, they committed to follow someone whom the religious leaders had branded as a heretic and demon possessed. But those early believers went into the world with such a degree of zealousness that by the year 300 A.D. they had turned the world upside down. Many of those first believers suffered great persecution and martyrdom. Even today in many countries around the world, believers are still suffering the same fate. Some years ago, I read a comment from a Chinese pastor when asked about the persecution the church was enduring there. His statement was simply, "Do not pray for the persecution to stop; pray that we will be faithful to our call." Perhaps it is that very element of belief that Platt saw as missing from the present day American church. Nan and I never perceived ourselves as radical, merely obedient.

In *The Daily Study Bible*, William Barclay when commenting on John 3:1-6 states that one element of the "new birth" is sonship. He then says, "The essence of sonship is love;

and the essence of love is obedience." Years later, Charles Colson added to this concept in his book, *Loving God* by stating that the greatest, most complete demonstration of our love for God is through our obedience to his commands.

While serving at Blue Mountain, there were often opportunities to hear guest speakers from various places. One of those was Major Ian Thomas, a speaker and author from England. One day when talking about God's call in our lives, he said something like this: "Once you reckon with God, where you serve is merely a matter of geography." I interpreted that to mean once you submitted to God's authority in your life, He had the freedom to direct you wherever He wanted you to be so you could do whatever He wanted you to do.

All that sounds really good, for who among us would not want to demonstrate our love for the God who saved us from sin and destruction? But I discovered what many others have learned – there cannot be complete obedience without relinquishing something else. To be sure, there can be an outward manifestation of obedience without the concomitant attitude of submission. But if there is submission to the authority, then obedience naturally follows. In my case, that meant when I submitted to the sovereignty of God, going where He wanted me to go was easy. At least it was easy to make the decision. Every person struggles with this issue on some level The basic question we face is this: "Is what I desire worth giving up what I must relinquish?" One's true answer to that question is revealed through his or her actions.

I pray for you that you will be willing to step away from anything that might hinder you from fully committing to follow God wherever He leads you.

You Are Not Accepted

"For I know the plans I have for you," declares the LORD, "plans to prosper you and not to harm you, plans to give you hope and a future." Jeremiah 29:11

When we moved to Blue Mountain in January, 1969, we intended to stay there for two years and then go overseas as foreign missionaries. We made no secret of our plans and everyone who knew us was aware of our goal. Due to life and the arrival of children, it was about two and a half years before we finally completed the application process. Early on, we were assigned a candidate consultant named Dwight Honeycutt, who guided us through the different steps we had to take. One big part of that process was to list five people who were to recommend us for service. Then each of the five would be asked to list other people who might serve as a reference. The net result was that there must have been at least forty people in that small community who knew the time had come. Of course, when we sent in our list of five people, we contacted those and asked them to serve as a reference for us and told them that they would soon be receiving a form to complete. Naturally, in a small community even those who had not received a form soon knew what was going on.

The process called for our names, along with those of other candidates, to be presented to the personnel committee for a final approval and then recommendation to the entire Foreign Mission Board in one of their regular meetings. For us the Board meeting that examined our application was held in late spring or very early summer of 1972. The Board was made up of representatives of the different state conventions, so it was a large number of people. We had been told the specific day they would meet and were promised that Dwight, who would represent us at the meeting, would call us once the Board made a decision. We had told some of our closest friends the date of the meeting.

On that day, I was at school as usual, but left around two pm so that I could be home when the call arrived. Nan and I were on pins and needles waiting for the news that we had been accepted and what the time line would be for us to make our move overseas.

The telephone finally rang, and Dwight delivered the bad news. He said that we had not been approved. The two reasons he gave were that first, and most important, the Board felt our marriage was not stable and they feared the stresses on the mission field would lead to a divorce. The second reason, which was totally overshadowed by the first, was that I was serving in a very atypical situation that did not provide the range of experience I would need for working with students in a large urban setting. I was working in a very small college in a rural setting, but was expected to serve in a large metropolitan environment on a much larger campus. But the main reason was our marriage.

To say we were shocked and devastated would be an understatement. After a few moments of staring dumbfoundedly at each other, I picked up the phone and called our pastor, Douglas Clarke.

"Did the call come?" he asked eagerly.

"Yep." I replied. "We weren't accepted."

There was dead silence on the other end of the line for a long moment, before he said, "I'll be right over."

Lessons from the Journey

When he arrived, we were able to vent some of our hurt and frustration with him, still in an attitude of disbelief. He pointed out that it was possibly the first time in either of our lives that we had ever been faced with not being accepted and able to do whatever we wanted.

We walked around in a daze for quite a long time not knowing what to do. After three or four unsettled months, we finally reached a point where we could at least talk about trying to find a marriage counselor. Even though Douglas was trained and certified in that area, he said he was too close to us to be our counselor. But he put us in touch with someone in Tupelo, and we began making the 45-minute trek over there. At first we went weekly. After about six weeks, we made the shift to every other week and continued to receive counseling for somewhere between nine and twelve months.

The counselor identified the basic problem in our relationship as unmet expectations coupled with unclear communications. Several factors contributed to this problem, and almost all of them revolved around our home environments. Added to those factors were our personality differences. Nan was an extreme extrovert and I was an extreme introvert. We worked on those issues during the sessions with him, as well as trying to find new ways to communicate at home. Finally, the counselor said we had reached a point where he felt we were stable enough to proceed on our own. Accordingly, he wrote a report to the folks at the Foreign Mission Board and said we had completed the marriage counseling.

The counseling process revealed that we had covered up and denied our problems without realizing it. Our denial was due largely to our inability to communicate with each other our feelings about what was happening. In other words, we knew there was a problem, we just didn't know what to do about it. The few times we did try and talk things out only led to increased tension in our relationship, so our response was to just not talk about misunderstandings. The counselor pointed this out to us and, simple as it sounds, the biggest thing he did was to help us see that we needed to talk about our feelings and to ask each other if there was a problem when we sensed things were not right. Strange we didn't have enough sense to do that anyway, but we didn't.

The whole experience of being rejected, having to go to a marriage counselor, and learn new ways of relating to each other was painful, embarrassing, and humbling. To quote a well-known saying, "What doesn't kill you will make you stronger." This process resulted in better communication between us and a much stronger marriage, which in turn opened my eyes to see that God had indeed given me an invaluable companion for life. We shared a vision and worked together to achieve that vision. Due to the unique crucible of the mission field, we worked together as a team for over three decades. During that time, Nan was my faithful companion, my constant encourager, and a source of great strength when the going got tough. She was much more than a helpmate; she was my true soul mate. I like to think I preformed the same role for her.

As Douglas pointed out to us, when we were turned down by the FMB, we had to deal with rejection like we had never previously faced. It was a shocking blow to our self-perception that made us examine ourselves in a new light. One part of that examination was questioning whether or not we would ever serve on a mission field. In the following months, we discussed several options for ministry. One was to just stay in Blue Mountain and work there. We even purchased a plot of land on which we hoped to build a home. I thought about moving to another campus in a large city in order to gain a different kind of experience that would qualify me to serve overseas. I thought about leaving BSU work altogether and going somewhere as pastor of a church. In that mix of feelings, every spring

I would pray seriously about staying in Blue Mountain or moving somewhere else. Every time, it seemed clear that God was saying, "Stay put." So we stayed.

Through the experience of working with the marriage counselor, we realized that God had indeed put us together. In the beginning, we struggled to know which flesh we would be. Gradually, as the years passed, we realized that both of us helped shape the other. Our identity as a couple was a little bit like her and a little bit like me. She became a little more introverted while I became a little more extroverted. Apparently, we were linked so closely in heart and mind that many of our friends seldom referred to us as individuals, but often said "Rob and Nan" go together like "sugar and cream" or "apple pie and ice cream" or "hot dogs and the Fourth of July." It was a wonderful journey even though at times it was hard. What ultimately came out of our union was a testimony to God's wisdom and His sustaining grace. The result of the struggle of our growth together was a marriage and ministry that was neither mine nor hers; both truly belonged to God. God put us together, melded us into one flesh, and gave us a ministry in which we both contributed. To God be the glory.

To be honest, that does not mean that everything was peaches and cream after we completed our time with the marriage counselor. There were still times when tension would rise and communication was difficult. But now we knew what must be done to put things right, and we would do the hard things to reconcile and regain harmony.

I pray for you, my grandchildren, that when you marry, you will be unwilling to settle for the status quo in your marriage, but will commit to work to make it a union that will honor God. It is not always easy, but it is well worth the effort.

Take My Son

"If you remain in me and my words remain in you, ask whatever you wish, and it will be given you. This is to my Father's glory, that you bear much fruit, showing yourselves to be my disciples." John 15:7-8

As I mentioned previously, I had a lot of time to develop my spiritual life during quiet times in my office. On a regular basis, I saw God give answers to questions people asked that were beyond my own wisdom. Those answers always applied directly to the issue that raised the question, and often provided comfort and direction to those with whom I talked. It was not always students, either. Sometimes it was a staff member or a person from one of the churches where I had been invited to preach. To be honest, I was frequently surprised by what came out of my mouth and often wondered, "How did I know how to say that?" Of course, after only a brief moment, I knew it did not come from me, but from my Father. The rejection by the FMB and the following months of counseling and application of those insights provided ample opportunities for God to work on my understanding of who I was.

Fall normally brings colds to children, and 1973 was no exception. Robert was about two and a half years old. He had been born six weeks early and as a result, his lungs had not completely developed. The day after he was born, we were sent to Memphis to check him into Lebhoner's Children's Hospital. After three days there and lots of tests, they told us about his lack of lung function. While there, they administered oxygen and he seemed to be all right. They said his lungs were functioning normally and released us to return home. Then when he was about eighteen months old, he got a cold and it developed into pneumonia. He had to spend several days in the hospital for treatment. The doctor said it was because of his weak lungs. Now he was sick again and since I tend to assume the worst in any medical situation, I feared he would again have pneumonia.

Nan was pregnant with Carroll and we were all excited about her arrival, even though we didn't know if the unborn child was male or female. Robert's cold did not seem to be getting any better. We were treating him with the usual stuff, but it didn't help. We did not take him to the doctor because that trip would take anywhere from four to eight hours. It required a trip to Ripley, and the doctor's office there didn't make many appointments. So you walked in, registered, and waited.

I could tell his breathing was getting more and more labored and was afraid of where it would lead. As usual, Nan said he would be fine. One night, after we were all in bed, I could hear him breathing hard even though his room was twenty-five feet down the hall from ours. Consequently, I lay awake listening to him struggle for air. After about an hour, I got up and walked down the hall to his bedroom. I stood at the door and listened, trying to decide whether to take him to the emergency room or not. While I stood there, I was praying and trying to get a sense of leading from God about what to do.

Finally, I walked into his room, picked him up, and held him above my head. I prayed and offered him to God. Among the things I said were that God had given him to us and now I was giving Robert back to him. I guess I expected an immediate result; I hoped I would hear his breathing ease. It did not, but I felt I must trust God to take care of him through the night. I decided that if he was not better in the morning, I would take him to the doctor.

The next morning, he was breathing normally and my heart was full of praise to God for taking care of him. From that point on, he never had another problem with breathing and never had pneumonia again.

I want to encourage you to pray with specific requests to your heavenly Father. He loves you and wants the best for you. When you pray, be sure and ask for insight to recognize God's answer. You don't want to miss the things He does..

The Journey Continues

F ollowing the news from the Foreign Mission Board that we could not be appointed at that particular time, we just continued doing what our life and job called for. Now that our life goal seemed unreachable, my constant prayer was focused on trying to discern what God wanted us to do. Of course, in my natural way of thinking, I examined other options. Since one reason the Board did not want to appoint us was that my work experience was atypical for what I would face overseas, I considered the possibility of moving to another BSU position at a larger campus. Since there was no opportunity for that to happen in Mississippi, we even discussed whether or not we needed to move out of state to be in a very different environment. I also wondered if perhaps I needed to find a way to let it be known that I was available to serve as pastor somewhere. Additionally, through a rather odd (for me, at least) invitation from some of the students, I wound up driving them to Ole Miss to take the GRE exam and, at their insistence, took it myself. To my surprise, I made a high enough grade to be accepted into graduate school. So the possibility of more study at Ole Miss was also an option.

One interesting development was that while Blue Mountain College was a female school, there were some male students attending. The rule for allowing males to attend stated that if they were currently employed by a Baptist church and could not reach another Baptist college, they could be admitted as day students. That procedure had been in place for at least ten years prior to our arrival. During that time, the number of male students had slowly grown, probably due to the influence of Dr. James Travis. He was the head of the Bible department and was gone somewhere every weekend preaching, which gave him numerous contacts in North Mississippi. He was the one encouraging the men to attend.

As the number grew, the men increasingly complained about the requirement that in order to obtain their BA degree they had to take a language. French and Spanish were the only options, and both of the language teachers did not want men in their class. The men discussed with Dr. Travis the possibility of getting someone to teach Greek, arguing that this would meet the language requirement for the degree while helping them in their ministry at the same time. Dr. Travis said he was not prepared to teach Greek, so one day he asked me if I could handle that. In my exaggerated opinion of my abilities, I responded "Of course." It took some time to convince both the Dean and the President that I could in fact teach Greek, because I had studied it in college and seminary. Finally, they relented and I was "employed" as an adjunct Bible professor. I taught Greek each semester and often one other Bible course, either Old Testament Survey or New Testament Survey. I think those were courses Dr. Travis did not want to teach.

We continued to wonder what we would do and where we would do it. Then one day our pastor was talking to us about our future and we indicated that, among other things, we were even considering staying in Blue Mountain. He put us in touch with a fellow church member who had three acres of land he wanted to sale. We purchased it with the idea of someday building a house on it. That was a pretty ridiculous idea since my salary just barely paid enough for me to feed and clothe my family. Thank goodness it was okay for us to wear things from Fred's Dollar Store.

All these options were swirling around in our minds, but nothing seemed solid. I continued to pray, Nan continued to pray, and we prayed together. All we knew to do was just keep on keeping on.

Sometime in the early spring of 1975, we both got the feeling that God was telling us it was time to contact the FMB again. When we did, we found that our previous candidate consultant, Dwight Honeycutt, was still there. We brought him up to date on what we were doing and what we felt God was telling us. The result of the conversation was that he reviewed our files, discussed our status with others in the office, and after a week or so reported back to us. He told us that since they had the report of the marriage counselor, the only three remaining matters were to update our biography, attend another candidate conference and then to send out references again.

We started working on the updates immediately, finished them and mailed them in. After waiting for a couple of weeks, we were contacted with the news that it all looked good. We were invited to another candidate conference to be interviewed again. Also called a GIC, or Group Interview Conference, the Board invites anywhere from eight to eighteen candidates to go to Richmond for a long weekend. There are multiple meetings and interviews with different FMB personnel, and after the candidates return home, the FMB folks meet to discuss what they learned. Following the weekend, they did not immediately inform the candidates of their recommendations so we were anxious until we were finally contacted again and Dwight told us everything went well. He also said that he would be flying through Memphis on a certain date and asked that we meet him at the airport. He assured us that it all looked good and that we were just going to talk about the timeframe of concluding the process.

On the appointed day we drove to the Memphis airport and met him for coffee. He said again that all was in order, the staff was convinced that we were qualified and all we needed to do was to update the list of people we wanted to use as references. Once that was done, they would work with us on the date to send out the reference forms. The whole process was looking good and almost complete.

A couple of weeks after that meeting we were surprised by a visit from two men from Fellowship Baptist Church in Bellefontaine, MS. They had been somewhere up in the area visiting a prospective pastor for their church, and they stopped by to see if I would be available to preach for them the following week. I agreed, and on the appointed Sunday, we drove down for the day. It all went well and after the evening service, they invited us back the following week.

The next week, following the morning service, we went to Perry and Mary Sprayberry's home for lunch. That was normal in a tiny community which had no restaurant. Perry was chairman of the deacons that year. We had just finished dessert when the front door opened and several men, all church deacons, walked in, obviously arriving for a meeting. We adjourned to the living room.

I was then, and continue to be, rather naïve in a lot of matters. I thought they were coming to tell me that they were having trouble locating a replacement pastor and to ask if I could I help them locate a possible candidate. I was framing my response to their request when they told me that the church had decided that they wanted me to be their pastor: they were there to invite me to move to Bellefontaine and pastor the church. I was so shocked I had trouble speaking for a moment.

When I recovered enough to speak, I told them about our long term vision to serve as missionaries and that we had been in contact with the FMB. The Board had informed us that things were moving right along and we anticipated being appointed that summer and going overseas sometime in the fall or winter. After some uncomfortable murmuring, they finally left. After the evening service, we drove home.

The next night, Mom and Dad called just to catch up on things as they usually did. As the conversation was moving to a close, I said, "Oh, you will be interested in this." I told them the church had asked me to be the pastor. When Dad asked what I told them, I responded that I had said we were pointed to the mission field and could not come. Dad surprised me by saying, "I am surprised that you would not even pray about it."

Have I mentioned that sometimes I am so single-minded that I only see one thing?

His comment sparked us both to start praying about it. After a couple of weeks, we both felt God telling us that it was his plan for us to move to Bellefontaine. After skipping two or three Sundays, the church invited me back to preach again. Nan asked what I was going to tell them about our decision. I told her I didn't know how to bring it up since I had been so adamant about going to the mission field. But God went ahead of us. That afternoon in a deacon's meeting, they told me they had prayed and prayed and felt that I was the right man for their church. They asked again if we would come. That time, we said yes.

Soon after that weekend, I sat down with President Fisher and explained my decision, and I resigned effective at the end of the semester. In early June, some men came up from Bellefontaine and helped us move. We used a horse trailer and several pickups, but made it all in one trip. Nan and I agreed that was much easier than moving gradually across town.

The whole process introduced us to a principle we eventually came to recognize and depend on. When you are following God and know you are doing what He wants you to do, but you ask for some kind of guidance about a next step and don't hear anything and know you don't have unconfessed sin or blatant disobedience, you are supposed to keep on doing the last thing God told you to do. In His time, He will give you the next step. The short version is, "When you pray and do not seem to hear from God, keep doing the last thing He told you to do." We found that to be true many times in the years that followed.

There are several examples of this in the Bible. For example, God promised Abraham that He would give him many descendants, but it was twenty-five years until Isaac, the child of promise, was born. Joseph was given a dream about his family bowing down to him, but before it happened, he was sold as a slave and then put in prison. David was anointed as king as a teenager, but had to endure several years of testing until he actually became king of Israel. Paul spent three years in Arabia following his conversion. Even Jesus lived on earth thirty years before beginning his earthly ministry.

When we sense God giving us a direction to follow we must begin the journey and walk by faith until the promise is fulfilled.

I pray that when something like that happens in your life, you will remain faithful to God while continuing to focus on your relationship with Him. Then I pray God will grant you the vision to see the next step, and give you the courage to take that step.

Let's Have a Chat

"I have much more to say to you, more than you can now bear. But when he, the Spirit of truth, comes, he will guide you into all truth. He will not speak on his own; he will speak only what he hears, and he will tell you what is yet to come." John 16:12-13

It was late fall in 1975, and I had been pastor of Fellowship Baptist Church for about four or five months. We had completed our move in early June, settled into the parsonage, and were getting comfortable with life in Bellefontaine.

I quickly discovered that most of the normal pastoral duties were very light because the church was small. Besides preaching, all I had to do was visit the sick and shut-ins, attend the monthly deacon's meeting, and prepare the weekly bulletin for the Sunday morning service. During that time I developed the practice of praying for the church members. I put their names on note cards and would begin my office time with prayer. I split the list into five sections, praying for one section each day so that all members were prayed for every week.

For a while, sermon preparation was easy. The excitement of the new position and the opportunity to preach regularly was appealing. If I did get in a tight with my schedule and not have time to adequately prepare, I had some sermons I had preached in various places while I served in Blue Mountain. Even though I didn't want to do it, in an emergency I could always pull one of those out and kind of re-work it. There was also a backlog of ideas for sermons that had emerged but never developed as I prepared for the Bible classes I had taught. They were just floating around in my mind.

However, after a little while, I started to run out of ideas and I was beginning to feel the pressure of preparing three sermons a week. It was so regular and seemed so difficult to find a passage and topic that conveyed the message I felt God wanted to deliver to His people. Perhaps I had an exaggerated idea of the role of the pastor; I tended to see the pastor as similar to that of the prophet in the Old Testament. There, the man was chosen by God to deliver His message to His people. As I read some of the passages from Isaiah and Jeremiah, I was always impressed with the force with which they could say, "Thus saith the Lord." I felt the pastor should have the same level of confidence and authority. Of course, that was my own idea: they certainly did not teach that in seminary.

I found myself wishing that I could just sit down with Jesus for a few minutes and talk with Him. Not long before leaving Blue Mountain, I had read a book on meditation in which the major premise was that a person was encouraged to picture in his or her mind a meadow with a stream flowing through it, and Jesus, the Good Shepherd, sitting there on a rock. That would be a good comforting picture with me right in the middle of it. Then the person was encouraged to imagine the conversation they wanted to have with Jesus. Sounds simple, right?

I had difficulty doing this. Sometimes, that type of abstract exercise doesn't really make sense to me. But one day in the office, in a time of desperation, I pulled a chair from across the room and placed it right in front of my chair. Then I invited Jesus to have a seat so we could have a little chat. I said to that chair the things I wanted to say to Jesus. I told Him about my frustration with the sermon preparation and that I often felt like I was just preaching out of my own understanding, and that what I said did not really have anything to do with what He wanted to tell His people. I felt quite foolish and was glad that there was no one else in the church. No one else was there because until I came to Fellowship Baptist, no other pastor had tried to keep "office hours." They always worked at home and only came to the church at the designated meeting times. I knew myself well enough to know that with three children at home, that would not work for me.

I thought the "conversation" between me and Jesus would be brief, but He was such a good listener, that I talked a long time. At the end of the time, I asked Him if He would kindly help me see and understand the message He had for His people. He did and from that time on, those conversations were a regular part of my weekly preparation. In time the format changed a little: I didn't always use a chair to represent Jesus' presence. I would pray asking for God to speak to me and then read the Bible. Using this process, God would often place a particular scripture on my mind and then I would develop it into a sermon. At other times, I would hear folks in the church talk about some matter that they did not understand or were concerned about. That is basically how I started developing sermons. Later, there would be times when I would do a series on a particular topic or a short study of one book.

There were still times when, due to unexpected hospital visits, sickness, or other events that my preparation was not all that it should have been. The result was that I would exit the pulpit feeling like I had missed the message God intended to be delivered at that time. Fortunately, as I gave more time to the spiritual side of preparation, the times of feeling like I had nothing to say grew less and less. The way God used that time to prepare the messages became very special to me, and showed me that He still desires to communicate with His people. This experience became a foundational part of my personal theology, and I later included it into some teachings on the importance on learning to hear God when He speaks. Much later, Nan and I built on this truth and used it to help prepare mission teams that we sent out from First Baptist Church of Jackson.

Additionally, I began to experience another part of this verse - the part where Jesus said the Spirit "would guide you into all truth." There were actually two facets to this truth. One was that I gained more confidence that the sermons I preached were biblically sound and presented spiritual truth on which people could build their lives. The other facet was that from time to time, I would be in conversation with someone and say something that could only have come from God. At times the statement seemed to reflect a knowledge of their situation that I could not possibly know, while at other times, the statement seemed to pull a scriptural truth "out of the air" that applied directly to their need or problem.

This whole experience served as a great motivator to me to do my best to not neglect the personal reading of God's word and time in prayer. All of these practices put together served to heighten my openness to God's Spirit moving in me. It is an awesome experience.

I pray for you that your own relationship with your Heavenly Father will develop to the point that you will be able to communicate with Him. You must always remember that real communication involves two people speaking. Too often, we tend to say what is on our mind and then leave. We must learn to wait on our Father and allow Him to speak to us.

I Will Show You a Miracle

"Whoever has my commands and obeys them, he is the one who loves me. He who loves me will be loved by my Father, and I too will love him and show myself to him." John 14:21

Among those we met at Fellowship Baptist Church were Jim and Ola Yarbrough. Jim was a farmer and I thought he was old. Looking back, he may have been in his early sixties and right now that seems young. Jim was one of those people with whom I made an immediate connection. He was easy to be with and easy to talk to. I enjoyed being with the Yarbroughs, and looked forward to getting to know them better and spending more time with them.

Sometime in early September, Jim went into the hospital for surgery on his stomach. It was expected to be routine. After a few days, he was released and returned home. I visited him regularly, and it was soon apparent that he was not recovering as anticipated. After a couple of months, he and Ola told me about a strange swelling in his stomach. No one could explain it. He was losing his appetite and consequently losing weight. But his stomach continued to grow.

Finally the diagnosis came through: liver cancer. That news sent shock waves through the small community, for Jim Yarbrough was both liked and respected. Everyone was caught off guard and for a short time became very introspective. It seemed a lot of energy was gone from the church.

It was very difficult for me personally, since I did like him very much. But more than that, it was the first time I faced the death of someone I knew outside my family who was not real old. There was also the reality that I would have to handle the funeral. I had never had to do that and didn't think I was ready.

I prayed long and hard for Jim and Ola without really knowing how to intercede for either of them. After a few weeks, one morning as I prayed, I felt or heard a voice in me somewhere that said, "I will show you a miracle." I knew it was God speaking.

It was not an audible voice: it was just somehow in my head. But it was as real as if it had been spoken out loud. That was the first time anything like that had happened to me and I didn't know how to understand it. But I believed it and began looking for the miracle. Of course, I expected it to be that Jim would be healed and we would all be amazed at how God worked in our midst.

As time passed, Jim got weaker and weaker. When I visited him towards the end, we did talk about heaven and about his faith. He was secure in knowing that he was saved and would be going to heaven. Finally, the disease won and took his life.

As I prepared for the funeral, I wondered without having the courage to ask, "Where is the miracle in this?"

Across the street from the church, there was a gas station run by our neighbor, Bill Sisson. Every afternoon during the week around three o'clock, a lot of the farmers would gather there for a Coke and small talk. On the day after the funeral, I went over to join them and was amazed to hear what they were saying. They were talking about Jim Yarbrough and his faith. They were all impressed to the point of amazement with the manner in which he approached death. He had a lot of farm equipment, and he sold it all before he died. He did a lot to tie up the loose ends of the business side of his life so that his wife would not have to handle it after he was gone. These men, who were good men, but kind of rough and self-sufficient, were all saying they hoped that when their death came, they would be able to face it as Jim had done. Even though most of them attended the Baptist Church and I knew them, I had never heard anything like this come out of their mouths. Unfortunately for all of us, I didn't know how to follow up on their expressed thoughts.

In retrospect, I concluded that the miracle God wanted to show me had two parts. The first was how a person who was secure in his salvation could face death. In the years that followed, I saw more examples of this faith and the peace it produced. The second part, which might have been the bigger miracle, was how the death of a righteous man could have such a big influence on those who knew him. I had never seen anything like that previously.

Until that time, in my spiritual relationship it seemed that God would somehow make his plans for me known either by giving me some kind of inner conviction or by leading me to a particular scripture verse and then impressing me with the need to act on it. The circumstance of praying for Jim and Ola was the first time in which I could say God actually spoke to me. I know it was not an audible voice, but even so, the certainty of the experience was no less real.

This event helped me understand that there are times when God wanted to communicate something to me just to help and comfort me. I had to learn that not everything God revealed to me was to be made into a sermon or told to someone else.

I pray your relationship with Jesus will develop to the point that you will also have the same experience, comprehending the joy of knowing God has revealed something precious just to you. That adds a deeper dimension to your relationship with your heavenly Father that will carry over to all your other relationships.

Hospitality is a Gift

"Now to each one the manifestation of the Spirit is given for the common good." 1 Corinthians 12:7
"We have different gifts according to the grace given us." Romans 12:6a

As time passed, we grew more and more comfortable with life in Bellefontaine. After Thanksgiving I noticed a little restlessness in Nan. About that time, Mom and Dad called us and told us they planned to come visit us before Christmas and bring the Christmas gifts. They no longer lived in Eupora because in 1971, Dad had been appointed to fill an unexpired term on the Mississippi Supreme Court. They moved to Jackson so he could do his work there. Since he had lived in Eupora, only twelve miles from Bellefontaine, he knew many people there and many of them knew him. Nan said this would be a wonderful time to have an open house and invite folks to come see them.

Nan grew up with all kinds of parties around Christmas time and while we lived in Blue Mountain, there were regular events that allowed us to dress up and visit in other folks' homes. In Bellefontaine, that was not the case. When I announced in church that we wanted to invite everyone to the house on a Friday night for an open house, they all wanted to know what an open house was. We explained it was a time for them to drop in for some coffee and cookies or candy and say hello to us and to Mom and Dad. We had to explain that it was come and go; no one had to stay long. In fact, it was expected that a person would come and only stay for a short period of time. It was a new idea to them.

On the appointed day, we had been working quite hard to get the house and refreshments ready. That included having all the rooms in the house ready for folks to walk through it. From what we later learned, this was the first time some of them had ever been inside the parsonage. After Mom and Dad arrived, Mom helped Nan put the finishing touches on everything.

Finally folks started arriving and we could tell some of them were nervous about this unfamiliar event. But they soon adapted, found some refreshments, and had a good time visiting. I am sure some of them stayed longer than they had thought they might.

At one point late in the evening, I was standing in one room with Johnny Crutchfield, a deacon and longtime member of the church. He told me that he had helped build the parsonage and I told him I was not surprised to find that out. He then said that anytime the church was between pastors, he would come and help get the parsonage ready for the new pastor. Again, I was not surprised. But then he said, "In all the years that I have lived here, this is the first time I have been in this house when the pastor actually lived here." I was dumfounded. The fact that he had been invited to come was very meaningful to him. The fact that this was the first time it had happened was meaningful to me also, but for a very different reason. I could not imagine that no other pastor opened his home to the church members, even if just to the deacons. Even in small town Eupora, I remembered visiting in the pastor's home from time to time.

After Christmas came spring, and as the time passed and summer was getting close, Nan got the itch to host another party. She told me she wanted to have a pie party. She wanted to invite the church members over one Sunday afternoon to visit and have pie. We discussed the logistics: when to hold the party, what kind of pies to make, how many pies to make, etc. We chose a time in late spring before it got too hot and the bugs got too bad, and I think Nan made about fifteen pies.

When I announced our plan to the church, again we had some explaining to do. On the designated Sunday, we canceled church that evening and had the members come over in the cool of the afternoon. I am sure I had help from a couple of the men to bring some tables and chairs from the church to accommodate the crowd. This time people stayed for quite some time and we all had some wonderful visiting time. There was a sense of ease and comfort in being together and passing the time like that.

I mention these events because they show Nan's penchant for entertaining. I believe it was because she had the gift of hospitality. It is not likely you will find that gift on a list of spiritual gifts, but I think it is one. She had the ability to make people feel at ease in our home no matter what the situation was or how little we knew each other. This carried over to the mission field. While serving in Tainan, often other missionaries would come through town and we would entertain them. Many times, it was new missionaries, and they commented later how comfortable they felt being in our home.

Speaking of spiritual gifts, there are many different lists of gifts. Some are very short and some are longer. The list I like has only two: the gift of eternal life and the gift of the Holy Spirit. Paul indicates that the Spirit will bestow the ability needed to the person actively serving Christ to meet the situation they face at the time. I remember one man I met who came from America to minister in Taiwan. Perhaps one would say that he had the gift of exorcism and the gift of healing. I watched him pray for both needs and saw God bring healing and freedom to the person in need. But one night following a service, a Chinese woman came to him for prayer. He prayed for her in Mandarin and didn't even know he was not speaking English. The Spirit always does his work.

No doubt a person will have one or two gifts that are the primary way they function in ministry through the church. But God can manifest in different ways as the need arises. We should also remember that we are encouraged to use and develop the gifts God has bestowed upon us.

Forgive the digression, but again, that is what old people do. I pray you will discover how God wants to use you and how He has equipped you to serve. May you always serve in joy.

The Next Step

Fellowship Baptist Church was a loving church with loving people. It was satisfying to work with them, getting to know them and their families. We all grew to love each other a lot as they welcomed us into their church and homes. God ministered to all of us during those days. There were some members who had been hurt by previous experiences in life and church who found healing during those precious months. Others had their faith strengthened as they focused on God's word and ministry to each other. Nan and I both grew in our faith walk and found new, deeper levels of communication with our Father than we previously experienced.

Sometime around mid-January of 1977, I was sitting in my study one day praying and looking out the window at the harvested cotton field. I was thinking it would be easy to just stay right here and continue to grow and minister. Then God began to impress me with the memory that he had a different plan for me. For the next several days, I prayed about that other plan and very soon realized it was time to contact the FMB again and see if we could actually get appointed. The whole thought was scarier now than it previously had been. We had not talked much to the folks about our dream of being missionaries, the children and we were comfortable here, and the unknown of moving somewhere around the world seemed more dangerous now that I had three children to think of. Even so, God was firm in His reminders of His plan for me. So I promised I would follow up. But I did say that He would have to work on Nan since it was obvious that she also was comfortable and not much interested in moving.

In mid-February, she joined some other women in attending a young pastor's wives retreat at Camp Garaywa. I had not even mentioned to her how God was working in my heart; I was praying for the right time to bring the subject up for discussion.

The afternoon she returned from the retreat I had some supper ready. After playing with the children and getting them to bed, she said, "We need to talk." She then told me that while at the retreat, God reminded her that He had called her to be a missionary and now it was time to take the next step. She was nervous about bringing up the topic since we had not discussed that phase of our life for quite some time. I was able to tell her that God had been telling me the same thing and we rejoiced about how God was working in our lives. We prayed together and agreed it was time to contact the FMB again. We made that agreement with some excitement and some trepidation. Our first experience with the FMB had not been positive and even though the follow-up a couple of years later was more positive, we still were not eager to go through that process again.

I called Richmond (yes, no email then) and discovered that Dwight Honeycutt was still working with candidates. He was glad to hear from us and he promised to check our record and check with the other candidate consultants to see what we needed to do in order to take the next step and move towards appointment.

When he called me back a few days later, he said the FMB felt the first thing we needed to do was update our biographies. We had anticipated that would be necessary, so we already were working on those. A couple of weeks after we mailed them, he called us again, saying they looked good and the personnel up in Richmond felt the only things left were to tell them where we felt God was leading us to serve and then to update the reference forms.

Lessons from the Journey

One interesting development was that when we applied previously, I was in student work, so that meant I would be appointed as a student minister. But now since I had served as a pastor, I could be appointed as a general evangelist, which was the classification the FMB had for people in my category of ministry. I was a little uncomfortable with the title, since I knew I was not very evangelistic. But they assured me it was just a classification, and I fit the description quite well. This title also expanded our options by allowing us to go anywhere in the world where the FMB had missionaries.

When Nan was young, she met some missionaries from Indonesia with whom she connected, so she liked the idea of serving there. I wanted to go to Africa so I could shoot elephants. Later, when Nan and I were dating and first married, it became a kind of family joke that she was going to Indonesia and I was going to Africa. The family laughed that we could spend furloughs together! Ha, ha. When considering student work, the requests seemed to be centered in South America, Asia, and Europe. We had settled on a school in the northern Italian city of Perugia with a large concentration of students from several European countries, some of which were closed to any kind of missionary presence. Now we had the opportunity to look at other places.

It seemed that God was placing Asia on our hearts. There was not any kind of special light or voice or anything like Paul experienced on the Damascus Road. It was just a feeling that God wanted us somewhere there. So we focused our prayers on Asia. The more we prayed, the more two countries came to mind: Japan and Taiwan.

The Board helped us by sending us some job requests from both countries. From what we read, it appeared to us that in Japan, the missionary would serve as the associate pastor in a Japanese church. In Taiwan, it seemed the missionary was expected to work with local pastors to plant new churches. That was more appealing to me and seemed to fit more with my expectations of what being a missionary was all about. After considering all the options and spending much time in prayer, the quiet conviction grew quite strong: Taiwan is the destination.

Once we settled that question and communicated it to the Board, we were given the good news that we would not have to attend another candidate conference. We were overjoyed with that! Candidate conference, or Group Interview Conference, was stressful and we discovered when we got to orientation we were not the only ones who didn't like it. We met several couples who were not immediately appointed because of what came out in GIC. That is what had happened to us, so you can be sure we were happy to skip that weekend designed to reveal any little weakness or flaw!!!

The last remaining step was to send out references again, which we agreed would be sent out sometime in late April. We came up with the list of five people and contacted them to let them know our plans and what to expect. The FMB's practice was to send forms to be completed and ask those five people for other people who could serve as a reference. So in this small farming community, many people quickly knew of our plans.

A few weeks later, I ran into a man who hadn't been on my list of references. His name was Carl Hardy and he was a long time member of the church. He was not regular in attendance because of health, both his and his wife's. I always suspected there was more to the story since he got around at will, and she was one of the hardest working people I met while in Bellefontaine. Anyway, he bumped into me one day at the post office and told me he had gotten a form to fill out. I said, "That's good. They want to hear from anyone who has anything to say." He said, "Preacher, I told them the truth. I said you are a pretty fair preacher, and a good pastor. But you ain't no evangelist!" I said that was fine, and I was sure they appreciated hearing from someone who told the truth. He asked how I was going to make it "over there" since I was not that great of an evangelist. I assured him I would not be standing on the street corner preaching to folks (at least I hoped I would not have to do that!), that I would be working with pastors to help them start new churches. He was concerned that I didn't know how to do that either. (So was I.) But he finally decided that if I wanted to go, he would not stand in the way of it. I thanked him and went on my way.

We were informed sometime around the middle of May that we had been accepted and would be appointed when the FMB had one of their regular meetings. We were asked to make arrangements to attend the meeting in Glorietta, New Mexico. Once we got that news, Nan and I talked about when to offer my resignation to the church and decided it would be at the end of June.

Those last few weeks were filled with tending to details and saying goodbye to dear friends. It was a time of mixed emotions. There was excitement, sadness, joy, and fear all mixed up together. We had to dispose of a lot of things, primarily furniture. Even though we didn't have much, the pieces we had were special to us. That was before yard sales, so a few pieces of it went to family and the rest went to friends there in Bellefontaine. We packed what we needed and moved in with Mom and Dad in Jackson.

Dad and Owen decided to make a family adventure out of the whole thing. They decided they would rent a camper and we would drive together to New Mexico. That was my family of five plus Mom and Dad and Harriet and Owen: nine of us in the camper together. True to form, Mom and Harriet planned plenty of food. We had sandwiches, cookies, chips, snacks of any kind and things to drink. The camper had a bathroom on board so there was no need to stop for potty breaks. Whenever anyone got hungry, the little fridge would open and something would pop out. The children had a great time because this was well before the days of mandatory seat belts for everyone in a vehicle. There was a very narrow little kind of day bed that extended over the cab of the camper and it provided just enough room for the children to crawl up there and look down the road. They loved that.

The first day, we drove from Jackson, MS to Amarillo, TX. Nan's cousin Frank lived there, and we spent the night in his house. That is, all of us except Harriet and Owen. They wanted to sleep in the camper for some reason. I think they had the idea (never verbalized) that they might like to own one since Owen was now retired. But after sleeping in it, they decided against it.

The next day, we drove on to Glorietta and I was fascinated by the different countryside. It looked like the scenery from all the cowboy movies I watched growing up. I expected to see Indians or cowboys come out from behind every rock. But they never materialized.

We were appointed as missionaries to Taiwan in a very moving service. FINALLY!!!! Twenty-three years after God first placed the desire in my heart to be a missionary, now I was one. Of course, I was still in the USA and had a few more months before I would actually get to the field. But it was a significant moment for both Nan and me. In a lot of ways, it was the culmination of a dream.

To me, a sad note in all this was the knowledge that I was taking Mom and Dad's only grandchildren to the other side of the world. I knew how much they enjoyed the children and I knew how much they would miss them. I found out that my cousin, Lynda Lou Hatchett and her family (husband David and two children) were moving to Jackson about the time that we would be leaving. I prayed that those children would help fill the void created by the absence of my children. God worked that out and Lynda's family did indeed fill the hole that our departure created.

Lessons from the Journey

Through this whole process, once again we saw that there is often a gap between the time God gives us a command until the time when it actually happens. Eventually, we learned not to be surprised by the waiting and preparation period.

I pray for you that you will discover this truth as well, and not be anxious when God gives you a direction to follow. When you don't see things developing as quickly as you thought they would or even in the way you expected them to develop, be patient. God is always at work and does things in His own time.

The Next Step

FIRST TERM

Transition

F ollowing the appointment service, we returned to Jackson for a brief period. We were scheduled to be in Callaway Gardens, Georgia around the middle of September for our orientation/training period. We looked forward to that with great anticipation. We had no idea what to expect, but assumed they would be teaching us how to be missionaries.

From the time we knew we were actually going to be appointed, we started trying to prepare the children for what was ahead. That was difficult since about all we actually knew was that we would move to Taiwan to live and work with the Chinese people.

Nan found pictures of Chinese people to show the children and we talked about differences in living. She also planned some Chinese meals, which was a challenge since we knew nothing about what they ate or how they cooked. Options for any kind of Chinese food were very limited where we lived at that time. She did find some La Choy Chow Mein noodles in a can and put that along with a can of chicken meat and a can of Chinese vegetables (basically bean sprouts and bamboo shoots) and served that along with rice. In time, we got to where we could eat it. The noodles were especially good and I still like them for a snack. In Jackson, we found a Chinese restaurant and ate there a time or two with mixed results.

Finally it was time to head to Georgia, and all of the clothes and other little things we needed to take would not fit into the car. We rented a small U Haul trailer to pull along behind us. It was too far to drive in one day so we stopped that first night in Alabama. We parked at the motel and then walked to a restaurant. Carroll (at three and a half) took one look around and asked, "Where are all the Chinese people?" Pretty logical if you think about it. We had to explain it would be quite a long time until we actually saw Chinese; we had to go to Georgia and stay there a while, then we would return to Jackson to catch an airplane to fly to Taiwan and that would take several days. She was not impressed. We had left home and should be there.

We did make it to orientation and met some wonderful people there. There was one other couple headed to Taiwan, Tilden and Linda Bridges. They had no children and we were with them some. Then there were two couples headed for Japan, and I think one couple headed to Korea and another one to Hong Kong. Another couple was Rich and Janis Dickerman who were headed to Macau. We developed a good friendship with the Dickermans, and we had the opportunity to visit them a couple of times in Macau and they visited us in Taiwan. In orientation, those of us headed to East Asia (Japan, Korea, Hong Kong/Macau and Taiwan) got together a time or two to get to know each other since we were going to the same part of the world.

After forty years, I can't remember a lot of what we studied and discussed while there. Two things do stand out because they were repeated ad nauseum. But they became bywords for us once we reached Taiwan. One was "It's not wrong; it's just different." That could apply to pretty much anything that was not like we knew it to be wherever we were from. It was quite handy when we had to eat strange and different foods, or when we saw six people on a motorcycle or when we sat shivering in the winter in church with all the windows open or any number of other things.

43

Lessons from the Journey

The other statement was that a good missionary has to be flexible. That is necessary because no matter how well you plan, plans have a way of changing. That was often the case. If one remained flexible, then the temptation to get angry lessened a little. That was very needful when dealing with Chinese culture and the sometimes closed-mindedness of certain folks in the church. Oops, seems like I didn't learn the lesson too well. (My coach often told me I had a rebellious streak. More on that later.)

There was one other teaching emphasized that seems to be lacking in today's church. At least I don't hear it preached. That is that wherever we go, we are an incarnational presence. It was pointed out in different ways that wherever we went in a pagan culture, we were a visible witness of God's love. We were encouraged to go to one place, learn the language and culture, and invest ourselves there. We were expected to make relationships with people and in time they would want to know about us. That would open the door to talk about Jesus and His death for our sins. That did work to a limited extent. There were two brothers who became good friends (because they wanted our children to help them with their English), Robin and Chhong-ho (Stephen) Huang. We became friends with their family, but they were the only two of their family who professed faith in Christ.

During the two decades we served in Taiwan, I saw radical change in the philosophy of being an incarnational presence and investing yourself in one place to build long term relationships. But that is another long story not to be discussed here. It has to do with a huge change in mission philosophy by our mission headquarters.

There were many positives to orientation. Along with us, the children made some good friends, like the Dickerman's. They still keep up with each other to a certain degree today. There were some good worship times and some good Bible study times and some really good missionary sharing times. Those of us who had struggled to get appointed could share our stories and receive support and understanding. Knowing that we were not alone and that it was a shared experience took a lot of the pain away. There was some good food we did not have to cook. That caused most of us to gain ten pounds or more in the short time we were there. We did get some good, practical information about moving, shipping stuff, international travel, and other things.

One weekend really stood out. We were not far from a big military base, Fort Bragg, which often had personnel from other countries there training with the US forces. One weekend during the semester, orientation would host an international weekend and invite the soldiers from various countries to visit and meet missionaries going to their country. There was a captain from Taiwan named Ben Song. He came with one of his fellow soldiers, and they brought two stewardesses from China Airlines with them. We had a delightful time meeting them and listening to them talk about Taiwan. But Ben told me one thing that caused me concern. When we went through the serving line, I helped myself to mashed potatoes. He said "No potatoes in Taiwan; only rice. But when you taste Taiwan rice you will never want potatoes again." I doubted that I would never want potatoes again since I really like them. And, to my good pleasure, I discovered that they did in fact have potatoes there.

After we got to Taiwan, we met Ben a couple of times. We even received an invitation to one of the stewardesses' wedding. It was our first wedding and was a very different experience for us. It was held in a big hotel in Taipei, and we had been in language school for about a year. While killing time in the gift shop prior the wedding feast, we knew the two women behind the counter were speaking Taiwanese and talking about us. We didn't understand much of what they were saying, but when we left, Nan turned to them and in

Taiwanese said "Thank you." They were surprised and embarrassed that we apparently knew what they were saying.

While in orientation, we talked with the people in the office who planned our trip to Taiwan. They helped arrange our flights, and they told us we needed to plan on staying a couple of days in Hawaii. In those days, one option for getting to Taiwan was to fly from Los Angeles to Hawaii. We could schedule a late flight out of LA and arrive in Honolulu after the flight for Taipei had departed. That way we could interrupt our travel at no cost to us. The Board had some kind of agreement with a hotel in Honolulu where we could stay for a reduced rate. So we planned that and stayed two nights there. It was a fun time and we enjoyed getting to see the Pacific Ocean. It was all very new and different.

Orientation was finally concluded, and we returned to Jackson for a brief visit and to celebrate Christmas. We had planned to arrive in Taiwan on December 31, 1977. That meant we left Jackson on December 26. I was sad to leave family, but happy to be on the journey at last.

The long period from the time that we decided to contact the board in late February until the time we finally departed in late December had its moments of frustration because it took so long. But we counted it as a natural process of preparation, seeing once again that when God calls, there will be a delay in the decision to act on the call and it actually becoming reality.

I pray that you will remember that little tidbit and don't allow yourself to get frustrated when you have to wait on God. He has a purpose in all things – even in waiting.

In Transit

We shipped the household goods we were allowed to take by ocean freight. That left us to pack suitcases with our clothes and any other small items we would need until our crates arrived. We each had two overseas sized pieces and were allowed seventy pounds in each one. Additionally, since we were going to be three days in transit in two different cities before arriving in Taipei, we also had one carryon bag. Five people and we had fifteen suitcases, ten of which were huge and heavy.

The morning we left Jackson was stressful for me; watching all those bags to make sure they all were tagged correctly and put on the flight; trying to tell all those who came to wish us well on the journey good bye; worrying about getting into the airplane on time…all those things and more were hard on me. Until that morning, I didn't realize that pre-departure nervousness and stress was a problem for me. However it was so noticeable and continued so long that it got to be a family joke: if we were traveling, Daddy was stressed.

We faced a minor delay in travel that I think occurred when we changed planes in Dallas. When we arrived in LA, according to the schedule, we had less than an hour to catch our flight to Honolulu. We didn't know anything about that big airport so we tried to follow the signs as best as we could. We had five suitcases, three little children, I was wearing an overcoat because they told us we would need winter clothes in Taiwan, and we were running through the tunnels trying to find the international terminal and I was afraid we were going to miss our flight. It was not an easy transition. We finally made it, found our gate and discovered that our flight had been delayed by about two hours. Welcome to international travel.

We arrived in LA in the middle of the afternoon so by the time our flight for Honolulu left it was getting close to the time when the children normally went to bed (in Mississippi anyway). We had about a five hour flight. I had not seen our checked bags since we put them on the plane in Jackson. The closer we got to Honolulu, the more stressed I became worrying about collecting our luggage - all fifteen bags - and then getting transportation to the hotel. It was the first time this boy from rural Mississippi had made this kind of journey, and it was all new and unknown to me.

On the flight, Nan, being true to form, had struck up a conversation with the people across the aisle from her. They were a couple from LA going to Honolulu for a vacation. The wife was chatty and the husband was enjoying the free booze. When the plane landed, folks started getting up and opening the overhead bins to get their stuff. Suddenly, the man who had been listening a little to Nan's conversation with his wife stood up in the middle of the aisle and shouted, "Everybody just slow down! We have a missionary here and he needs to get off first!" He then blocked the aisle so people would not push past us. I was able to collect all our carry-on bags and guide the children out of the plane towards baggage claim.

I thought, "I never dreamed a drunk man could be a helping angel." Maybe he was not a real angel, but it sure seemed like one to me at the time.

Our overseas suitcases did not arrive; they had been put on the wrong flight out of LA. So we spent time waiting on them and then filling out forms to identify them. I was assured they would show up and the airline would contact me the next day. After the delay, we somehow made it to the hotel and it was delightful.

We enjoyed our time in Honolulu. The weather was a welcome change from December in Jackson and we thought if this was the climate we would find in Taiwan, we could be happy there. We walked from the hotel to Waikiki Beach. We were all amazed at seeing the unending ocean and the big waves. And the children, being children, got too close to the water without knowing how far up the shore the waves would come when they broke on the beach. Waves didn't run up the shore at the lakes we had visited in Mississippi, and within minutes the children were soaked to the skin. They needed dry summer clothes, so we purchased some Hawaiian things, which they enjoyed wearing in Taiwan until they outgrew them.

This was also our first taste of jet lag. Since we had no schedule, we just slept when we were tired and went out to see the sights when we were not. The folks at the FMB had told us that breaking the trip to Taiwan like this would help us with the jet lag. They were not completely truthful about that, at least for me. We all battled it the first couple of weeks in Taiwan.

After two days in paradise, we boarded a Japan Air Lines flight to Tokyo. Hello, different culture. We were among the very few Caucasians on this flight; it was just us and a lot of Japanese people. Harriet made a friend - or was adopted by a Japanese girl about her age - who spent a lot of the flight showing her how to fold paper: it was her introduction to origami.

One thing about air travel in those days was that the food was good. In addition to the regular meal, they brought snacks around and the meal trays had rolls, butter, cheese and chocolate. If the children were asleep or not hungry when the meal was served, we collected the things that we could stuff in a bag or purse. Those tidbits came in handy when one of the children got hungry later and there was no meal available.

When we left Honolulu, our overseas luggage was not in sight. The agent said, not to worry, it would catch us in Japan. When we got to Japan, those bags were still not in sight. Again the agent said, not to worry, it will catch us in Taiwan. I began to doubt them and wondered how we would replace the items that were lost.

Somehow we made it to a hotel in Tokyo and all passed out. Carroll woke early the next morning around three. I got up with her and she had some rolls and butter. We sat in a picture window and watched it snow. It was quite a lovely sight.

Later in the day, we made it back to the airport and boarded the short flight to Taipei, Taiwan. When we came out of the passport control area, there were our ten huge bags sitting in the middle of the waiting area with a net over them. We then cleared customs and were met by some missionaries. We had finally arrived.

NOTE: What I have written so far and what follows is from memory and follows the theme of significant scriptures that shaped and led me through the years. When we left for Taiwan, both our mothers encouraged us to keep a journal of our life on the field. We both said we might not be able to do that, but we would be writing home often and our letters would be our journals. They thought that was a good idea and promised to keep the letters. So I have two large boxes of those letters in my closet, and perhaps transcribing them will be my next project. Those letters provide more of the daily activities, more of our growing insights into the culture, and more of the children's lives in Taiwan. They were regular until sometime in 1994 when we all got email. From that point forward we depended on email, which was more convenient and quicker, but unfortunate in that those letters were not saved. That was doubly unfortunate because the most dynamic and fruitful years of our service were from around 1992 until 1996. Perhaps God will refresh my memory to recall the most significant events He wants you to know about. You must also be aware that it is a fact of life that as the years pass people tend to forget or block out memories that are hurtful, negative, or stressful and remember things that bring joy and pleasure. My letters home will reveal more than a little frustration about life in Taiwan but here I am focusing on positive memories.

Arrival in Taiwan

"The LORD appeared to Abram (at Shechem) and said 'To your offspring I will give this land.'"
Genesis 12:7

After leaving Jackson, Mississippi and making stops in Hawaii and Japan, we finally arrived in Taipei, Taiwan on December 31, 1977. We were met by some of the missionaries who lived there and transported to what was called Grace Compound. We spent a couple of days there recovering from jet lag and beginning our lives in our new country.

When the business matters in the mission office were complete, we flew again to Taichung. This was our new home for the next year and a half. Following a brief stay in the home of missionaries on furlough, we moved into the Chien Hsing Compound, a series of apartments on Chien Hsing Road. Our neighbors were fellow Southern Baptist missionaries: Sam and Marion Longbottom, Ben and Betty Tomlinson, and Ann Thomason. A very significant missionary lived across town. Her name was Mary Sampson. She had worked briefly at First Baptist Church in Jackson and knew Nan's family. She is the one, along with a Chinese language teacher, who gave us our Chinese names. She also became a good guide and interpreter of Chinese culture and customs for us. Sam and Marion were our official hosts and were a great help in teaching us how to navigate around the city. They helped Nan and me enroll in language school, introduced us at Morrison where the children enrolled and also helped us find a nursery school for Carroll. She decided if Harriet and Robert were going to school, she would as well. There we met Bob and Judy Long and their daughter, Becky, who was the same age as Carroll. Bob and Judy were friends of Sam and Marion. They had served together in Vietnam until they had to leave in 1975. Even though they were veteran missionaries, they had not been in Taiwan much longer than we had. We formed strong bonds of friendship with those two families that lasted through the years.

Sometime in the first couple of weeks, we were told we would have to select a language to study. We thought, "That's easy; we choose Chinese." But it was explained that the Taiwan Baptist Mission worked in three languages: Mandarin, Taiwanese, and Hakka. Mandarin was the language of education and government. Taiwanese was the language of the majority of the population, but was in something of an unacceptable status by the government. Hakka was the language spoken by some farmers who lived in the more rural areas and only a very small minority of the population spoke it.

A little more explanation followed and we were told that prior to the end of World War II, Taiwanese was and had been the predominant language since the first Chinese arrived sometime back in the mid-1600's. When the Japanese began expanding their empire in the late 1800's, they occupied Taiwan. That happened in 1895. They imposed their style of government and education on the Taiwanese people and ruled until the end of World War II in1945. Apparently, the Taiwanese just accepted their presence and did not fight them. As a result, the Japanese gradually relaxed their iron-handed rule and started allowing some municipalities to elect their own government leaders. They also took some of the smartest students to Japan for further education, and when their education was complete, they returned to Taiwan to live and work there. Of course, that all ended when the Japanese were defeated in the war. As a result of that occupation, many of the older Taiwanese people spoke Japanese as well as Taiwanese. It was really interesting to meet people who spoke Japanese, Taiwanese, and English. Some of them were illiterate, and when asked how they knew which language to speak, they said something like, "We don't know languages. We only know that you speak one way to this person and another way to that person." I often thought "Too bad it didn't work that way for me."

At the end of the war, Chiang Kai Shek, who had been leading a battle against the emerging Communist party in China and sometimes attacking the Japanese as well, fled to Taiwan when his army was defeated. The Allies rewarded Chiang Kai-shek by giving him Taiwan as his country. He brought with him about two million refugees from China, which included the remnants of his army and those who were in government. In this way, the Republic of China moved from China to Taiwan. All those who came with the authority to rule spoke Mandarin, and that is why Mandarin was the government language and official language of Taiwan.

We were told that out of the population of sixteen million, approximately fourteen million were native Taiwanese. At the time we arrived, it was estimated that around 80% of Taiwan's residents had Taiwanese as their first language. We prayed about which language to study and chose Taiwanese. I know we discussed the choice a lot, and one deciding factor was that we wanted to speak the language that the majority of the population spoke. Perhaps that was not a real "spiritual" decision, but it was a factor.

We knew that the Foreign Mission Board's major goal for first term missionaries was learning the language and acquiring knowledge about the culture. It would not be possible to minister effectively without these skills. We knew that meant our first term would primarily focus on these two things.

The annual mission prayer retreat was in mid-February and met in the middle of the week. The adult missionaries attended, but the children stayed home because they were in school. Some of the wives with young children also stayed home with their children and that is what Nan did. I went with the other missionaries from our compound to Sun Moon Lake, a resort center in the mountains.

The prayer retreat and mission meeting were the two times during the year that all the Southern Baptist missionaries got together. It was customary in these meetings that the new missionaries would give their testimonies and tell how they had arrived in Taiwan. I was asked to tell a portion of my story in the meeting and Nan would tell her story in the mission meeting that summer.

I was nervous about the whole thing. What did I have to say to veteran missionaries, some of whom had served in China until they had been run out by the Communists? As I prayed, God reminded me that they wanted to hear how I got to Taiwan. Through prayer, God led me to this verse, and I remembered how He appeared to Abram and led him away from his father's home and country. When he left home, he did not even know where he was going. All he had was God's word that He would show him where He wanted Abram to live. I knew that was my story as well. God gave me the desire to serve Him in a foreign country. Now, just like Abram at Shechem, I felt I had arrived. I knew I was where God wanted me to be. That certainty, along with the certainty of God's call, were significant forces that worked to send me to Taiwan and to keep me on the mission field when I was tempted to give it up and return home.

I am convinced God wants all His children to live with the same degree of certainty I had that they are doing what He wants them to do in life. Of course, that is not to say that everyone should be a pastor or missionary. Some are called to be teachers or doctors or business men or home makers. But I feel they should have the peace that they are doing what God wants them to do. I don't understand how anyone can live with peace in this world and function effectively unless that belief is firmly in place in his or her heart. I pray that you will find that certainty and the peace it brings – if you have not already found it.

Meeting Taiwan's Culture

"Abraham replied, 'I said to myself, There is surely no fear of God in this place, and they will kill me because of my wife." Genesis 20:11

During those first few weeks in Taiwan, while the children were in school and Nan was doing her thing in borrowed housing, I would take the car left behind for us to use and drive downtown to try and get a sense of where we lived. One day, I parked the car and was walking down the street, country boy come to town, staring at all the strange sights. As I approached a corner, I heard a large dog growling just around the corner. My first thought was, "German Shepherd." I moved over as close to the curb as possible to avoid the dog and turned the corner. There I saw, not a dog, but a man. He was on his hands and knees swaying back and forth, drooling all over the street, and he was chained to a water faucet sticking out from the side of the building. My heart stopped, adrenalin pumped through my system, and the short hairs all over my body jumped to attention. I was too shocked to even make a mad dash to safety. But the man ignored me and continued to sway and growl. It did not sound like a man imitating a dog's growl, but sounded like a real dog. I was too shocked to even attempt to think what this could be or what it could mean. Needless to say, I did not tell Nan and the children about it; I didn't want to frighten them.

A few weeks after that, when the move to the Chien Hsing apartment was complete, we were enjoying a leisurely breakfast on a Saturday morning. Suddenly we heard the sounds of a parade of some sort on the street in front of the house. We all went out to take a peek.

It was a parade all right, but one unlike any we had ever seen. At the very front walked a man wearing blue warm up pants and a red sash around his waist, with no shirt and no shoes. He looked like he was in some kind of daze or trance as he walked slowly along. I later found out the man in the trance was what the Taiwanese called a tang-gi or spirit medium. He was put in the trance in the temple and then led the parade.

The man was followed by a couple of men who were some kind of helpers, a band of sorts playing Chinese musical instruments, and a crowd of a hundred or so people. The people were all jovial, laughing and waving at the spectators that collected to watch. Some of the crowd carried baskets of some sort of cakes which they handed out to the children or other people on the street. Of course, our children were handed this treat. After the parade passed, I asked a man who was obviously a missionary if the cakes were safe to eat. His response, "Yeah, if you don't mind eating food offered to idols." We later threw them in the trash when we went back inside.

As the parade came to the front of our house, they stopped. The half-naked man (tang-gi) stopped and another man walked up to him and handed him a short-bladed ornamental sword. The tang-gi took the sword and started hitting himself on the forehead with it. After he hit himself a few times, the man who had handed him the sword took a swig of something out of a bottle he carried and spewed it into the tang-gi's face. He stopped hitting himself. Then the man with the bottle and sword took some little squares of yellow paper, wiped the blood from trance man's face, folded them into a kind of triangle, and dropped them into a box his helper carried.

Then he handed the tang-gi a short red baton with short nails sticking out of the last few inches of it. It looked like a studded baton and the tang-gi started hitting himself on the back between the shoulder blades. After a few licks, the helper spewed him in the face with the liquid again, wiped the blood with more yellow paper, folded it, and added it to the box.. (Much later I found out that the papers were taken to the temple where the parade originated, and would be sold to people who came asking for prayers of healing. The papers would be burned along with packets of "spirit money" as an offering to the spirits to effect healing on the afflicted person.) Then the parade marched on for a few hundred yards and stopped again where the process was repeated. I don't know how far they marched in this fashion, but we went back inside.

As I viewed this, my first thought was, "I never saw anything like this in Mississippi." My second thought was, "Seminary did not prepare me for this." That was my introduction to the Taiwanese world view, which included a belief in multiple spirits that could regularly visit the living and had power to bless or curse. But as we discovered later, one of the spirit's visits usually caused negative disruption to daily life because they had not been properly worshipped. The Taiwanese lived in a religious belief system where they knew they had to appease the spirits, but never knew if they had done enough to actually achieve that. Consequently they lived in a state of anxiety and fear, longing for a peace that they could not find.

We knew that idol worship was an important part of the Taiwanese folk religion, and learned that most of the population had one or more representations of some kind of spirit in their homes. It could be pictures of ancestors, an ancestor tablet listing the names of their ancestors, or the idol which represented the particular god this family worshipped. Often these items would be kept together on a worship table or shelf, becoming the center of the family's worship that took place in the home. The family would visit a temple only a few times a year, usually on the birthday of the god they worshipped or to pray for some special need. We did see temples in Taichung, but not too many. Our lives centered around language school and Morrison where Harriet and Robert were enrolled. That changed after our move to Tainan.

The god parade introduced us to a very different worldview, and our understanding of that viewpoint was fed in the following years with more knowledge and additional experiences. Some were mildly interesting and others were downright frightening. The Bible teaches that some people have the spiritual gift of discerning spirits. Often I was glad I didn't have that gift, for I wondered how I could live and function in this world so negatively influenced by spirits intent on harm and disruption. We did see people possessed by these evil spirits and actually had to minister to some later in our time in Taiwan. Eventually, I would meet people on short-term mission trips who would go to churches to share the Gospel and pray for those in need. But they saw so many demons that they could not function if they were on the street all the time. They could only go directly from where they were staying to the church, and straight back again. Nan and I both had a certain awareness of that level of spirit activity, but not to the point that it paralyzed us.

The continuing question I faced was, "How does one make an impact in this culture? What will it take to show God's reality to a people who regularly see negative manifestations of spirit power?" The answer was a long time coming.

Of course, you who read this face the same question. The society around us is increasingly antagonistic to our Christian world view and value system. How will you make an impact in your own circle of friends? How will you communicate the Gospel to those who have not heard it or have not accepted it? Only God can answer that question, and to receive the answer all of us need to nurture the spiritual side of our life.

"I Want to Find That Road"

"Consider it pure joy, my brothers, whenever you face trials of many kinds, because you know that the testing of your faith develops perseverance." James 1:2-3

I confess I didn't think of this verse at the time, but it seems appropriate for many things that happened during our time in Taiwan. The following event was the first of our many trials and seemed large at the time. Perhaps that is because the first trial is new and you don't even realize that it is a trial when it starts. In life, the first of anything is often the most stressful.

Sometime in late summer I was upstairs in our apartment with Carroll (now 4 years old) and she was staring out the window. I asked her what she was looking at. She made no reply, but seemed a little quieter than usual. Her normally happy demeanor was absent and this new quiet, almost moody demeanor lasted several days until she finally told me "I'm looking for that road."

I asked her what road she was looking for because there are a lot of roads in this city and we have seen many of them. She could not tell me which road she was looking for.

Then one day at mealtime, it came up again and I asked again which road she was looking for and she said, "You know, that road that goes to the airplane."

I said, "Oh, do you want to go to the airport and watch the planes take off and land?"

"No," she said. "I want to find that plane that will take me back to Gran."

By then, she had everyone's attention. Harriet and Robert were not saying anything, but I could feel their eyes widen and their ears pop open. They wanted to hear the answer to this.

As best we could, we tried to explain to little minds how we believed that God had a purpose for each of his children and we believed that for us that purpose was to be in Taiwan and serve him here. We reminded them that I was a preacher and that now I would be doing that same kind of work in Taiwan. The hard part of the answer was that we would be here a really long time, but promised that we would eventually return to Jackson for a while. Fortunately we didn't try and explain how long it would be because we knew that to a four year old, three years would not compute. We were not real sure it would compute even to Harriet and Robert so we just stuck to "a long time."

If the truth be told, it is likely that both Nan and I were also feeling a little homesick about that time as well.

Earlier I mentioned that growing up my family often had daily devotions and read from a little book titled "Open Windows." Nan's family had read from this as well. This devotional book was published by the Women's Missionary Union of the Southern Baptist Convention, and every Southern Baptist church member could receive it. One unique feature of this little book was that at the end of each day's devotional there was a list of the Southern Baptist missionaries serving around the world. Each missionary was listed on his or her birthday. That way each missionary was prayed for on their birthday by millions of church members all around the world. When we were in orientation talking with other newly appointed missionaries, we discovered that many were eagerly anticipating their next birthday to see what God would do for them. Frequently during our training, we had visiting missionaries address us, and many of them told us that they would purposefully plan some difficult or significant event for their birthday so they could be sure it would be covered in prayer.

Carroll wanted to find "that road" about the time for school to start. Harriet and Robert were looking forward to returning to school, Nan and I had already set our language school schedule to study in the mornings, and Carroll would return to kindergarten. But when it was time for Carroll to go, she announced she was not going. We tried to encourage her to go, but realized we should not force her to go against her will. Consequently, Nan changed her schedule to be at home in the morning with Carroll. I would be at home in the afternoon and Nan would go to school then. We made all the other adjustments we had to make.

While at orientation, there had been many questions about how the children would adapt to the mission field. We were always told that they will adjust better than the parents, because they are very resilient. Now I started to think they just didn't want to tell us the truth in fear that we would leave before reaching the field. My cynical nature shows up sometimes. That may well be the spot where the first seed of distrust in all institutions was planted. That seed was joined by others through the years and made me struggle at times to keep them from bearing fruit. I knew the fruit would be bitter and disruptive to all that I wanted to do.

Time moved on and we adjusted. I frequently had the feeling that all was not well in our family. I knew Nan and I were struggling with the intensity of trying to learn a very difficult language and making other adjustments to living in this culture. We didn't talk much with the children about how they felt, but I sensed that they were struggling as well.

The days and weeks passed and finally we were at Christmas. It was kind of fun, but it also made us realize how much our holiday centered on the Christmas decorations in stores, Christmas music on the radio, the anticipation of everything about the holiday, and most of all, time spent with family on Christmas day. This first Christmas away from home was kind of a letdown, at least to Nan and me. But we made it through.

January arrived and with it some birthdays. Nan's birthday is January 5 and mine is January 19. I remember wondering briefly if we would see anything unusual on our birthdays, but we didn't have anything in particular that we were praying about. At breakfast on Nan's birthday, Carroll came downstairs and announced, "I like Taiwan. I think I'll stay." What a relief. Her announcement relieved a lot of tension at least for Nan and me. Then on my birthday, she came down to breakfast wearing her kindergarten uniform and announced, "I'll go to school today." So she did.

It seemed like things got a lot easier and happier in our family after that. To be sure, there were still struggles with the language, understanding the culture, learning how to do without certain things and all that. But life was better.

God answers prayers. Jesus said *". . . your Father knows what you need before you ask him."* (Matt. 6:8b) I pray that you will live always trusting that God is watching and working in your life. I have come to believe that most of the time, we are totally unaware of His watch care and protection.

Find Your Place

"Go walk through the length and breadth of the land for I am giving it to you." Genesis 13:17

I chose this Scripture not because I thought God was giving me the whole island of Taiwan, but because it symbolized the principle the Taiwan Baptist Mission followed for new missionaries. Sometime during their first year, the new missionary family would be taken on a tour of Taiwan to introduce them to some of the work being done and the people they could be working with. Usually the tour would include introductions to pastors, missionaries, and locations of churches. The tour also included a look at the Baptist Book Store, the Baptist camp, and the Mass Communications Center. Mass Comm did some publicity for the mission and the Chinese Baptist Convention and some radio programming.

The annual mission meeting was always held on the Morrison School campus located in Taichung. The school had dormitories because they did provide boarding for students who lived in various parts of the island with no high school. It was an event our family came to eagerly anticipate.

During the meeting, the missionaries who had arrived since the previous meeting would be introduced. The first summer we were present, we were introduced along with Tilden and Linda Bridges, our friends from oorientation, and Walter and Jackie Dildy and their two children. (The Dildys were living in Taichung also.) If there were others introduced, I can't remember who they were.

Sometime during Mission Meeting, Walter and I approached Hunter Hammett, our mission administrator about the possibility of us leaving from Taichung to take our trip around the island. At the time, there was no veteran missionary available to lead us, and for some unknown reason, Hunter gave permission for us to take our own tour. Of course, he arranged for the missionaries in the various cities to host us and show us the work there. We left Taichung for Taipei, our first stop. Then we headed from Taipei to Hualien on the East Coast. That is where the adventure began.

Taiwan is an island, and the eastern edge of it is on the Pacific Ocean. The coastal highway was terribly misnamed. It was not a highway; it was more like a gravel road that was one lane most of the way from Hualien to Taitung. We left Hualien headed south for Taitung. The traffic would move along all in one line until it reached a designated stopping point, where traffic police controlled the flow. At these wide places, all the southbound vehicles pulled over to one side, and everyone got out to stretch their legs while the northbound vehicles drove by. Once they passed, the southbound traffic started up and moved along. There were three or four such stops.

We were traveling in two cars, and I was in the lead because Nan had her map and was confident she knew the way. Walter was following me, and I noticed he was mighty close, so I sped up to create a little space between us. But when I sped up, he did as well. That meant we were racing along this narrow road carved along steep mountains with no guardrails. Just feet away from our tires were sheer cliffs that dropped a hundred feet straight down to the ocean. It was quite tense. At the third stop, I got out and asked him why he was following so closely. Jackie laughed out loud and said it was because his face was sweating so bad, the spots under his eyes where his glasses rims touched his face were getting a rash. So he took his glasses off and was trying to stay close enough to me to see where we were going. Frightening. After that, I slowed down and just hoped he could see my brake lights and stop if I needed to stop.

We liked Taitung. It was smaller, quieter, and moved at a slower pace than the other cities which we visited. After a couple of days there, we crossed back over to the west side of the island and spent a few days in Kaohsiung before driving north to Tainan. To me, Tainan seemed more crowded, louder, and dirtier than the other places. In our short time in this city, we saw more temples than we had seen in Taichung, and they seemed somehow more sinister and dangerous. Their more visible presence created a sense of foreboding for me. I didn't want to end up there. But even while we were in town, it seemed God whispered to me, "This is where I want you." I didn't say no, but I didn't clap my hands with joy either.

After Tainan, we returned to our starting point in Taichung. We finished the summer and started the fall routine again. Sometime early in that school semester, we read an article by some noted linguist who said that no one should start learning a new language after age thirty-five. I was thirty-five when we were appointed, and celebrated my thirty-sixth birthday a couple of weeks after we arrived in Taiwan. Nan was thirty five. We already knew that many linguists ranked Taiwanese as one of the two most difficult languages to learn. Russian was the other one. It was not an encouraging article.

We were settling in and getting more comfortable with life in this new country. The children were happy with school and things were good. We celebrated Christmas and then it was time for Mission Meeting again. This time we were all looking forward to it.

As the date got closer, it seemed to me that God's whisper got louder. I couldn't shake the feeling that I should be in Tainan, and now it seemed God was saying it should be this summer. I prayed about it a lot and discussed it with Nan. She didn't have any strong feeling one way or another.

About half way through Mission Meeting I asked Hunter if we could have a talk. I told him I was convinced God wanted us in Tainan. He was happy to hear that. Then I told him I felt like God wanted us to move that summer. I told him I knew we had to complete the language requirement prior to moving to a new city, but felt strongly that we should move now. I asked if that was even possible. He said it was not out of the question. I am sure he discussed it with others in the mission leadership, and we were given permission to move. There was one condition, and that was that we continue with language study since we had not completed the required course work.

After Mission Meeting was over, we started preparations for another move. In late July, we moved into a new house on University Road, built by the mission, which became our home for the next twelve years. Many years later, after we left Taiwan, we looked back and realized that although we moved around a lot and were always in transit, we had lived longer in that house than any other since our wedding.

Through that whole process, God showed me again that He does desire to communicate with His children, and that His plan for me to be a missionary had more dimensions than simply committing to follow the call to Taiwan. Three of my foundational truths were reinforced again: God has a plan for His children, He communicates with His children, and obedience is the normal response to God's communication and leading.

I pray that you will learn to depend on God's leadership in your life and that you will experience the same joy I often felt and still feel when I know He is leading and I am following.

In Tainan

The Taiwan Baptist Mission expected the missionary assigned to a city to concentrate on building relationships with the local pastors and their churches. The mission hoped that the missionary would be able to encourage the pastors to lead their churches to plant a new congregation. When that happened, the missionary would be there to assist in any way possible. That philosophy, while good in concept, did not actually work out as planned.

In Tainan, there were six Baptist churches; five were Mandarin-speaking churches and one was a Taiwanese-speaking church. I was to meet all the pastors, but would focus primarily on the Taiwanese church since that was the language I was studying. That presented a problem since the Taiwanese pastor was in jail for actions against the government. No one expected he would ever be released. His wife and family still lived in the apartment over the sanctuary, which prevented the church from getting another pastor.

We moved into our new house in late July of 1979, barely in time to get settled prior to the children starting school. There was no Morrison Academy in Tainan, but there was a school. During the Vietnam War, roughly from 1966-1975, the US military had a large presence in Taiwan primarily centered in Taichung and Tainan. Due to the large number of military dependents, the Department of Defense started a school on the airbase in Tainan. (The children of military personnel in Taichung attended Morrison.) The DOD schools allowed any child of an American citizen to attend, so that is where our children went. Carroll started kindergarten, Robert was in third grade and Harriet was in fifth grade. The results were mixed: some teachers were good and some were not; some classmates were good and some were not. But they survived.

I continued my language study by driving to Kaohsiung (about an hour's drive south from Tainan) after dropping the children at the school. The mission arranged for Nan to have a tutor who came from Kaohsiung so she could continue her studies as well.

After the children completed their school day, there was a bus from the Asian Vegetable Research and Development Center that brought some of their children to school, and our children would catch a ride home after school with them. The AVRDC was about five miles north of Tainan, and we made friends with several families there through the years.

Even though at times the routine was hectic, we soon adjusted and became comfortable there. The children greatly enjoyed exploring the area around our house. We lived directly across the street from one of the major universities, and at that time it was easy for them to walk over to the campus or ride their bicycles there and just look around. They found one of the old city gates on a back part of the campus, and what we believed was an old Japanese pill box left from World War II. There were also plenty of students around, and some of them were bold enough to approach our children and ask to practice speaking English. In that way we met Robin Huang and later his younger brother, Stephen. They both came to be very good friends and remained so until they graduated from the university. Even following their college days when they went to America to study, we maintained contact with them. Their family sort of adopted us and we got to know their parents as well. Their father spoke good English, but their mother didn't, so we got a lot of practice speaking Taiwanese with her.

Lessons from the Journey

Trinity Baptist Church was started by some American servicemen a number of years prior to our arrival. It started as an English congregation, but they soon acted on a vision of also starting a Chinese congregation. Both congregations were meeting when we arrived and we visited the English service a time or two. By that time, there were only one or two Americans left in the community who attended the church; the congregation was all English-speaking Chinese. President Jimmy Carter had recognized China as the only legitimate government of all the Chinese people effective January 1, 1979. Following that, the US military started leaving Taiwan and by the time we arrived in Tainan that fall, there was only a small contingent remaining. The English congregation had no pastor, so most of the preaching was done by Bob Beard who was the principal of the branch of Morrison Academy in Kaohsiung. The pastor of the Chinese congregation was Peter Wang and we developed a good relationship in the following years.

He introduced me to the other Baptist pastors in the city. I discovered that they met once a month, usually at one of the churches, to discuss events in their churches, pray for each other, and then go out and have lunch together. The host pastor chose the restaurant, the menu, and paid for the meal. It was a good way to get to know these men. In these lunches, I was introduced to some food I hope to never have to eat again. That list was led by bitter melon, sea slug and chicken intestines. Nan and I began to think that the Chinese ate such weird foods due to the numerous famines in their history. When a person is hungry they will eat anything that will not kill them. I guess over the years they developed a taste for some of those strange things.

It was not long until I was asked to serve as pastor of the English congregation. Mission policy was that new missionaries were supposed to focus on language learning and were allowed one hour a week of ministry that was not language-related. Even though I knew the church's request went against that policy, I asked anyway. For some reason, I was given permission to pastor that congregation. Perhaps because the mission leadership knew the history of the church, or perhaps because they knew that my only responsibility would be preaching on Sunday morning, they allowed it. I did have to agree to continue my Taiwanese study. In retrospect, I must admit that my language acquisition did suffer. I studied, but lacked the opportunity to worship in a Taiwanese church and regularly engage in using Taiwanese in conversation. That really hindered my understanding of spoken Taiwanese.

Nan's day centered around her language study and keeping house. She thrived by studying with a tutor. She chafed under the methods used by our language school. Their philosophy was to memorize the vocabulary, memorize the sentence patterns, memorize everything. Don't try to understand it, just memorize it and practice it. Then when you speak, it will come out. One of my friends said "Learning Chinese is a lot like throwing mud on a wall. Most of it slides off, but over time, it begins to stick. Then you can use it."

Nan learned in a different way, and now she had more control over how to study, as well as the subject matter. She noticed early in our stay in Tainan that it was an old city and had some old historical sites. There was actually an old city gate we drove by regularly. She wanted to know more. As a result, over time, she began telling her instructor, "We need to take a field trip!" She would have already picked out the spot, whether it was a historical site or an old temple. Her tutor would explain what Nan was seeing and why it was significant. I believe the teacher got really interested as well and did research herself. This really opened the door for new insights into our adopted home for Nan, and we all benefitted from her knowledge in this area.

In Tainan

We noticed there were a lot of temples in Tainan, and it seemed that many of them were old. As Nan researched the historic sites and architecture, she included a few of the old temples. One was the Confucian Temple, the oldest in Tainan and one of the oldest in Taiwan. Confucianism as a religion grew from the teaching of the ancient philosopher Confucius, who was born some five hundred years before Christ. One of the primary tenets of his teaching was family loyalty, and that led to the veneration of ancestors. From there it was a short step to ancestor worship, which is a major element in Chinese life and an important part of all their religious practices.

Another temple in town seemed to be a mix of Buddhism and Taoism, and emphasized the worship of spirits prevalent in both of those religions. Those spirits could be spirits of gods or spirits of departed ancestors. This temple seemed to be well known by many missionaries, even those who did not live in Tainan. Its walls were covered with pictures showing in graphic detail the tortures in the different levels of the Buddhist hell. It was a scary place indeed, and caused our children - and even some of the missionaries - to have nightmares. The missionaries called it the Temple of Hell. Until Nan found it out, nobody knew that its real name was "The Temple of the Kind and Holy God of the East Mountain." We found the contrast in these two names to be both comical and sad, because they emphasized to us the dichotomy of the Chinese worldview: the disconnect between the original worshipful intent and the actual fear-filled practices.

A third temple she researched was a temple complex with two parts connected by a narrow alley. One part was the Temple of Matsu, a female goddess of the sea worshipped enthusiastically by those who lived along the coast. The other was dedicated to the God of War, Guan Gong, who was considered one of the stronger gods in Taiwan. There was a large courtyard as a part of the temple complex on one side of the God of War temple, and it was located on a street filled with shops where one could purchase worship paraphernalia. The street was wide, but had little vehicular traffic. There were shops where one could stand and watch idols being carved and painted for sale. Other shops sold candles, brass incense pots, incense cones and sticks, and paper money to be burned as an offering to the spirits. There were a couple of shops that specialized in making articles out of bamboo strips covered with colored paper. These items included cars, televisions, clothing and houses. They would be burned as offerings to the ancestors, so the departed ones would be happy wherever they were. When asked how the dead people would use those things, the pragmatic answer was quite simple: "The departed ones are spirits who live in the spirit world. When the items are burned, the smoke goes to the spirit world and there the ancestors can get the things we send them. They will know we love and remember them by those offerings."

Nan's research made us more aware of the pagan environment in which we lived. It was sobering to understand we were "in Satan's backyard" trying to witness to God's grace and love.

She found the local markets and shopped for all our meals, practicing her language skills in the process. It was not long before she got a bicycle and would ride to the market, where she built some relationships with the vendors. As her language skills progressed (and even before they did), she would often entertain the ones who knew her. They soon learned they could joke with her and she would joke with them. Even though the routine of having to prepare all the meals from scratch got tiresome at times, she loved it. She did relish a challenge and took great joy in discovering ways to use local ingredients to make things we could no longer get. She experimented with multiple ingredients to make favorite foods, even inventing a taco sauce that we all still like. But she refused to serve it when we were in the States because "it was not real Mexican food." She figured out how to make wide pasta noodles so that we could have lasagna, cooked up a delicious sauce for it, and even used dried Chinese fruits to make fruit cake. And this was all before the day of Google!

Since there were very few expatriate children in town, she became quite inventive about making times for family games and filling summer days with all kinds of activities. She read a book entitled *Super Summer,* which gave her the idea of transforming our summers into times of fun productivity. The children delighted in setting summer goals like which books to read, how long to practice their instruments or sports, and what projects to work on. Once a week, they planned an outing somewhere. She reasoned that since we were on an island and since we were on the western side of the island, there should be a beach on the west side of town. She explored until she found it, and then took us out there for special picnics.

The most famous – or infamous – activity was the Bike Hike. This happened at the beginning of our second summer in Tainan. By then, Nan had driven around town enough to get a sense of how the city was laid out, where the different roads led and how they connected. She found a little park on the south edge of town that looked like it would be a good place for a picnic. So she planned a bike hike to ride bicycles down to the park, eat a picnic lunch and then return home by a different route. It sounded like a grand adventure. Little did we know.

What she thought would be about a three-hour outing turned out to be more like six hours. Six hours in the hot Taiwan tropical sun, riding along on the edge of roads crowded with traffic, and wondering if the trip would ever end. The children had a friend, Nora Lin, whom they enticed to accompany us. When the trip was over, I wondered if she would ever speak to any of us again.

After we finally returned home, tired and hot, but safe, I got on my motorcycle and traced the route. When I returned, I asked Nan how far she thought the hike was. She thought it was about four miles. I said, "Try FIFTEEN miles!" It was quite a test, but provided many, many different kinds of comments for years to come.

Late that fall, the lone remaining American in the church approached me after the morning service and told me there was an American lady in the hospital and I needed to visit her. I did and met Ruth Lin, a Texan. She was a Baptist nurse who had come to Tainan some years previously to work in a leprosarium in Tainan. One of the patients was a Taiwanese man named Frank. Long story short, they fell in love and married and she remained there with him. By the time I met her, Frank had been cured and was quite healthy. Ruth was very happy to meet a fellow Southern Baptist, and in the course of the conversation, she said that we needed to get all the missionaries together. I knew Nan and I were the only Southern Baptist missionaries in town, but assumed there were missionaries of other denominations around somewhere. Ruth knew them. We agreed it would be good to get together, so once she was released from the hospital, she contacted those she knew and we had our first meeting at hers and Frank's house. That began a regular meeting each month for fellowship, shared meals, and mutual encouragement among all of the missionaries in Tainan. Every month, we rotated the meeting venue, so eventually we visited in all the missionaries' homes. All of us enjoyed those times together.

During that first term, both our parents came to see us. Mom and dad came while we were still in Taichung, and Harriet and Owen came while we were in Tainan. They both visited more than once while we lived in Taiwan and their visits always encouraged us.

In Tainan

As I said earlier, the house we moved into was new. There were actually two houses built side by side sharing the same back yard. They were directly behind En Tze Baptist church, and the original intent had been for the missionary to live in one side and the local pastor to live in the other side. I don't know how it happened, but the house next to us had been rented out to a family who had opened a cafeteria for students. This meant that beginning around 11:00 am the students gathered, and the little lane on which we lived was almost impassable until around 12:30 pm. The students rode their bicycles and would block our front gate and the entrance to our garage. It was an irritation that we tried to learn to accept and live with. Practicing patience is never fun. Most of the time it was all right, but sometimes it was troublesome enough to make anger rise up in me. This was a challenge for someone who came to tell the "lost and dying world" about a God who loved them, but we lived with this situation for the final two years of our first term.

A Far Country

*"... the younger son... set off for a distant country and there squandered his wealth in wild living. ...
When he came to his senses...."* Luke 15:13, 17

During our second year in Tainan, things were not real good in the Sugg household, at least as far as Nan and I were concerned. For reasons we didn't understand, the whole family was feeling some level of discontent, anger, and fear. Possibly it was the constant pressure of our living conditions, because they were so different from anything we had ever experienced. No doubt, the separation from our family was wearing on us. We weren't aware of it, but we were under spiritual attack from the enemy, who didn't want us in his territory trying to share the good news about Jesus. All these things and more combined to create the phenomenon of culture shock, which we adamantly denied we were experiencing. And the straw that broke the camel's back was the daily presence of flocks of students around our front door, which made it extremely difficult for us to even walk down the lane in front of our house around noon. Maybe it was just Nan and me, but I think all of us felt it to one degree or another. As a result, we continued to take it one day at a time and try to make the best of a bad situation.

Dealing with the constant presence of all those students gathering around the front door was wearing. And then one day, the city decided that the benjo (a type of open sewer) opposite our door was too narrow and needed to be widened. So they dug a ditch there and for a couple of days it was open and receptive to whatever came its way. Added to the ever-present bicycles, this made our already-narrow lane even more cramped. The next time I needed to run an errand, I knew it would be a challenge to get the car into the lane. But I had to go, so I carefully backed out of the garage. As I was turning the wheel to straighten out, it happened. The front wheel on the driver's side dropped into the ditch. I could envision my car being stuck in the road for hours blocking all traffic while I tried to find some wrecker to come pull me out of the ditch. I was furious and getting madder by the second. I was so mad. I went inside and asked Nan to come help me. She saw my plight and was at a loss for words. I told her to get in, start the car, and when I picked up the front a little, just ease forward and then I would be on my way. She looked at me skeptically, but she complied.

She got in and started the car. I put my back against the driver's door, my hands in the wheel well, planted my feet on the edge of the ditch, and lifted. I was able to lift it enough that she could ease forward out of the ditch. Then she got out, I got in and drove away on my errand.

I had always heard that an adrenaline rush would give a person superhuman strength. That day, I found out that anger could do the same thing.

A lot of the Chinese were a little afraid of me anyway because I was so much bigger than they were. I am sure that when they looked out their windows and saw me pick up the front end of our van, their fear increased a lot. So much for being a "gentle giant."

Several months later, I had to attend a lunch meeting with the local pastors. By this time, I was aware that our lane would begin filling up with students on bicycles. It was basically impossible to get the car out of the garage from about 11:00 am until around

12:30 pm. The meeting was scheduled for 11:30 am, so I planned to take the car out around 10:50 in order to avoid the rush.

Due to a phone call from the mission office, I was later leaving the house than I had planned. When I opened the garage door about 11:20 to back the car out, the driveway was already filling up with bicycles. I tried to move them, but it was like bailing water out of a hole dug on the beach; every time you pulled out a bucket of water, another one poured in. Finally, I was able to stop a couple of young men in their mad rush to be first in line, and they assisted me by keeping the tide back long enough for me to back out. Then I had to slowly force my way through the oncoming waves of students headed for lunch. Finally, I made it out of the narrow lane and turned onto the main street where the crowd thinned out some. Even so, it was lunch hour, and students were slowly making their way to wherever they were going. When there were that many of them, they paid no attention to the bicycle lanes on the sides of the road; they just took over and filled the entire width of the street. If you were in a car, you moved at the pace of the students.

I made it to the red light and could see freedom just on the other side of the intersection. Once the light changed, I would be able to drive at a normal rate and be only a few minutes late for the meeting. There was a line of female students on their bicycles stretching across the entire width of the traffic lane immediately in front of me. They were having a wonderful time chatting and giggling about whatever.

Just as the light changed and the bicycles started out, the young lady in the middle of the line got her skirt caught in the chain of her bicycle. She stopped, giggling about it, and all of her friends stopped as well. They all giggled a lot. Only a quick stomp on the brake prevented me from driving into them. They took their time – standing in the middle of the lane, giggling – and finally extracted her skirt from the chain. Then they drove on. I only missed two light changes.

I was fuming and suddenly I heard God say, "You are in a far country."

I responded, "That's right and you are the one who put me here!!!"

"No, that's not the country I am talking about."

"What kind of country are you talking about if not Taiwan?"

"You are in the far country of anger."

I had no comeback to that statement.

I drove on to the designated church, met the pastors, and had lunch with them. Following lunch, I returned home and went on with my daily routine. But the memory of that conversation lingered in my mind for weeks. God and I had several more conversations about the experience.

The gist of those conversations was always basically the same. God encouraged me to let the anger go and return "home," that is to my relationship with Him. I brought up people I knew who were also displaying anger, or sorrow, or laziness, or a general bad attitude. Always His response was the same: "I am not talking to them; I am talking to you."

Finally, after too long of a time, I gave in to His persistent plea. I offered Him my anger and asked that He take it away. Looking back, I am not sure exactly when it left. I don't know if it was immediately or if it took a few days. But very soon, my attitude changed radically for the better. And I never knew of anything specific that triggered the anger. Of course, being late for the meeting and the frustration over the situation in the lane in front of my house and almost running down those students was the catalyst that brought it roaring to the surface. I guess it was just the accumulation of a lot of things that had been needling me for some time. Whatever it was, it was now gone.

Lessons from the Journey

This experience emphasized for me in a very personal way that separation from God is not geographical; it is attitudinal. God desires a deep, intimate relationship with all His children, but there are times when our decision to hold on to feelings that do not honor Him hinders the relationship we should enjoy. In His sovereignty, God gives us the freedom to choose between holding on to negative feelings and attitudes or releasing them. That is really an amazing freedom if you think about it.

I also discovered that in order to release the negative attitudes, I must be willing to give it up. That sounds so easy, so simple that it should not have to be stated. Yet in reality, it often is extremely difficult. The flesh is strong and is always demanding attention. Sometimes we justify our anger or sadness or loneliness or whatever else by focusing on what caused it. Usually it is some offense done to us by someone else. It feels kind of good to hang on to it. But that interferes with our relationship with God and, ultimately, with our relationships with everyone else.

Choosing to release that anger reinforced the pattern that was set the first time I chose to obey the command of Christ and be baptized. The pattern of submissive behavior was fed each time I chose to obey any command or chose to "do the right thing" in my Christian life. I am convinced that this pattern, once set, became stronger and stronger each time I chose the right attitude and obeyed a direction for holy living. I also believe that as the pattern grows stronger, each act of obedience or right choice makes it easier to recognize the need for such decisions in the future and enables one to continue to follow the direction that is already set.

I pray that you will be quick to identify any attitude that comes between you and your heavenly Father and quickly give it to Him. He is able to take it from you if you are willing to let it go.

Winding Down

By early spring of 1981, we knew we were almost through our first term and I think we were all happy about that. Soon we would be returning to Jackson to see family and friends again. We had experienced a lot, learned a lot, and now knew that we could indeed handle life on the mission field.

The children had adapted to the different schools and had done well. There were struggles, to be sure, but they had worked just as we had worked. Our family was a tight knit unit and we shared a lot of good times together.

About six months before we were scheduled to leave for our first furlough, our business manager told us that Art and Ruth Robinson were discussing leaving Morrison where they had worked for many years. They wanted to focus their remaining years in Taiwan on working with local pastors and churches. Art would become the pastor of Trinity and Ruth would teach English in the churches. If everything was approved, the house next to us would be their residence and we would be rid of the cafeteria. That was wonderful news! It was also good news to me that I would no longer be serving as pastor of the English language church and could focus on what I had come to do – working with the Chinese and hopefully helping to start a new church. After a month or so, we were informed that it was definite – Art and Ruth would move following Mission Meeting. We planned on departing as soon as Mission Meeting was over and they would live in our house until their goods arrived and their house was all set up.

A couple of months prior to departing Tainan, one of the pastors asked me to preach in his church. He said it would be good for me to preach one time in Taiwanese before I went home and it would be a good way for the people in his church to get to know me. I reminded him that his church was a Mandarin speaking church and I was studying Taiwanese. He informed me that the only reason it was a Mandarin church was that the missionary who started it was a Mandarin speaker and all the members spoke Taiwanese. I knew then I had to get a sermon ready.

I was still in language school and could enlist the assistance of my teachers to guide me in how to arrange the words for the sermon. I made my sermon outline with the scriptures I wanted to use and then tried to put it into Taiwanese. I was shocked to discover how poor my Taiwanese was.

The teachers worked hard with me, and finally I had a draft of the sermon. It was written out, and I planned on going over it until I could preach without the manuscript. I had never preached using a manuscript and was uncomfortable trying to preach that way. But try as I might, I simply could not remember the word order and sentence construction.

The appointed day for the sermon arrived, and I was really nervous. We were about ten days away from departing Tainan for almost a year. Due to my inability to grasp what I had written in order to preach without the written notes, I read the sermon. When I finished, I wondered if even God knew what I said. I could tell by the looks on everyone's faces that they surely had no idea of what this crazy American was mumbling about. It was awful. What was intended to be an encouragement turned into a source of failure and fear. That was not a good mindset in which to go on furlough!

For the next ten months, I wondered how in the world I was going to do what God had called me to do. Dread filled my mind whenever I thought about returning to Tainan.

Lessons from the Journey

When we arrived in Jackson, First Baptist Church had rented a furnished apartment for us, and God arranged for that apartment to be very near family members. Not only were all four grandparents within a ten-minute drive, but also the home of Nan's sister Georgia was practically in our backyard. It was easy for the children to get with their cousins, who were similar in age, whenever they wished. We enjoyed visiting with family and other friends we had not seen in some time.

One of the main reasons for the FMB to provide time away from the field for us, in addition to just getting away from the stress of living in a different culture, was to promote missions in local churches. The state Baptist paper would list missionaries on furlough and the Mississippi Woman's Missionary Union had addresses for us all. Churches contacted us to arrange for us to speak to them about our work and the need for support. We both enjoyed doing that, and from around the middle of October until late December, most of our Sundays were spent away from Jackson. Sometimes we would be together, but often we would be in separate churches promoting missions and our big mission offering, the Lottie Moon Christmas Offering. That one offering provided about half of the mission board's annual budget so it was important to have good support.

SECOND TERM

Park Road Church

"I came to you in weakness and fear, and with much trembling. My message and my preaching were not with wise and persuasive words, but with a demonstration of the Spirit's power, so that your faith might not rest on men's wisdom, but on God's power." 1 Corinthians 2:3-5

Our first furlough was wonderful. We enjoyed good times with family and friends. The children participated in lots of school activities, while Nan and I enjoyed going to different churches to talk about missions and encourage the members to support the Lottie Moon Christmas Offering.

While on furlough, I frequently remembered the very traumatic experience of preaching that first sermon in Taiwanese. I knew that when we returned to Taiwan I would be expected to preach regularly and also knew I simply could not do that. Sometime during the first three months at home, God led me to this verse. I could identify with Paul and I took this as God's promise to me that my preaching would not depend on my own wisdom and ability, but on His unique power. This may have been the first time I took a verse and claimed it as God's promise to me. I clung to it like a drowning man clinging to a life preserver.

We returned to Tainan in February of 1982. The first Sunday we were able to do so, we attended Park Road Church. I had located it previously and knew how to find it. When we went in, our family of five doubled the Sunday morning attendance. One man there was named Deacon Ong, and he was the only member of his family who was still attending. When I returned that night, by myself I doubled the Sunday night attendance. There was only me and Mrs. Gau, the pastor's wife. As I mentioned previously, her husband was in prison for sedition: he had brought some forbidden printed material into Taiwan and it was discovered during the customs check. Mrs. Gau and two of her three children still lived above the church sanctuary. Their oldest daughter was already married and living elsewhere in town.

Mrs. Gau's position was that she and her husband had used their own money to construct the church building and the apartment was their home. She refused to vacate it to allow another pastor to come lead the church. Consequently, Park Road could not get another pastor, so other Taiwanese pastors and speakers would come and preach at the regular worship times.

When I arrived, she was insistent that I begin preaching every Sunday immediately. We discussed that expectation for some weeks and I started to preach but not on her schedule. At first, I would preach once a month on Sunday morning. My sermon preparation was the same as it had been for that one Taiwanese sermon I had preached right before furlough: I worked out what I wanted to say and then translated it into Taiwanese. It was written out and I had to preach from that cursed manuscript. It never went well.

One night after I had been preaching once a month for about three months, I arrived for the evening service. Mrs. Gau met me at the door and said, "The pastor who was supposed to preach tonight cannot come. You will preach." She kind of laughed. I tried to explain that was impossible because I needed time to prepare. She laughed again. But I knew when the singing was over she would call on me. I was so flustered I had great difficulty even finding the book of John in my Taiwanese Bible. But finally I did and located one verse I could read. I hoped I could make some kind of understandable comment on it. I may have stood up talking for five minutes - certainly no longer than that. I was mortified. Much to my dismay, the same thing happened again about four weeks later. It had the same result.

Sometimes I am a slow learner, but I do learn. Following that second Sunday night farce, I went home and found a scripture and worked up a short devotional on it. I wrote an outline for it and stuck it in the back of my Bible. Sure enough, about a month later, the same thing happened. But this time, at least I knew what I wanted to say. It still didn't come across very well, but I had a minor degree of satisfaction in knowing that I had made a valiant effort. One of the consequences of those spontaneous Sunday night talks (I would never call what I did a sermon) is that today more than thirty years later I still feel unprepared if I go to any church anywhere without a sermon outline in the back of my Bible. If you think those were traumatic days, you would be correct.

There was another consequence to the repeated requests. After six or seven months, I was still using a manuscript to preach and still knew nobody understood what I was trying to say. On another designated Sunday that I was supposed to preach again, I had been praying hard in my study prior to departing for church. The family gathered and headed to the car. I lagged behind to lock the front door. In that moment, with the key inserted in the lock, filled with dread yet again over preaching from that manuscript, a series of thoughts flashed through my mind:

I have never preached from a manuscript.

I am uncomfortable preaching from a manuscript even when I am speaking in English.

I hate using a manuscript.

I don't like the constriction of the manuscript.

I like to feel free for God to whisper to me about a verse or thought in a spontaneous way.

And finally...

If that woman is stupid enough to continue to ask me to preach with no preparation, then I am stupid enough to preach without this blankety-blank manuscript. With that, I threw the manuscript through the front door and locked it. That day, I stepped up into the pulpit without a single note. I couldn't tell that the "sermon" was any worse than if I had used the manuscript. Freedom at last!

Early in my time in Taiwan, during a regular Evangelism Department meeting with other missionaries, I heard some of the men joking about how long it took them before they could preach and the congregation could understand them. I remember one veteran who spoke both Taiwanese and Mandarin – a man I respected – say laughingly that it was two years before anyone could understand his sermon. When I heard that, I thought, "I hope I don't have to wait that long." For me, it was somewhere around the year and a half mark.

By the time that term was complete, I was preaching three times a week in Taiwanese using only the notes I made in English. I counted that as a direct result of the promise God made to me before that term began. I know I did not preach with signs and wonders as did Paul, but I did gain a lot of freedom and confidence in doing what God had sent me to do. It was quite satisfying.

Obedience Brings Blessings

"Why do you call me Lord, Lord, and do not do what I tell you?" Luke 6:46

After we began attending Park Road Church, former members started coming back, including Deacon Ong's wife and three sons. He and I developed a good relationship, and I was able to depend on him to gain understanding about the situation at the church. Things were rocking along pretty well until one Sunday when I arrived at church and discovered there had been an incident.

The Gau's son Chhong-Chi often did things with the young people in the church, especially the boys. There was a side building that was part educational and part recreational. The thing that made it a recreational building was that it had a ping pong table on the ground floor.

On Saturday afternoon deacon Ong's son was at the church playing ping pong with some other boys, and Chhong-Chi was supervising. Deacon Ong's son said he had to use the bathroom, so he went into the house to the second floor. Apparently he was there for some time, and finally Chhong-Chi went to find him. He found the boy in his room poking around. One thing led to another and Chhong-Chi accused Deacon Ong's son of stealing money from his dresser drawer. Of course, Deacon Ong's son denied it, and I never found out if any money was actually missing or if it was just misplaced. But the result was that the son of the deacon was accused of stealing and that disrupted everything at the church.

Deacon Ong was understandably embarrassed to the point that he announced he was going to stop coming to church. He said the Bible says that if a man cannot control his own family then he cannot be a deacon. That meant he could no longer be a deacon and there was no reason for him to come to church. Mrs. Gau got one of the pastors from the next city to come up and try to sort things out. He must have done a good job, because the end result was that Deacon Ong decided to take a month off from the responsibility of being a deacon. His family would continue to attend church, but he himself had very little to do with it. He would come into the sanctuary just before the sermon began and leave during the closing prayer.

This happened sometime in early 1983, and by this time I was the main preacher. I was preaching almost every week on Sunday morning, every Sunday night and most of the Wednesday night prayer services. As I prayed about what to do during that month, I preached every sermon I could think of on forgiveness and reconciliation, all to no avail.

I well remember getting up one Monday morning and thinking, I have to preach again on Sunday and have no idea what to preach on. I went into my study and began praying. As I prayed, I felt led to John 13. So I got up from my knees and looked at John 13. This is where Jesus washed his disciple's feet. Well, that shocked me. I closed my Bible and said, "No way. I have never even seen a foot washing ceremony." I left the study and went about my other activities.

Tuesday, back in the study and in prayer again, John 13 came back to me. Again, I closed my Bible and walked away.

Lessons from the Journey

By Wednesday, I was getting a little anxious. So as I prayed I did actually read the chapter. I even prayed something like, "Lord, you know I have never done anything like this. I don't know how to go about it."

Over dinner that night, Nan asked as she often did what I was thinking of preaching Sunday. I was evasive and didn't tell her what was going on.

By Thursday, it was getting serious. By now, I was even looking back through sermons I had previously preached to see if there was anything I could resurrect. Nothing.

Friday. It was time to do something. So I got on my knees and said, "OK, Lord. You win. I'll do it." So I began thinking about how it might work. The rest of that day, I prayed and tried to figure out the logistics of the ceremony.

On Saturday, I told Nan what I was going to do. Of course, she pitched in with her suggestions and helped me collect the things I would need: a basin for the water, something to catch the water in, and lots of towels.

On Sunday morning, I arrived a little early and rearranged the furniture. We had wooden pews made from slats so they were light and easy to move around. They normally were arranged in rows. I put the pews we would need in a sort of circle. Of course, when the people came in, they wanted to know what was going on. I just told them they would see.

When I started to preach, I read the appropriate parts of John 13. The sermon was basically, "Jesus washed his disciple's feet and now I am going to wash your feet." This was totally unheard of in a Chinese church. It was very unusual for a pastor to do anything like this and unthinkable for a missionary to do that.

I filled the basin and went around the room washing everyone's feet. All the way I was thinking, "Lord, help me get through this." When I finished, I returned to the pulpit emotionally spent and was about ready to lead the closing prayer when Deacon Ong jumped up.

I don't remember all he said, but the main thing went something like this: "When Pastor Song said he was going to wash our feet, I thought, 'he will never wash my feet' and I wanted to leave. But it was like I couldn't leave; something held me in place. So when he got to me, I allowed him to wash my feet. And when he did, it was like something started in my feet and went up through my body and right out the top of my head. You all know there have been some bad things said, and now I apologize. I feel so free! I want to take everyone out to lunch." And he did.

I was in shock. I don't know what I expected, but it was not this. Deacon Ong and Mrs. Gau got their difficulties straightened out and things were good at Park Road again.

One thing I learned through this process was something I should have already known. God is not afraid to push you out of your comfort zone. (After all, He sent a country boy to urban Taiwan!)

The second lesson, which is very important, is that when we determine to obey God, He will give us a test to see if we actually mean it. And it will most likely be to do something we would never think of doing on our own. If not that, it will be something that offends us in some way. The offense comes when we feel like God wants us to forgive someone for hurting us or letting go of a bad attitude. It is not easy, but this is a part of our "being conformed to the image of Christ."

Another thing I learned is that when we obey God, someone is going to be blessed. It may be you or someone else. But God is certainly going to bless. I found that to be true many times. I pray for you in your life that you will learn to identify God's voice when He communicates with you and then determine to follow His leading. In this way you will give honor to your heavenly Father.

New Routines, New Experiences

W hile we were on furlough, the Tainan International Dependents School closed because of lack of students. We had known when we left for furlough that this would happen, because there were no longer any military dependents in the city who needed the school. When we got back to Taiwan, the children started attending Morrison Academy in Kaohsiung, the next city south of Tainan. The Asian Vegetable Research and Development Center just north of Tainan was sending their children to Morrison and we made arrangements for our children to ride their bus to school. It worked out quite well although it made for a long day.

Art and Ruth Robinson did make the move to Tainan the summer we were gone, and Art took over the responsibility for Trinity Church. I introduced them at their first Co-worker's Meeting, which was a gathering of all six Baptist pastors in the city. From that point forward, the three of us continued to attend the monthly Co-workers meeting. (Ruth was the only wife that attended these meetings.) Every year, I also attended the annual Chinese Baptist Convention meeting and the annual island-wide Coworker's meeting, which was a spiritual retreat. Both of these were meetings that missionaries would normally attend, in part to know what the Chinese Convention and pastors were discussing and in part to connect with these church leaders. An unwritten portion of the missionary job description was to be a chauffeur and bus driver for the pastors, who did not own cars. They usually traveled around town on motorcycles. This transportation responsibility was often time-consuming, but did provide an opportunity to continue to build relationships.

One of the realities that we faced was how to provide a meaningful church experience for our children. Nan and I felt it would be easier for them to go to Trinity Church, since the services were in English, than for them to attend the Taiwanese church with us. We tried that for several months, but finally decided it would be better for them to go with us to Park Road. They studied Mandarin in school, but now were regularly hearing Taiwanese. By the time they started attending with us, some of the former members had returned, so the group was a little larger. Deacon Ong's three sons helped pave the way for their participation in the church. Gradually, they became involved in various activities, and this aided their language development.

They grew in other ways as well. The more comfortable they were at Park Road, the more Mrs. Gau, included them in special programs. All of the children were taking music lessons and were good singers, so from time to time they were invited to either sing or play their instruments in church. They also participated in some of the Christmas programs. This involved performing before a small group of people that they knew, so it was low pressure. It helped them learn how to present themselves on stage as well as giving them opportunities to interact with Chinese young people in a natural environment.

Morrison in Kaohsiung only went through 8th grade. That meant boarding school for our children once they entered 9th grade, which happened for Harriet in the fall of 1983. Now our routine included driving to Kaohsiung for programs with Robert and Carroll and driving to Taichung (a two hour drive from Tainan) for special events for Harriet.

New Routines, New Experiences

I really enjoyed going to Taichung for very un-spiritual reasons. The different classes at Morrison were always trying to raise money for one thing or another. To accomplish this, they sold food – hot dogs, hamburgers, cookies, cakes, cotton candy – it was almost like going to the fair. We also enjoyed being in a comfortable place where no one stared at us and we could easily communicate with everyone in English. It was like a brief visit to America without ever leaving the country.

Sometime during the second year in Park Road, some young people who formerly attended church begin returning. They had been away at school or in the military or something like that. They wanted to participate and requested an English class. Nan and I both preferred not to teach English because we observed those classes could take on a life of their own and seldom yielded any fruit in the church. However, we had now been in Taiwan long enough to discover that there was a series of Bible story books developed by Chung Tai English Broadcasting specifically for English Bible classes. I agreed to teach English if they would accept the lessons from these books. They agreed, and I found if we handled the material properly, it could lead to some very interesting discussions. I was able to explain some Biblical truths to the group and felt this justified the class.

The English class led to an event that was extremely traumatic. The fall of our second year, before Harriet moved into the dorm, we started discussing American holidays in the English class. It was around the first of November and someone asked about Thanksgiving; what was the reason for it and what did we eat. In the discussion, Mrs. Gau said, "You should invite the English class to your house for Thanksgiving dinner." In her mind, that settled it – they were coming. I talked it over with Nan and she agreed to host it for the eight to ten members of the class. But the following Sunday, Mrs. Gau announced to the church that the entire congregation would be eating Thanksgiving dinner at Pastor Sugg's house. I almost fell off the pew. The children were totally surprised and Nan got a shock as well. That was not the only shock.

Fortunately, we had found a place to purchase a turkey, so we prepared for the group to come. We had no idea how many would be there, but planned for about forty. I think around thirty showed up for the meal, and they were happy to taste an American Thanksgiving dinner. Our biggest shock came when they started leaving, and some of the women pulled plastic bags out of their purses and started stuffing the remaining food into the bags. (This was normal behavior when the Chinese went out to eat in restaurants, so they were just doing what they always did. It hadn't occurred to us that they would do this even in a private home.) Of course, we were shocked and didn't really know what to say. Naturally, we had counted on eating delicious Thanksgiving leftovers for days. The good news was that since we didn't know how many would come, we had over-prepared, so there was more hiding in the kitchen. The biggest hit was Nan's Parker House rolls. She had to make more of those the next day, to go with the few leftovers we managed to keep. The Thanksgiving meal with Pastor Sugg was an annual event for the rest of the time I was at the church.

While I was doing all the normal "pastor stuff," Nan continued researching Tainan history. She became quite an expert on the subject. I have mentioned earlier that the mission planned for new missionaries to take a tour of the work around the island. Now that we were second term missionaries, we were veterans. Even though we might not feel like we had a lot of things figured out yet, to these families who had been on the island for less than two years, our word and experiences were valued. We knew from our own "round the island trip" that once a new missionary visited about two or three cities, all the churches kind of ran together. We came up with a different plan. Nan's tour did include showing them some of the churches, but did not include interviews with the pastors. The main part of the tour was to lead the groups to some of the historical sites, which included a couple of the older temples. During these tours, she encouraged them to learn as much as they could about their own cities and the Chinese culture, telling them it would increase their appreciation of Chinese history and give them a deeper understanding of the people with whom they worked.

It seemed that many new missionaries arrived in Tainan with a curious interest in seeing the Temple of Hell. The look into that aspect of Taiwan life often led to discussions around the supper table about spiritual matters and the reality of the Taiwanese spirits and gods. We had learned that there were over 120 gods in the Taiwanese pantheon, and that did not include the various spirits worshipped in nature or the ancestral spirits of all the ones who had died. It was quite a lot to try and understand.

Sometimes, these new arrivals would mention their struggles in adapting to Taiwanese culture. We always treated those struggles as a reality that had to be acknowledged and worked through in some way. In those conversations, we discovered that often their concerns had been downplayed by other veterans with comments like, "Just hang in there and it will pass." Or "That's just the way it is. You have to live with it." Since both Nan and I had wrestled with some of the same issues – homesickness, lack of spiritual resources, a measure of fear about the reality of spiritual oppression in Taiwan, and the struggle with language – we knew that often a person had to make an intentional effort to overcome those feelings and fears. We also learned that to have someone take serious those feelings meant a lot so a listening ear and prayer for the suffering one was a tremendous help. Those missionaries who felt brave enough to share their feelings always thanked us for listening and understanding. We developed lasting friendships with some of them and were able to have a kind of informal ministry to them in the following years.

It was also during this term, while serving on one of the mission's various committees that I heard a veteran missionary complain about the new missionaries whining about their troubles. She said, "We all went through that and came out all right. They need to do the same thing and not bother us with their problems." I thought that was pretty callous, and felt that some compassionate understanding would go a long way toward helping ensure that these new arrivals might survive their first term.

Towards the end of our second term when my language proficiency was getting pretty good, I was accompanying one of the groups. We were in the courtyard of the Temple to the God of War, and while Nan led the group around explaining things, I stopped to watch two men play Elephant Chess. It is a complicated Chinese game kind of like chess, but with different pieces and different moves. As I watched them, one of them looked up and asked the three questions any foreigner could expect to get:

Are you an American?

Is your wife Taiwanese?

Why are you here?

I had been asked these questions quite often in the past and had been working on my answers. The first one was easy. The answer was yes.

The second one was also easy. Most of the Taiwanese thought the only reason an American would speak Taiwanese would be because he had married a Taiwanese woman. So I could say that my wife was also American and she also spoke Taiwanese.

The third question was what I was waiting for. When they asked that question, "Why are you here?" I responded, "I came to Taiwan to tell the Chinese people about a God who loves them." I was not prepared for their response.

They both burst out laughing. When they stopped, I asked, "What's so funny?"

One of the men said, "That is a really good joke. Everyone knows gods don't love people!"

All my life, I had heard that people all over the world were dying to know that there is a God who loved them. Now I was here to give them this good news and they thought it was a joke! I knew then I would have to come up with a different approach to sharing the Gospel. After much prayer and other considerations, I realized that the Taiwanese longed for peace but seldom found it. So I began emphasizing the peace that God gives.

In addition to her interest in Tainan's historical sights, Nan had another interest. While on our precious furlough, we were introduced to Master Life, a Bible study designed to help believers mature in their faith. We both thought it would be good to use this in Taiwan. Nan enlisted the assistance of the young lady pastor of the church next to us, and through her broken English and Nan's not-yet-fully-proficient Taiwanese, she taught herself how to teach that course. I no longer remember how she did it, but she met a pastor from Makung, which is in the Peng Hu islands just off the Western coast of Taiwan. He invited her – or agreed to allow her – to come to his church and teach Master Life, and she went once a week. In my estimation, that was quite an accomplishment. She would fly over there on Wednesday, teach the class that night, spend the night, and return home the following day. I know she derived a lot of personal satisfaction from that experience.

On a side note, something happened during the time she was teaching that brought a lot of pleasure to our family. Well, mostly to me, but we all benefitted. It had nothing to do with ministry: it was personal. I had always wanted a motorcycle, but never had one. (In high school, when I asked my dad about getting one, he said, "I'd sooner see you carry a live rattlesnake around in your pocket!") After arriving in Taiwan, I discovered that the motorcycle was a primary mode of transportation and started thinking maybe I could find a used one to learn how to ride. Through a strange turn of events, Mr. Hwang, Robin and Stephen's father, found a brand new one on sale for about half price, and he encouraged me to purchase it. I did, and gave Nan the surprise of her life when she returned home from one of her trips. She accepted my impulsive purchase, and we often enjoyed riding together downtown. It was much easier to find parking places for the motorcycle than for the van.

One day towards the end of the term, Mrs. Gau announced in church that we would collect clothes to take to an orphanage in one of the counties south of Tainan. It was in a remote location and was run by a pastor. About a week after the church started collecting clothes for the donation, I was informed that we would also deliver the clothes. I asked when this would happen. The answer was that in two weeks we would meet at Park Road, load everything into cars, drive to the orphanage, distribute the clothes, eat with them and worship with them. That sounded pretty simple and straightforward.

On the appointed day, we gathered at the church, where Nan and I witnessed frantic activity. It seemed that everyone knew what was going on except us. Boxes and goods were stuffed into three other cars and my van. Nan, Robert, and Carroll got into the van with me, and Mrs. Gau and one or two other church members also rode with us. Mrs. Gau had to lock up and then load herself. By the time we were ready, the other cars were long gone. I had planned on following Deacon Ong, who assured me he knew the way. Now, with no one to follow I asked, "Who knows the way to the orphanage?"

Silence.

Finally, a quiet voice in the back said, "God knows."

Nan had a map of the county, and none of the Chinese knew anything like that existed. After we set out, we had to stop several times – at the insistence of our Chinese passengers – so they could ask directions. The trip took longer than I had anticipated; it was almost three hours. I was afraid they would be waiting lunch and worship on us, and I was embarrassed by that. No need to be. After we arrived, I discovered that I was the preacher for the day. They couldn't start without me! (By this time in our second tour I had learned to always travel with a sermon tucked in my Bible.) After worship, we ate. Somehow during the worship and meal, the clothes magically disappeared from the cars.

Then I was told that some wanted to go visit Mrs. Gau's son, Chong-Chi. He had recently joined the army and was at the base in Kaohsiung. I worried that we could not see him, but was told visitors were allowed on Sunday. Nan wanted to take the children home, so she took our van, the children and a couple of Chinese folks, and headed out with her map. (She really trusted those maps.) I went with the group to see Chong-Chi. When I finally got home and asked how long it took her to return, I wasn't surprised to hear that it was a much shorter trip: one hour and twenty minutes. She said the Chinese protested the entire time that she was going the wrong way and that you could not get to Tainan the way she was going. They were quite surprised when she drove confidently into city of Tainan. I wished I had been with her.

We all learned a lot during those three and a half years at Park Road. It was a good experience even if it was a bit traumatic at times.

Forgiveness Produces Peace

"If you forgive men when they sin against you, your heavenly Father will also forgive you. But if you do not forgive men their sins, your Father will not forgive your sins." Matthew 6:14-15

Harriet started her life in the dorm and everything went well. She enjoyed being there and had some wonderful suite mates that remained life-long friends.

We also benefitted from her going to the dorm. For several months prior to her departure, she began to display some symptoms of being a teenager, like anger and sullenness, and she stopped playing with Robert and Carroll like she'd always done before. They couldn't understand what was happening, and quickly learned to avoid her outbursts of temper. Family relationships were more tense, and we tried to assure the younger two that things would work out. If it hadn't been for her going off to boarding school, the transition through the teen years probably would have been longer and much more unpleasant. After just a few weeks at school, the first time she came home for a visit, there was still a lot of argument. But this time it was over who would get to sit by her. We had to work out a seating rotation. The radical change in Harriet later prompted Nan to offer surprising advice to parents dealing with their teenagers' angst: "Just send them off to boarding school!"

It was sometime around late January when we received a phone call from Dr. Brooks, the superintendent of Morrison. He told us that something had come up with Harriet and we needed to be in his office the following morning at 10:00. That is all he would say other than to assure us she was all right and it would all be explained the following morning.

Naturally we were concerned, worried, and troubled. We didn't know what had happened and we could not discuss it very much for soon after the call, it was time for Robert and Carroll to come home from school. We picked them up and did the usual things that afternoon and evening. Nan and I talked briefly about it after they went to bed, but with so little information, there was nothing we could say. We prayed about it and asked God to guide us.

The next morning after we dropped the children off to catch their bus to school, we headed to Taichung. During the night Nan and I both had arrived at the conclusion that somehow Harriet had been sexually molested. We spent the first hour of the trip trying to figure out when it could have happened and who it could have been. It was useless, so we just stopped talking and withdrew into our own minds.

As I thought and prayed, I arrived at the conclusion that if indeed someone had done something to Harriet, I was going to have to forgive that person. If I did not, I knew myself well enough to know that anger would well up in me, and have the potential of becoming a bitter root of anger and pain. I knew I didn't want that to happen because it would hinder, if not totally destroy, my relationship with God. If this happened, it would also impact my other relationships as well. So I started praying, asking God to give me grace, abundant grace to forgive whomever had done whatever to Harriet. I didn't actually feel any different when we arrived at the campus: I was just extremely nervous and tense.

When we got to his office, there were several people present. Of course, Harriet was there along with Dr. Brooks, Harriet's dorm parent, and a man from Hong Kong who was

81

the member care person for the East Asian missionaries. Thankfully, Dr. Brooks cut straight to the point and told us our suspicion was correct. Harriet had been sexually molested. It had occurred some years previously and she had stuffed it for years. But during the school's Spiritual Emphasis week, she had confessed to the speaker what she was dealing with, and he called in Dr. Brooks.

There was a lot of talking and crying, and I did my share of crying. But I can honestly say that there was no anger, only a deep sadness. We were told the circumstances - when it happened and who did it. Turns out, it was one of our own missionaries, and he and his family were sent back to the States the next day. He was ordered to begin counseling and stick with it until he was cured, or something.

Harriet assured us she was fine, and we didn't know what else to do, and we had to be home when Robert and Carroll got back from school, so we went home. We didn't tell them what had transpired that day. Later on, Harriet told them about it herself.

To say we were shocked and devastated would be an understatement. But I know God worked a miracle in my heart. Even to this day as I write this, I feel no animosity towards the man who did that horrible thing. I can honestly say I never did. Even some years later, when I thought I should have at least hit the guy, I knew that was not really what I felt: it would have only been doing what everyone else expected me to do.

When people are hurt, the natural reaction of the flesh is anger and retaliation. But obeying God's commands and precepts helps us choose to give grace instead and trains the heart to do things that please and honor God. I think of it as being similar to how the regular practice of exercise trains the body for participating in some kind of sport. We grow in our spiritual maturity when we regularly and consistently follow God's leading. In reflection, I can see that my prior experiences of doing my best to follow God's prompting in my heart and to reflect God's character helped me in this instance.

I hope anyone who reads these thoughts will follow God's leading in their hearts and not hold on to hurts and disappointments. True freedom and peace are found when hurt and anger are released so God can take care of those sentiments.

Experience Gives Other Opportunities

L ate in our second term, the Taiwan Baptist Mission received news that a Church Planting Conference was scheduled in Singapore. Our leadership decided someone should attend to see what was presented. They selected two men: Burton Cook from our Mandarin work and me from our Taiwanese work. I was excited to go because I had read about Singapore since I was in high school. To me, it was one of the exotic cities of the world. Like Hong Kong, it was an international city with a multi-ethnic population, and had been the setting of adventure stories I had read about spies and soldiers of fortune. Not a very spiritual reason for wanting to go, but anyway I was eager to see the city.

We arranged for lodging in a YMCA hotel to try and save a little money for the TBM. After our arrival, we discovered we were across town from the church hosting the conference and would have to leave our hotel before they served breakfast in order to register and be on time for the first meeting. We set out early and arrived with time to spare. When I asked about coffee availability, I was told the church would not be serving coffee.

I told my companion, "Burton, if I don't have coffee, by ten o'clock I'll have such a bad headache I will not get anything out of the conference." So we found a missionary who seemed to know what was going on and asked him about coffee in the vicinity. He was not encouraging.

"There might be some at the market about two blocks away – if you want to drink the stuff they serve here." We were willing to give it a try, so we walked the two blocks to the market.

As we approached the building, on the window of the corner shop was printed in large letters "Kap-Pi Tiam," which in Taiwanese translated "Coffee Shop." We entered to the wonderful aroma of good, strong coffee and ordered.

Our coffee came in thick white mugs with a small Chinese soup spoon in it. As we stirred the coffee, we discovered the spoon was filled with sweetened condensed milk. We were delighted by this new taste treat, and each had two cups. Thus fortified, we made our way back to the church to see what we could learn.

One of the speakers that morning was the same missionary who had spoken so disdainfully of the local coffee. In his presentation, he remarked that he had come to Singapore about a year and a half ago to study Mandarin to work with the Chinese. But he discovered that "everyone in Singapore spoke English" so he dropped out of language school. Having spent thirty minutes in the market ordering and drinking coffee, Burton and I both knew not everyone spoke English! We knew someone working in an English language church could have a good ministry and feel like there was no need for additional language acquisition, but if one had a vision of a broader ministry that really crossed cultures, then language learning was a must.

The second morning of the conference, we headed straight to the market for coffee. Walking through the park on the way to the church we stopped to watch a familiar sight.

Many Chinese were scurrying around busily setting up a stage for a Chinese opera, along with additional tables we knew would be for worship offerings. It was clear to us that the Chinese were preparing to celebrate the birthday of one of their gods.

In the next session, the discussion centered around the different religions practiced in Singapore and how to reach the population. The speaker, who was the same man we had heard the day before, was expounding on the different gods worshipped by the Hindus and Muslims. He also mentioned that the influence of the Catholic church was very strong there. In a lull in his presentation, Burton asked, "What about the Chinese cultural religions?"

"Oh, they are dead. They are not important because the Chinese have adopted the Western way of life and have rejected them."

I looked at Burton and he looked at me, saying, "Do you think we need to introduce this man to his city?" We both felt we should do that very thing, but wondered if he would even understand what we had to say about culture and religion. He was very secure in his own understanding and was not open to the views of someone who did not live in Singapore.

I mention this incident only because it showed me that my cultural awareness was growing. Even though I did not know how to break through the barriers Satan had erected through culture and religion, I was confident that God had a way to open doors to present His Gospel to the Chinese. God created mankind for fellowship and is always at work building bridges and opening doors so the Gospel can reach those who need it.

An Unusual Baptism

"God made him who had not sin to be sin for us, so that in him we might become the righteousness of God." 2 Corinthians 5:21

Mrs. Gau never spoke of her family, so I didn't know if she had siblings or living parents. Maybe she was from some distant part of Taiwan, or maybe because of her husband's arrest, they had chosen not to associate with her anymore in fear that they would also fall under suspicion. But one day she called me and said her brother was in the hospital and we should visit him. This was around late 1984 or early 1985, and I had been working at the church for at least three years. My experience had taught me that what she said on the phone was only a part of her request, and that I would discover the full story only as it evolved. This seemed to be a consistent pattern with many of the Chinese.

I met her at the hospital and she took me in to meet her brother. He was bedridden and had multiple tubes coming out of various places of his body. One was a tube coming out of his mouth so he could not speak. She explained to me in his presence that he had never trusted in Jesus, but she had been faithful to witness to him and pray for him through the years. She said he had now decided that he wanted to accept Christ. This was a new situation: I had never before presented the Gospel to a person who could not speak for himself.

I asked him some questions and he would nod in affirmation. Yes, he did know who Jesus was. Yes, he did understand what sin was and that sin separated us from God. Yes, he did know he had to ask Jesus into his heart or profess his faith in Him. Yes, he was ready to do that now. So I prayed for him, thanking God for giving him faith to finally accept Him as Savior.

After we left the room, Mrs. Gau told me more about his life. He was a real reprobate. His life was filled with gambling, smoking, drinking, and probably other things she did not mention. She reiterated that she had been praying for him for many years and witnessing to him whenever he would listen to her. He had repeatedly rejected her witness and refused to believe in Jesus. But now she was convinced that he had believed.

I left her at the hospital, and the next day she called me, telling me her brother wanted to be baptized. It was complicated because he was not expected to live much longer, and he could not leave the hospital room. He could not even get off the bed. She asked if it was possible to baptize someone in those conditions. I assured her it was possible. I just didn't tell her I had never done it.

Two days after meeting him for the first time, I returned to the hospital to baptize him. I had thought and prayed about it and had come up with a plan. Mrs. Gau was there as well as a couple of church members and possibly one or two of her extended family. I can't remember who was in the room, but have a vague recollection of there being around five or six people other than me and Mrs. Gau.

I read a scripture, made a couple of comments about the importance of believing in Jesus, and then related how Mrs. Gau had been witnessing to her brother for years and that now he had decided it was time to accept Jesus. Then I baptized him.

Never having actually seen someone be baptized by sprinkling, much less been trained in how to do it, I just did what I thought would be logical. I had a small pan of water and put my finger in it. I collected a few drops of water and said, "Because of your profession of faith, I baptize you in the name of the Father, and the Son, and the Holy Spirit." Each time I named one of the Godhead I put a drop of water on his head.

While in the process of baptizing him, suddenly I was overcome with a strong sense of God's grace and how it reaches out to touch a man totally devoid of any reason for ever thinking he could receive God's grace. Here was a man who had repeatedly rejected the Gospel and continued to live a life in opposition to all the teaching of the Bible. In the same second, I realized that I was in the very same shape – there was nothing in my life to commend me to God for consideration for any kind of grace or blessing. In that split second, what had always been a kind of intellectual acceptance of divine grace became a very personal, real experience of grace. It was so moving I had to pause for a moment to gather myself in order to lead a closing prayer.

Sometimes I have difficulty reading facial expressions, and this man was especially hard to read since he was lying on his death bed with tubes sticking out of various places. But it did seem to me that he had a more peaceful expression on his face.

He died two days later, but Mrs. Gau told me she had never seen him so peaceful.

It is always impossible for one person to tell what another person is thinking or feeling. I cannot tell when someone accepts Jesus just by looking at them. But in this circumstance, the peace that came on this man was proof enough to me that he had indeed received Jesus into his heart. But I knew that for me, I had a new and deeper sense of acceptance of God's love and grace in my life.

I pray that God will reveal to you the fullness of His grace and impress you with its wonderful truth in such a way that it will not just be in your head, but also imbedded deeply in your heart. His grace and mercy are impossible to explain or understand, but deeply soul-satisfying once it is experienced.

Furlough Number Two

This furlough was from summer of 1985 until May of 1986. We started this furlough differently from our first one and all the others that followed. Nan had been asked to lead the youth program for the Hong Kong Mission Meeting, and she enlisted me to assist. Their meeting was the exact same date as our Mission Meeting in Taiwan.

We had planned on traveling through Europe on our way home. Our friends Ray and Mandy Adams, Presbyterian missionaries who worked at the Presbyterian Seminary in Tainan, went home to England about a month before we left. They invited us to visit them in London on our way to the States and we accepted their invitation.

Since the Mission Meetings were at the same time, we left our teenage children in Taiwan, and afterward they flew to Hong Kong with a missionary who was returning there. Since we knew Europe would be cooler than tropical Taiwan and Hong Kong, we planned ahead for a shopping excursion. We met the children at the airport and then spent one day purchasing warmer clothes and repacking suitcases.

Before the trip, we had looked in travel brochures for a hotel in Amsterdam and could not find one that suited Nan. She wanted something local and quaint, not a chain like Best Western. I wanted the Best Western, something sure that I could depend on. But even more disconcerting to me than not using a name brand hotel was the fact that, since we could not find what she was looking for, she decided to book the hotel after our arrival in Amsterdam. Her reasoning was, "No problem: tourists arrive in Europe all the time looking for lodging. We will find something when we land." My usual travel stress was in the red zone!

After we collected our luggage and cleared customs in the Amsterdam airport, I went to change some money while Nan and the children visited the information kiosk to find lodging. When I caught up with them, Nan's eyes were glowing over having found a hotel named the Vincent Van Gogh. It turned out to be a delightful place that we all loved. The first morning, we went down for breakfast and found good coffee for us and hot chocolate for the children, accompanied by delicious bread, cheese, butter and jams. We decided perhaps we should have planned for more than two nights there. Then we were introduced to Nutella and talked about moving to Europe.

We enjoyed the time in Amsterdam and then flew on to London to meet Ray and Mandy. They entertained us royally for the five days we were with them. Then we took a train to Scotland. Our travels there included overnight stops in York and Edinburgh before reaching the end of the line in a fishing village called Oban. The trip took five days and we almost froze. The only thing that saved us was that the stores and wool shops were having their summer sales so we bought wool skirts and sweaters for the girls and sweaters for Robert and me.

We all enjoyed the whole experience. We had authentic fish and chips and our first taste of haggis, neeps, and tatties. We were told this was traditional Scottish food, so we tried it. It was better than I expected and much better than some objectionable foods I'd eaten in Taiwan. Haggis was a meat made of mixed organ meats from sheep and maybe some other scraps of regular meat. It was blended with oatmeal and was filling. Neeps were turnips, and tatties were potatoes, which I liked so that was okay. The children were not impressed with their taste. Nan and the children opted for fish and chips.

One morning, as we were leaving our bed and breakfast in Edinburgh, our hostess asked us where we were going. We responded just to town to look around. She asked if we had seen Arthur's Seat. We said no, we had not heard of it. She said, "Oh, you must see it. It is famous." She gave directions and we set off.

The morning was cloudy, windy, and cool (or to us, cold) and the sky would periodically spit rain drops on us. After walking about a mile, we saw a big grassy hill just ahead and knew Arthur's Seat was on top of the hill. We climbed up the path past gorse bushes and rocks until we reached the top. Carroll was the last to arrive. When she saw what we were looking at, she expressed all our feelings when she exclaimed, "A rock?!? We walked all this way just to see a rock???" I know it must have been at least a mile and a half from where we stayed. So we headed back to town and stopped at a woolen factory for another sweater. It helped redeem the trip when we found the tea shop and had something warm to drink with some scones.

Finally we arrived in Jackson, Mississippi and settled into our routine there. The children did their thing: school and sports. Nan and I did our thing, which was a lot of speaking in different churches about missions. One or both of us was somewhere almost every week, and there were some weeks in the fall when we would separately be in as many as six or seven different churches. One of my great joys was the opportunity to visit small, out of the way churches that had never had a missionary visit them before. Those visits were special to me, because I could remember how much a missionary visit meant to me when I was a boy.

The children always went to our "home church," First Baptist Church. Both sets of our parents went there, so it was natural we would furlough there. We also had plenty of time for good family visits: fish fry dinners on Mom and Dad's patio, family reunions, birthday parties… all the things we had missed. The children got to reconnect with their cousins, especially since they all went to the same school, and they had fun together.

THIRD TERM

A Turn in the Road

"In this you greatly rejoice, though now for a little while you may have had to suffer grief in all kinds of trials. These have come so that your faith – of greater worth than gold, which perishes even though refined by fire – may be proved genuine and may result in praise, glory and honor when Jesus Christ is revealed." 1 Peter 1:6-7

Our first two terms brought trials, tribulations, and tests. We always tried to meet those challenges as best we could. Both Nan and I were blessed with a stubborn streak, no doubt about that. But we chose to look at the positive interpretation of that trait and call it perseverance. We knew we had been called by God to be missionaries, so when we faced difficult challenges, we accepted them as obstacles to overcome. So far, we felt we had done that. We were not unscathed and had learned a lot, but we were still committed to our call and the task ahead of us. In hindsight, we came to realize that some of the difficulties we faced were indeed tests designed by God to lead us into a deeper understanding of Him, ourselves, and how He wanted to use us in Taiwan.

We returned to Tainan in the summer of 1986 for our third term, knowing that Robert would join Harriet in the dorm when school started. Carroll would be the only child at home with us, and that would present challenges. Our children were really close to each other and we didn't know how it would work with her being the only one at home.

I assumed that I would resume my responsibility at Park Road Church. I knew of nothing that had happened to change that assignment. The work we did there in our second term had been successful in many respects: my language had gotten pretty good and the church had grown a good bit. We felt there was room for even more growth and advancement.

We were barely unpacked when a visitor arrived – Pastor Peter Wang. It was not the first time he had visited in our home, but I was surprised that he came so early after our return. I was not sure anyone in town knew we were back. We hurriedly cleared space amidst the boxes in the living room so we could visit and Nan served tea, then left to continue her work. We had the pleasant conversation about our furlough and things at Trinity church. After about thirty minutes, he got to the real reason for his visit. (The Chinese always have to chit-chat a while about meaningless matters before getting to the point of the visit.) He told me very plainly that they (I guess the pastors in town) had received information that Pastor Gau would be returning to Tainan very soon and that I did not need to be at Park Road when he arrived. He didn't offer any explanation about why I didn't need to be there, but I knew if it was important enough to prompt this visit, I needed to pay attention to his advice. Even in my limited understanding of Chinese culture, I could see it would be uncomfortable for me to be there as pastor when he returned.

After he left, I told Nan what he related to me and we discussed it. Neither of us knew what it meant or what we would do if I was not at Park Road. There was no other Taiwanese Baptist Church in Tainan. I thought I could always do what the pastors wanted me to do and teach an English class every night. That did not sound appealing in the least and was a far cry from my idea of what a missionary should be doing.

Lessons from the Journey

We did visit Park Road the following Sunday and put off their invitation to step back into the role of pastor. I explained we would be going Mission Meeting the following week and I would see what the mission wanted me to do. They knew enough about the mission's workings to know that sometimes the missionary could be assigned to a different city so they accepted that explanation for the time being. I thought it was interesting that she gave no hint that she even knew her husband would return soon.

We did go to Mission Meeting, and we all enjoyed that week. Our Regional Leader, Sam James, told us about something new that was being done in various countries in Asia. He called it a Church Growth Study and said that several missions around the world had participated in this study and had witnessed a dramatic increase in baptisms and the number of churches planted. He wanted the Taiwan Baptist Mission to conduct such a study. His proposal was discussed at length and we finally agreed to participate. The expectations and explanations were very general at this point. Sam promised to send information to our Executive Committee, the committee that met monthly and handled a lot of business for the mission. This committee would come up with a proposal and suggest personnel to lead the study. I believed so strongly in the possibility of this potential work that I told Sam I would like to volunteer to be on the committee for the study. I knew it would be a long shot for me to be considered, but still that was my desire.

I was excited. This sounded like the very thing I came to Taiwan to do – not be in a long study, but be involved in church planting. I, as well as some others, felt we were not reaching our potential from the standpoint of winning the lost and starting new churches. This might just be what we had been waiting for. Yet even in my excitement, it seemed it would be a while longer in order for the leaders to finalize all the plans.

In the meantime, we returned to Tainan and I went back to Park Road that first Sunday after Mission Meeting. When Mrs. Gau asked if I would be available to fill the pastor's role again, I told her the mission had some things they wanted me to do and I could not do it right now. I did agree to preach one Sunday morning a month, rather than three sermons a week like before.

When fall arrived, we drove back to Taichung to put Harriet and Robert in the dorm. They were both very excited about this move. Carroll was a little let down, but she kept up a brave front when we returned to Tainan. We tried to make it up to her by planning some special things, but I fear it was not the same as having her brother and sister around.

We were in an unusual place for us; neither of us had a specific assignment. It was almost like we were starting over or perhaps we were waiting on something to develop. Watching and waiting for something unknown is not easy. When there are specific assignments to fulfill it is easy to just do the next thing that has to be done in order to accomplish the task. Most of our ministry so far involved doing certain routine things day after day until we completed whatever task we were working on. But this time, there was no specific, immediate task. There were some routine things to continue, like meeting with the pastors once a month and attending the Tainan missionary prayer supper once a month. The rest of the time we were praying and watching hoping to see how God wanted to use us. It was a new experience.

Late in the fall, Pastor Gau did return. Mrs. Gau called one afternoon and invited me to come to the church to meet him. I went, we met, and after a polite time, I returned home. He stepped back into the pastor's position and I didn't return to the church for several months. In time, as I continued to meet with the pastors in their monthly meetings and meet Pastor Gau in other informal ways, we gradually got to know each other. Sometime after he got settled back into the routine, he did invite me to preach a time or two and I did some visitation with him. But it was always at his invitation and it was not very often. In time we got to be friends. I was glad that the relationship developed naturally and he did not see me as a rival.

Towards the end of that first year, the Church Growth Committee was formed and I was invited to be on it. We all went to the first meeting to see what was expected and to get more complete instructions on how it would function. Leroy Hogue, one of our veteran missionaries, was asked to be the Steering Committee Chairman and he agreed. After our first meeting, when it was all explained what the goal was and how much work would be involved, he resigned. That was unfortunate since he had the confidence not only of our own missionaries but also of the pastors in the Chinese Baptist Convention. That was important since the committee was intended to be a joint committee and the Chinese needed to respect whoever led the project. Since Leroy taught at the seminary and also was the pastor of the English congregation of Grace Baptist Church, he said his plate was full and it would be impossible for him to meet the expectations for this project. With his resignation, Dr. James was very close to stopping the entire attempt.

When I heard the news that the whole project might be scrapped, I wrote Sam an impassioned letter begging him not to stop this project. I believed it had the potential to be a significant help in attaining our goal of reaching Taiwan for Christ. Against all common sense, he not only decided to continue with the project, but named me as the Steering Committee Chairman. And against all common sense, I accepted. This was a radical change in direction from how I envisioned this third term working out.

I had no idea what I was getting into.

I cannot say that I spent long hours praying about whether or not to volunteer for this project or whether or not to accept the position of Steering Committee Chairman. I had come to a point in life where I believed that if I was seeking God in my daily devotional time and was committed to following Him wherever He led, somehow the things I wanted to do were actually His leading in my life. I know there were many times when I would pray, "Father, help me love the things you love and hate the things you hate." I believed that if I lived in that kind of close relationship with God, the things I desired to do would somehow be what God wanted done. I had also learned an important lesson: when I started to do something, if it was not something God wanted me to do, I would not feel peace about the decision to take that action. I guess that was what some of my Pentecostal friends would call "a check in my spirit." I felt peace about accepting the role and knew I would work to the best of my ability to fulfill the job requirements. I also had every confidence that God would guide me.

"I Will Guide You"

"I will instruct you and teach you in the way you should go; I will counsel you and watch over you."
Psalm 32:8

I n the days that followed the announcement of the personnel of the Steering Committee for this Joint Church Growth Study, I was overcome with excitement about what could possibly come from it. We had heard stories of how this study in other countries had led to planting many new churches. There had been so many powerful and radical results that the Mission Board either coined or adopted a new phrase and began to introduce it to us: Church Planting Movements. In some countries the response to this initiative was so tremendous that the leadership was having difficulty keeping an accurate count of the numbers of new churches. There were reports of entire sections of some countries turning to Christ, hence the name Church Planting Movement. Some of us hoped the same result would be seen in Taiwan.

The euphoria I felt lasted until about three days prior to the first meeting. Then the excitement was replaced with reality and I realized I would be the one directing the entire project. Nerves took over. I found it difficult to eat, sleep and concentrate on what needed to be done. Since no one in Taiwan had any experience with this type of study, there was no one to turn to. It was all new and I was the leader.

The night before I was to leave for Taipei and the first meeting, I could not sleep. I lay in bed staring at the ceiling wondering why I ever agreed to do this crazy thing. Finally I got up and went downstairs to my study. There on my knees with my Bible in front of me, I opened my fear-filled heart to God. In His graciousness, he led me to this verse. In the quiet of my study I claimed that verse and told God I was depending on him to guide me through this process. Otherwise it would be a giant failure. That was May 13, 1987.

The next day I headed for Taipei and that first meeting. I was nervous and jittery all the way there and right up until time for the meeting to start. But once we had an opening prayer, a quiet calm settled over me. I was able to follow the agenda I had come up with and we made it through without any problem. I say with no problems; that may not be entirely accurate. There were four Chinese and four Americans on the committee besides me. Only one of the Chinese spoke Taiwanese, one of the missionaries did not speak any Chinese language, and the other missionaries spoke Mandarin. We were almost dealing with the Tower of Babel all over again using a mix of Taiwanese, Mandarin and English. But God granted grace and we somehow managed to communicate.

Many times in the following months I quoted that verse to myself as a reminder of God's promise. I knew unless God intervened, all was lost. But every time God guided us to clear communication and to the appropriate action.

The project was designed to take eighteen months. If we met that schedule, we would conclude all the work by sometime in November of 1988. Included in the planned activities were a questionnaire to be completed by every missionary and Chinese pastor, followed by interviews of those same people. Detailed reports were written on every institution we had in the mission and convention that gave their history and purpose, and tried to rate their effectiveness.

The plan called for an outside evaluation team to come in and oversee the project by offering suggestions on the development of the questionnaires as well as other aspects of the work. They were the ones to conduct all the interviews, visit all the institutions which included the mission and convention leadership, and then come up with a detailed list of their observations about all the work being done in Taiwan at the time. Their observations would also include insights gleaned from the questionnaires and interviews with the pastors and missionaries. Some of the pastors and missionaries were very candid in their remarks and some of those were pretty critical of present policies and practices. That is what the evaluation team said they needed.

While all this was going on, there was an internal committee reading and selecting articles to be reprinted and mailed out to the missionaries and convention pastors and leaders. The goal was to introduce new ideas to us on how to be more effective in our work. There were articles on anthropology and cross-cultural evangelism, articles on church planting, Bible studies on church development in the New Testament, and there were also reports from various countries on the results of these studies in their locations. Naturally, this committee was also composed of both Chinese and Americans and all of the articles had to be translated: some were in Chinese and had to be translated into English and some were English and had to be translated into Chinese. The missionaries were expected to read all of this material while the study was ongoing. It was hoped that this reading would help us begin to think in new ways and see beyond our established patterns and practices.

From all the data gathered, the Outside Evaluation Team made their observations and then they made a lengthy list of recommendations for the mission and convention to consider. They did not have the authority to force the implementation of the recommendations, but we knew our regional leadership would be watching us closely to see if we followed through on them.

All in all, it was a mountain of paper and a momentous task. And I was in charge of it all. The routine grind of the endless pressure was daunting. Through the whole two-year process, there were several times when the pressure got so intense, I was afraid I would break. In those times, I enlisted friends to pray for me. One of the main ones I depended on – other than Nan – was Charlie Hardy. He and I had not worked together: he was in Mandarin work and I was in Taiwanese work. But we had connected and I really respected his prayer life. He was a great encouragement to me in those dark times.

Those eighteen months were filled with numerous meetings all over Taiwan. I was gone from Tainan almost as much as I was in Tainan. It didn't take long for the pastors to realize that I was not in town and they did not expect me to be around very much.

Our annual prayer retreat was usually held in February. In 1989 we scheduled it to be held at our Baptist Camp at Lingtou, just outside of Taipei. This year, attendance for all missionaries was mandatory. Even if it had not been, I think there would have been very few who didn't attend. We all wanted to hear the report from the Outside Evaluation Team first hand. Since it was a joint committee and affected our work with the Chinese, they were invited to attend as well.

All of the reports had to be copied, bound, and reproduced in preparation for the meeting. That was my last responsibility. I found a copy shop in Tainan and contracted to have it done. Then the day before the meeting, I loaded all those copies in our van and headed north. I'm surprised we didn't break some springs or an axle because the van was so overloaded.

Lessons from the Journey

The books were passed out and then we read through them together. The OET led the reading and discussion. They would answer questions as they were asked. There were well over a hundred observations followed by over a hundred recommendations, so the reading took quite a long time. There were frequent interruptions often by someone angry at some observation or recommendation. But we made it through the entire process.

Looking back, there are three recommendations that stand out. They seem to be the ones that impacted our mission the most.

First, it was observed that the primary role of the missionary was to be a catalytic agent, and the missionary should use his or her influence to bring about change in the way church was done. The study emphasized what we already knew; the churches were focused on maintaining the status quo while they should be focused on outreach and church planting. This observation stimulated much heated discussion.

Second, the study observed that many of the missionaries lived in close proximity to an existing church and did most of their work through that church. That meant they were living in a neighborhood that technically was considered reached. In order to reach the lost, the missionaries had to move out of the shadow of the church buildings and into communities where there were no churches.

Third, it was observed that most of the missionaries were working in existing churches. It was recommended that the missionaries should focus more on planting new churches; therefore, they should leave the churches they were in and start new ones.

To be sure, these three points generated a lot of emotional discussion. But the emotions were not limited to these three alone. I mention them because they stand out to me as the ones that affected me the most.

When the conference was over, I was physically, spiritually, and emotionally spent. I was as dry as I had ever been. Fortunately we were scheduled for furlough as soon as school was out and I needed time away from Taiwan. But in yet another moment where pride – and stupidity – took over and drove common sense out of my life, I accepted the invitation to teach one semester at Southeastern Seminary in Wake Forest, North Carolina in the fall. The chair of their mission department had come to Taiwan to assist in the writing of the questionnaire we used to interview the missionaries and pastors for the church growth study. I should have politely refused the invitation and stayed in Jackson, but the desire to teach took over. (This is why we should never make major decision when we are tired; I was too tired to think straight.) I was scheduled to teach one course on church growth and one on comparative religions. The invitation was based primarily on the assumption that since I was in Taiwan, I could provide first hand experiences in the class on comparative religions, and the insights gained in the church growth study would be a living resource into a discussion on church planting. The first week in North Carolina confirmed that pride was strong and a very poor guide in how to select activities to put into my life. I wished I was in Jackson.

As a follow-up on the original reason for doing the church growth study, I'll give this brief report. In the ten years prior to the study, the combined efforts of the Chinese Baptist Convention and the Taiwan Baptist Mission planted an average of one church a year. In the six years following the implementation of the study, the mission alone averaged starting ten churches a year. We did it without the help of the Chinese churches because they didn't want to participate. Their reason for their lack of cooperation was that they knew what would happen: they said the missionaries would start the churches and then go on furlough. While on furlough, the convention would have the responsibility of keeping these weak churches going. They believed most of them would die and they would be held responsible. They were partly right. A lot of the churches the missionaries started were weak and did die. Perhaps somewhere between fifty and sixty percent died within the first three years after they were planted. But enough remained to convince the Chinese that we missionaries were serious about this new direction. They also reasoned that if they helped us, perhaps more of the churches would remain and the convention would grow. After all, they said, "You missionaries can't even speak good Chinese."

There was one other reason why most of the churches failed. It was more basic and is always the problem when planting churches. We were tied to a model of church that depended on seminary-trained leaders. In any church, whether it is new or old, growth is always dependent on the availability of leaders. If the church does not have a way to train and produce new leaders, they are doomed to remain static and ultimately begin to shrink as the current leaders pass from the scene. Historically, Southern Baptists grew rapidly because they followed a model that did not depend on seminary-trained pastors. That meant when the westward expansion in America began in the 1800's, any man who felt God had called him to preach could go and preach. Of course, that man was examined and approved by his home church and other churches that knew him. That philosophy created a large pool of pastors which allowed a large number of churches to be planted in the newly settled areas of our nation. In Taiwan, we did not have that option, because the Chinese mindset was that seminary education was necessary in order for a person to lead a church. Since the seminary only produced a limited number of graduates each year, there were not many pastors available to work in these new church starts.

The time from the conclusion of the Prayer Retreat until our furlough in the summer was a time when I tried to remain out of sight. I didn't want to do anything. At the end of the school year, there were lots of activities since Robert was graduating and Carroll was now at Morrison in Taichung as well. We enjoyed going up there for the end of school activities.

I have included all this information about the Church Growth Study because it was the focus of my ministry for that third term. Basically all I did was administrative work. I just thought whoever reads this would want to know that.

Salt Light Chapel

"Whatever your hand finds to do, do it with all your might, for in the grave, where you are going, there is neither working nor planning nor knowledge nor wisdom." Ecclesiastes 9:10

Nan and I grew up long before it was popular to select a life verse, but I am convinced that if she had one, this was it. She frequently quoted the first part of the verse and then tackled any project with great gusto. Therefore, it was understandable that while I was in limbo waiting for the mission to do something to initiate the church growth study and trying to stay out of Mrs. Gau's sight, she was looking for some meaningful ministry to fill her time. Carroll was still at home, the last chick to leave the nest, and she and Nan did some things in her room and in the kitchen. But most of that was early in the semester and she had a lot of free time.

Early in the second semester of Carroll's eighth grade year, we once again saw evidence of God watching over us and going ahead of us to provide help and support. One of Carroll's good friends was Yoshie Imai. Yoshie was Japanese and her father was one of the scientists who worked at the Asian Vegetable Research and Development Center. Soon after the semester started, he received the news that he had to return to Japan. Yoshie was devastated because she would not be able to conclude the school year with her classmates. She had been away from Japan for so long, she did not particularly want to return. Carroll told us of her plight and we offered to let her stay with us until the end of the school year. Her parents agreed, so Carroll had a good friend for the remainder of that semester. That was a very good blessing God gave us.

At some point early in that term, we met a man who was a teacher at a women's home economics college on the outskirts of Tainan. This man was a deacon in a church that was right next door to the college, and he was trying to keep the church doors open for the students there. They had been without a pastor for several years. Nan and I visited there a few times, and she really caught a vision to help this dedicated man. He was doing all the preaching and trying to minister to the young ladies at the college. Although he had repeatedly requested the seminary to send a young pastor to work there, so far none had come. He was scheduled to move to another city soon and did not want to see the work closed. After discussing it with the deacon and praying about it, Nan started preaching there.

I visited Salt Light when I was in town and not engaged somewhere else. She gradually took over the responsibility for that Sunday morning worship, which included all the preaching, and began reaching out to the young ladies who came to the church. In time, she built a relationship with some of them and formed a level of friendship. This ministry meant a lot to Nan and she poured herself into the sermons and relationships with the ladies.

It was not long until she decided that the generally unkempt look of the building was a turn-off to those interested in coming. She worked with the young ladies (and her family) to initiate a cleanup of the sanctuary. In the process, she discovered some printed material in one of the back closets. It was material that we had heard about, but never seen. There were some children's Bible story books and adult devotional books written in Taiwanese Romanization.

The first missionaries to Taiwan were Presbyterians from England. They arrived on the coast near Tainan sometime in the 1840's. Their first years must have been very rough: they were in a strange land where they could not communicate. They functioned much like Wycliffe missionaries do today, making contact with a group of natives and trying to learn the spoken language. As they gained familiarity with some of the vocabulary, they transcribed the sounds using the English alphabet. In time, they learned to speak Taiwanese and developed a system for identifying all the sounds of the words, as well as a way to indicate the tones of the words. (All eight of them!) This would later be called Taiwanese Romanization, and they ultimately translated the Bible into this system. Later, they developed Bible story books for children as well as devotional and discipleship materials for the adults. It is important to remember that most of the Chinese with whom they worked were illiterate. They had a spoken language based on the written Chinese characters, but they could not read the characters. The system developed by the Presbyterian missionaries allowed the missionaries to teach the new converts to read so they could read the Bible, as well as the other materials they translated and produced like hymnals. In 1895, the Japanese expansion into the rest of Asia came to Taiwan. For some reason, the Japanese allowed the Presbyterian Church to continue to use and produce this literature. That is what Nan found in the closet of the church. Interestingly enough, we learned about the early arrival of Presbyterian missionaries and development of Taiwanese Romanization during language school. Many of our teachers were Presbyterian pastor's wives who had grown up reading and speaking Taiwanese using this system.

In 1949, Chiang Kai-shek's Mandarin-speaking government took over the island and imposed that system of written Chinese characters for everyone. All the Taiwanese currently living there began to learn it, but by the time we arrived around thirty years later, there were still many Taiwanese speakers, especially in the older generation, who could not read the characters.

When Nan found the books in the back of the church, the discovery planted the seed for another, more far-reaching project in her fertile, active mind. In the previous term, she had met some ladies who could not read the character Bible in Taiwanese. She wondered if it would be possible to teach people how to read the Taiwanese Romanization, since Bibles written in that system were already widely available. Of course, those who were literate in Chinese characters had no need to learn how to read the Romanization. But the thought was there and it did not disappear.

On our previous furlough, we had seen that both Mom and Dad were involved in teaching English as a Second Language to internationals at First Baptist Church. The ESL methodology was based on a system developed by Frank Laubach, who had been a missionary to the Philippines. He developed that system and used it effectively to teach Filipinos to learn how to read. I think they were learning to read Spanish. Nan saw how he used pictures of common things to represent a letter of the alphabet and in this way taught illiterates how to read. She thought, "Why can't I do that with Taiwanese?" When she found those Bible story books, her creative mind kicked into high gear and she really focused on that project in her spare time. She continued to work on it for the next few years.

Robert was in Boy Scouts. One reason for his interest in Scouts was that his grandfather, Owen Gregory, had been a Scout executive in his early days. That interest carried over to his daughter, Nan, and through her to Robert. He likely would have joined Scouts anyway, but her interest was a great encouragement. He was working on his Eagle Scout badge and had to do a project. Nan and Robert decided a worthy project would be to reclaim the yard and grounds at Salt Light Church. That was a lot of work, but he accomplished it and we were all very proud of him for completing this task. We made a trip home that summer, and he was awarded the Eagle Scout rank through the scout troop that met at First Baptist Church in Jackson. That was special to us all.

Nan took up the former deacon's burden to get a pastor for the church and towards the end of our third term, she contacted all the missionaries in our mission who taught and worked at our seminary in Taipei. She told them about this little church located near a college and impressed them with the need to find a pastor for it. Finally a young couple accepted the call and moved down to Tainan. That was not long before we started our furlough. We all felt Nan had accomplished a lot during that three years and we left Tainan with a deep sense of satisfaction.

FOURTH TERM

A New Term

The furlough following our third term was unlike our first two. I was in Wake Forest, North Carolina teaching at Southeastern Seminary. Nan was in Jackson with Carroll, while Harriet and Robert were both in the dorms at Mississippi College in Clinton. Carroll was in her junior year at Jackson Academy and not real happy to be there. Before we ever went to Taiwan the first time, we had decided that it would be good for the children to have a full school year in the States during furlough years. We felt this would help them in their long term adjustment to life in America when they left Taiwan, assuming it was more likely that they would live in the US after college than somewhere else in the world. This well-intentioned decision seemed logical at the time, but we later discovered that all three children struggled to fit into American school culture. Harriet and Robert did better with the adjustment, but Carroll really had a hard time. She had lived in Taiwan the longest of the three children and had few memories of her early life in America. Taiwan was truly her home, and she deeply missed it, making it difficult for her to accept life in Jackson. When I concluded the semester of teaching and came home for Christmas and the remainder of the furlough, it was obvious Carroll was not doing well. We even discussed returning to Taiwan in time for the second semester of school in Taichung. But she said she would stick it out and she did.

That spring, Nan went to Dallas, Texas for a week to study informally at the Summer Institute of Linguistics, which was associated with Wycliffe Bible Translators. Their missionaries were trained in techniques for learning and recording a previously unstudied language, with the goal of translating the Bible into that language. She took with her the work she had done on her project of developing a method to teach people to read Taiwanese Romanization, and they were very supportive of what she had done. They also gave her suggestions about how to continue. She returned encouraged and ready to complete the project.

Perhaps it was the stress of our previous term coupled with the semester of teaching in North Carolina, or perhaps it was the awareness of the stress we always dealt with in Taiwan, or perhaps it was the fact that, in addition to leaving our parents and other friends, we were now leaving two of our children in the States. Whatever the reason, I was not looking forward to going back to Tainan, Taiwan. Added to these understandable reasons for not wanting to return, there was the additional realization that we were expected to do something we had no idea how to do – plant a church. It was difficult for me to make myself get on that airplane. In hindsight, I would say, and I think Nan would agree, that everything in our lives to this point had been working to place us in this exact position. Without a doubt, this fourth term would prove to be the most effective of all the time we spent in Taiwan when judged purely on a human level. It was also the most stressful term - for me, anyway.

As far back as I can remember, I had been plagued with the question of why we no longer see God do the miracles and healings recorded in the Bible. No one could answer that question to my satisfaction. As I got older, I started hearing about other churches with different practices and beliefs than what I was familiar with in my Baptist upbringing. These were Pentecostal or charismatic churches where they spoke in tongues and were reported to see other types of miracles on a regular basis. They often prayed in church for people to be healed of all kinds of illnesses and saw God answer those prayers. But I never actually met anyone from one of those churches that I could question about their beliefs and practices.

While in Blue Mountain, God led me on a spiritual journey and impressed me through real experiences that my questions were not outlandish; that He did indeed act in our lives in ways that differed from how I had been taught in my early Christian walk. (It was not that I had been taught that those things were not for today, it was just that the possibility of them happening was not mentioned and I certainly never saw them.) Nan and I both were interested in the activity of the Holy Spirit, which was never talked about or preached about in our home churches except in very limited ways. We stumbled on a couple of books that fed this interest.

A couple of years before we were appointed and left for Taiwan, Nan's sister, Georgia and her family moved to Jackson. Georgia had married an FBI agent from New Jersey, Gene Griffiths. He bought the business Nan's father had started before he resigned from the FBI. While she was living in other cities, Georgia had some experiences with the Holy Spirit in charismatic churches and people. When she moved to Jackson, she found and joined a brand new charismatic church that meant a lot to her. As our children graduated from high school in Taiwan and returned to Mississippi for college, they were often in Jackson and started attending her church as well. So it was not unusual for us to visit there from time to time when we were home on furlough.

A week or so before we returned to Taiwan for this fourth term, Georgia told us about a couple who would be in their church one Sunday night and invited us to attend. This couple, Scott and Kathy Webster, had a ministry of prophecy. I had never seen anything like this and was not sure how I felt about it, but thought it would be interesting to go and see what happened.

After the worship and sermon, the couple asked people to come forward for prayer, and during the prayer, they would "prophesy" over them. It seemed most of the time the prophecies were general encouragement coupled with the need for the recipient to be bolder or more consistent in their faith walk.

From time to time, one of the couple would say something like, "I sense there is someone here who needs..." and would issue a general word of motivation or encouragement. Then one of them said, "I sense that a couple here is thinking about starting a church in their living room." Well, that got my attention. Both husband and wife really were feeling something, for they prophesied in that vein for a couple of minutes. Among the things they said were that the church that came from this attempt would become a training center for new believers that would reach the nations. This church would send missionaries around the world and would also start other churches. There were other parts of the prophecy, but I cannot recall them now after all these years. Needless to say, this prompted a lot of discussion between Nan, Georgia, and me in the brief time before our departure.

It was also about this time that we were surprised to run into our old friends Danny and Judy Armstrong, who had been students at Blue Mountain College when I was BSU Director there. Back then, we had formed a good friendship, and I performed their wedding ceremony. We had lost track of them, but knew that they had been appointed by a charismatic ministry as missionaries to Indonesia. Now that we were reconnected twenty years later, we talked some about where we were serving and what we were seeing God do. Danny gave me a book, *On The Crest of The Wave,* by Peter Wagner. It was about how the Holy Spirit was moving in great ways around the world, and when He was working in your ministry, it was similar to a surfer catching a huge wave to ride to the beach and just hanging on. I found it an interesting read and added it to my growing collection of books about the Holy Spirit.

As I said, looking back, it is obvious that the most tangible result of our time in Taiwan took place during this fourth term, I would also say that this term produced the most stress I personally faced during all my time in Taiwan. I came closer to walking away and returning to Mississippi than at any other time in my ministry. When I was leading the Church Growth Study, there was also a high level of stress. But that was different from what I felt during this term. While working on the Church Growth Study, I had a committee with which to discuss concepts, plans and timelines. Once the goals and timelines were set, it was just a matter of doing the next thing. The stress in that situation came from setting and meeting deadlines. But now there was no committee, no agenda, no guidelines. There was only Nan and me trying to maintain a sensitivity to God's Spirit that would be keen enough to allow us to sense how He was directing us. We discovered that many times the only way to be sure that God had indeed led us in a certain way was to do whatever we felt He was directing us to do and then evaluate the results. We walked a lot by faith, which is how He wants us to live.

I had mentioned previously that both Nan and I had a very strong sense of being called to be missionaries. Now this prophecy added to the feeling that we could not leave – at least not until we saw what God wanted to do. These two factors strongly influenced us to remain on the field that term.

A New Thing

"Forget the former things; do not dwell on the past. See, I am doing a new thing! Now it springs up; do you not perceive it? I am making a way in the desert and streams in the wasteland, to give drink to my people, my chosen, the people I formed for myself that they may proclaim my praise." Isaiah 43:18-21

We returned to Taiwan in the summer of 1990. The Church Growth Study was history, and elements of the recommendations made from the Outside Evaluation Committee were being implemented by the mission. One of those was that missionaries should move out of mission housing and out of the shadow of existing churches into areas where there were no churches. Accordingly, when we left for furlough in 1989, we had packed our goods in crates, and they were stored until we could return. We landed in Taichung and arranged to stay in guest housing on the Morrison campus while we prayed about where to start over. Robert was home for the summer and Carroll had returned for her senior year at Morrison. They certainly enjoyed that summer: hanging out with friends, staying up late and sleeping late, and watching the World Cup.

Another decision made by the mission following the Church Growth Study was that missionaries would focus their ministry on starting new churches. As a part of that thrust, it was stated that the best chance for a new church to succeed was for it to have a sponsoring or mother church. That meant the missionary would be working with a pastor and his congregation that had expressed a desire to help start a new church.

Because we spoke Taiwanese, it was generally accepted that our work would be in the southern part of Taiwan, where we had lived for the previous twelve years. The Taiwanese influence was strongest there. After several weeks of praying, meeting with mission leadership and traveling south to talk with pastors and look over potential sites for new churches, we discovered that there were no Taiwanese churches in the south (or anywhere else in Taiwan) with any interest in planting a new Taiwanese church. Wherever we went, we would be on our own, which is the most difficult way to start a new church. Since that was the case, we opted for Tainan, where we would at least know our way around the city. But we did select a different area of the city in which to live. On the recommendation of one of our former neighbors and through much prayer, we located a potential area for a new church. It was just on the northwestern edge of the city in a developing area named An Lam Kho. We rented a store front apartment there.

The apartment was like most of the stores and dwellings in the city at that time. The first floor was the business, and the upper three floors were where the family resided. We intended for the first floor to be the place where the church met. It would be visible and we hoped it would generate interest from casual passersby.

Robert and Carroll helped us settle in before they left home for school; Robert back to Jackson and Carroll back to Morrison. We talked and prayed about what to do and how to start. Neither of us had any experience in starting new churches, but had read a lot of suggestions in the material handed out during the Church Growth Study. We came up with a plan and started trying to make inroads into this difficult task.

Even though I do have a rebellious streak, at the core of my being I desire to do what is expected from me and to please those with whom I work. Returning to Tainan put me in an awkward situation. On the one hand, the mission was telling me to start a new church in an unreached area using methods which were different from all the things we had done previously. The ideal method was to have a sponsoring church whose pastor supported the effort and who would give some members to work with us. On the other hand, all the pastors in Tainan disagreed with the mission's decisions and were quite vocal when they stated repeatedly that Nan and I were in the wrong place doing the wrong kind of work. They had their own plans on how we should be working in Tainan, which involved helping them by teaching English in their churches. We were caught between these two forces and it was quite uncomfortable. Early in the fall, we attended the Taiwanese Summer Camp. This was an annual event planned for the members of the Taiwanese churches and included pastors, missionaries, and church members. In the early days when Baptist work was new in Taiwan, it was probably important for this group to be together for mutual encouragement and support since there were so few Taiwanese churches. By this time, interest had dwindled a good bit. Even so, we went and were surprised by one of the speakers. He was not one of our Baptist pastors; he pastored an independent church and was coming to give us a report on the Year 2000 Committee.

Let me explain. Sometime around the mid-1980's, some influential denominational leaders, mission leaders, and other religious leaders in various parts of the world were looking ahead to the year 2000. They felt that the emphasis in this new millennium should prompt some bold plans from the Christian community. Consequently, in several countries, discussion was started about setting goals for church outreach, missions, and church planting. That worldwide interest also touched Taiwan, and some of the influential church leaders there felt they should also establish a Year 2000 Committee. That group set some very ambitious goals for the new millennium: two million Christians meeting in ten thousand churches. I don't recall the number of members and churches in Taiwan at the time, but I am sure there were less than 2,000 churches in all denominations. To reach such a bold goal would take a mighty move of God's Spirit. The committee felt that one way to help encourage and motivate pastors and churches to embrace this very high goal would be to secure good speakers to come to Taiwan to help us catch the vision of God's power and ability to work among us. It seemed to me that many, if not most of the speakers they invited had very strong Pentecostal or charismatic backgrounds. I mention this because as our new term developed, Nan and I attended a lot of these meetings, and were constantly encouraged to believe that God could and would do impossible things. That had a tremendous influence on our ministry, especially towards the end of the term.

Soon after the Taiwanese Summer Camp, we arranged to meet our good friends, Milton and Nannette Lites, for a mini-prayer retreat to start our new work. They were our prayer partners and we shared a lot of ideas with them. It was during our time together that God led me to this verse. I felt it was significant, but was not sure what it meant other than to emphasize something new was happening in our lives.

I must add that in the midst of all the other things that happened, Nan never forgot the burden she felt to develop a method to teach Chinese to read Taiwanese Romanization. Whenever she had time, she worked on it.

We returned to Tainan from our prayer retreat and tried all manner of outreach events. We even tried doing something we swore we would never do – teach English to children who were not even close to being a part of our church. Absolutely nothing worked. We had zero response to all our efforts. Needless to say, we were discouraged.

In the early spring of 1991, our long-time Mission Administrator, Hunter Hammett, announced he was stepping down from his role in mission leadership. He had been appointed to work with churches and he wanted to conclude his time in Taiwan by returning to that original assignment. He was one of my heroes because he had started in Taiwanese work, but then had learned to speak Mandarin as well. I harbored a secret hope that one day I might also do that, but knew I'd had such a difficult time learning Taiwanese it was a really long shot. As a part of his announcement, the mission leadership made it clear that we needed someone to step in and be the next mission administrator. In the discussion that followed, three names were mentioned as possible replacements and I was one of them. I also had a secret hope that I could one day become mission administrator because I felt that role needed someone to act in some ways as a mission pastor, especially to the new missionaries.

Later in the spring, the mission leadership announced that for our annual mission meeting, they would like for all the church planters to prepare a poster that showed their work. They hoped it would serve a twofold purpose. One would be to show what was being done and the second result would be to encourage everyone about what was happening in the follow-up of the Church Growth Study. Nan and I knew we didn't have anything to show.

The guidelines were to show the mother church, the church members helping us, the new members, etc. Our poster was a series of shots that showed only our building, the empty room where we hoped to hold services, the empty room where we hoped to have a Sunday School class, us and our little white dog, Biscuit. We included blank spots for the pictures of our mother church, our sponsoring pastor, and the church members who were helping us. Biscuit was our only member after a year of trying everything we knew to try.

As Mission Meeting neared, I was hoping that I would be selected as Mission Administrator. That would be a legitimate excuse for leaving this work that was sucking the life out of both Nan and me. No one would blame us for walking away from a church start with no results to fill the role of Mission Administrator.

We looked forward to Mission Meeting and were anticipating it because we always enjoyed it and I was especially anticipating the election. On the day we were scheduled to vote, I went out early for a morning jog. As I made my way around the track, I was talking to God and wondering how the election would work out. As I concluded my jog and was walking an additional lap to cool down a little, God spoke to me and said, "You can do the job of administrator if you want to and I will be with you. But that is not what I want for you." I was shocked. But I responded, "I want what you want. I don't know what it is, but that is what I want." Once again I experienced God communicating with one of His children in a personal way. I was encouraged.

It started to drizzle a little and as I walked in the rain, I lifted my arms and praised God for His graciousness. It felt as if a mighty weight was lifted from me. I felt noticeably lighter and happier, freer than I had been in weeks.

The election took place and I was not elected. But after that early morning talk with God, I did not expect to be. I was happy and excited about what He wanted to do. We returned to Tainan to continue praying about how to proceed.

Pray for Us

"And pray for us, too, that God may open a door for our message, so that we may proclaim the mystery of Christ, for which I am in chains. Pray that I may proclaim it clearly, as I should." Colossians 3:3-4

I n the summer of 1991, Harriet and Robert had come home for Carroll's graduation from Morrison. After we had attended Mission Meeting and I was not elected as Mission Administrator, we heard that Peter Wagner was in Kaohsiung leading a conference on something like power in ministry. Robert and I decided to attend so we could hear this great teacher and see what we might learn. During the conference, Wagner talked a good bit about the importance of intercession. He explained his belief that intercession was a spiritual gift, because he had met people who could pray for hours on end, and he said that could only be because they had a gift for it. He relayed experiences in his own life of how people had prayed for him and the results he had seen come from it. Both Robert and I were challenged and discussed his points a lot on the way home, and then related to the girls what we had heard. It was quite an interesting time.

In mid-summer, we made a quick trip back to Jackson for Robert's wedding and to put Carroll in college. This trip marked another step in the life journey; our first marriage and our last child leaving home. I sometimes wondered if the last child leaving would have had the same impact on us if we lived in the States and she had the freedom to come home on weekends, or if it would even matter.

After Nan and I returned to Taiwan following that hurried trip home, one Sunday morning I was on the ground floor where we hoped to hold services. For whatever reason, I felt someone needed to be present just in case a Chinese passerby happened to stick their head in the door and ask about the church service. Of course, no one ever did. I had been doing this for months, and so far not one curious Chinese person had entered. That morning, Nan was upstairs doing something, and I sat in a chair looking around and wondering. Maybe I was feeling sorry for myself. But I do remember that was the closest I ever came to packing my suitcase and walking away. We had been working here for over a year and had not one tangible result to show for our efforts. I wanted to be like Abraham who never wavered in his faith (Romans 4:19-20) but I surely didn't feel that way at the time. When I went upstairs and told Nan what I was feeling, her response was, "But we haven't seen the prophecy fulfilled yet. We can't leave until that happens." To be perfectly honest, at that moment, I didn't think we would ever see it fulfilled.

A couple of weeks later on another Sunday morning, Nan and I were interrupted in our meditations by a very raucous sound. We immediately knew what it was – a god parade. We looked out the window and the parade was starting right in front of our house. It was small, but we knew an active temple would draw worshippers from the neighborhood, and there would be constant noisy activity, with ongoing rituals and sacrifices. We also had come to understand that the presence of a temple meant more demonic activity in that area. It should have been discouraging, but instead it made us angry. We knew we had prayed long and hard seeking God's direction about where to locate, and felt quite strongly that we were where He wanted us to be.

Lessons from the Journey

We went outside to see where this parade would stop. To our consternation, it stopped just about four houses down from our own house. There was a little tiny building there, and they were conducting opening ceremonies for a new temple. Nan asked a few questions and found out the name of the temple: Ngo-hok-twa-ti. It was a temple to the god of prosperity.

We returned home, and Nan pulled out our Christmas card list and drafted a letter that afternoon. I went to the stationery shop to purchase envelopes and paper. We printed the letter, stuffed the envelopes, addressed them and got them ready to mail all in one afternoon. The next morning, I took them to the post office and mailed approximately 125 letters home. In the letter, we told our friends we needed people who would pray for us every day. We promised to send them a letter about every six weeks with a new list of three or four prayer requests, and would include a report on how God had answered the previous requests. Our first request was that God would close the new temple that had opened just four doors down the street from us.

In a couple of weeks, we heard back from twenty-seven people who covenanted to pray for us daily. We were happy to report to them that God had closed the temple, and it never opened again.

We also made the decision that from now on, we would pray about every opportunity that came our way. From time to time, we would be invited to do various things, often involving teaching a Bible class or teaching English. Since we were trying anything to see if God would use it to open some doors, we were doing a lot of different things. I was preaching in some of the local churches regularly, but we never saw any direct positive result in our own attempt to start a church come from that involvement. I did have a statement from two of the pastors that they might be in a position to start a Taiwanese work in the future, but the hopes I had for that never materialized. From this point forward, we planned on seeking God's direction about every invitation, even if it was only for one evening. In all honesty, there were times when we would still accept invitations against our desires to turn them down.

We both had difficulty saying no. But we did get better at it as time went on. We also learned to accept responsibilities for only a limited time and then evaluate the results to see if we wanted to continue. The only problem with the "trial period" was that the Chinese almost always wanted it to continue until Jesus returned. It was an extremely rare situation when both I and the sponsoring pastor would agree that the endeavor had not produced the desired results and it should be discontinued. I think that happened once.

From the incident with the temple, we established the new practice of sending letters to the intercessors about once a month. Our challenges and struggles continued, but in the midst of them we had an unusual sense of peace and rightness about where we were and what we were doing. It was not rational or logical that we should feel so at ease when nothing was happening that we could see, but we did. We commented on that feeling often to each other and attributed it to God answering the prayers of His people as they lifted us to His throne.

"I Will Build My Church"

"And I tell you that you are Simon Peter, and on this rock I will build my church and the gates of Hades will not overcome it." Matthew 16:19

The time from September of 1990 through the rest of 90 and 91 was very difficult. Both Nan and I believed that God is always at work, and we needed to recognize what He is doing and join him in His work. We were trying to do that, but were having great difficulty discerning exactly where He was working. All we saw was blatant idol worship representing the stranglehold Satan had on all the inhabitants of Taiwan. We lived in a dark, oppressive atmosphere in which it was difficult to spot a ray of hope. Perhaps that was a measure of our lack of vision, or perhaps it was indicative of the relentless, grinding pressure of the reign of the Prince of Darkness. Whatever it was, we were having difficulty seeing anywhere God was working. Consequently, we would try almost any opportunity that came our way. We could always imagine how God could use that to open doors and reach the lost with the gospel of His love. That philosophy led to involvements which tended to drain our energy, both physically and spiritually.

I continued to attend the monthly co-workers meetings and they continued to tell me that I was in the wrong place doing the wrong work. They said I should be living next to a school and teaching English. The unspoken part of their constant message was that the work should be done in one of their churches, and I would live nearby rather than out in the boondocks where God had called me. However, this was the type of activity that the Church Growth Study and our mission had directed us away from. So there was not a lot of encouragement from local pastors.

The co-workers also were not shy about expressing their belief that if a new church was started, the pastor of the mother church would be in charge and would make all the decisions. Any offerings from the new church start (the chapel) would go directly to the mother church and they would in turn give an "allowance" to the chapel. That is not what I envisioned, not by a long shot. Consequently the incipient seed of rebellion tucked away in the deep recesses of my heart was pulled to the surface, nurtured and cultivated by these attitudes. By nature, I am conservative and traditional. But the rigid traditionalism apparent in the pastors and some of our veteran missionaries was a constant thorn in my flesh. I struggled hard to control it, and for the most part, did keep it in check, thanks to God's grace at work in me.

While there was no overt public support or encouragement from the Chinese coworkers, two of them privately indicated that they were contemplating starting a new work and that their deacons had told them it should be in Taiwanese. Consequently, they both said it might be possible for us to work together. One of the pastors was located in a little village north of Tainan, and he wanted to start a Taiwanese service on Sunday nights. I agreed to go there and preach for six months and then we would evaluate the interest and results and decide what to do in the future.

The other pastor was in downtown Tainan, and his church was the oldest Baptist church in the city. His wife was involved in Child Evangelism in Taiwan, and they said they would help us reach out to the children around where we lived to see if anything would develop.

In early 1991, our friend Milton Lites introduced us to a young man he knew who was from Tainan. Milton's focus was music and he had met this church musician, James Ngo, who did agree to come and help us with worship. He was a great encouragement to Nan and me. His fiancée, Jessica, came with him, and they worked with us most of 1991.

About the same time, we rented a hall near our home and showed the Jesus film. Most of the attendees were children between the ages of six and twelve. We invited them to come to Sunday School and some of them did for a couple of weeks. Fortunately, James had worked with children previously and knew how to handle them, which was a good thing since neither Nan nor I had good results working with Chinese children.

There was one other result of showing the Jesus film. We picked up a young man named Chhoa Han-seng who became one of our first members. He was faithful in his attendance as long as we were in Tainan and continued in the church after we left.

When we returned to Tainan in late August of 1990, I visited Park Road church and continued to work on building my relationship with Pastor Gau. In turn, he would invite me to preach there once a month and visit prospective members with him. I preached at a couple of other churches with some degree of regularity as well. I was also teaching an English class at one of our Baptist churches whose pastor had said he wanted to cooperate with us and perhaps start a new church. Perhaps I was just doing some things in order to be active and not appear to the Chinese to be doing nothing. But nothing we did produced anything that we could say was lasting results for our church start. Discouragement was starting to creep in. Even so, we continued to believe God would do His work and we continued to pray for enlightenment and guidance and trusted in God to act.

In her spare time, Nan continued to work on her project to develop a method for teaching people to read using the Romanization system we had been taught. Interest among the Chinese ranged from none at all to outright ridicule. Undaunted, she pressed on. She called the project Lo-bat-ji, which translated into English meant Romanization.

While we were away on furlough, a couple from Singapore, Earl and Sherry Bengs, had come to Taiwan to study Chinese. They had been missionaries in Viet Nam and had to leave around 1975. They were good friends of our friends, Sam and Marion Longbottom, our neighbors when we had lived in Taichung. Earl was studying Taiwanese and Sherry was studying Mandarin. We met them early in our fourth term and it was immediately apparent that we were kindred spirits. In the course of time, we found out that in Singapore, even though most of the residents spoke English, there were still quite a lot of ethnic Chinese who only used their native language. Both Taiwanese (which was the language spoken in the Fu Chien Provence of Southern China) and Mandarin were commonly used. The situation was that many Chinese Christian young people had come to Christ and learned Christian concepts through English ministries. They could not communicate the truth of the Gospel to their parents in their native language, since the parents did not speak English. Earl and Sherry wanted to know how to speak Chinese in order to help the young folks with whom they worked communicate the love of God to their parents.

Nan talked at length with Earl about what she was doing and showed him all she was working on. He got so excited about it that he urged her to hurry up and complete the project, and then come to Singapore to use it to teach young Chinese people to read Taiwanese (Fu Chinese). This was the first encouragement she had received to work on the project; everyone in Taiwan told her it was not needed.

"I Will Build My Church"

We were very busy, but as far as we could tell, nothing we were doing would contribute to a new church start. It was discouraging. At some point in the fall of 1991, our discouragement bled into our letters home and Robert's wife Tracy shared our feelings with her dad, Phil Harris. He was teaching a Sunday School class and told her to tell us that he was asking his class to pray for us to have twelve people in our church by the end of December. That was only a few months away, and based on what we had seen so far, I felt like that was a pretty bold prayer.

I would also add that during this time I suffered with the most severe allergy attacks I had ever experienced. They seemed to get worse when we started that term. At times they were so severe I would spend two or three days in bed.

At the same time, I reconnected with a young man whom I had known at Park Road Church. When he came back to Tainan after his military service, he searched me out. When he returned to Park Road, all his friends were gone. Almost all of them were married and some had moved to other cities. He started dropping by the house almost every afternoon to chat. He would always start the conversation with "Pastor Song, I am lonely." It was so sad; it seemed I was his only friend. I tried every way I could to encourage him, but all to no avail. His constant depression finally had an effect on me, dragging me down to his level.

Perhaps it is a mark of my own spiritual insensitivity that I did not recognize either of these two factors - the draining young man and the health issues - as part of an attack on me by the evil one. I discovered that spiritual warfare is real and personal. Combined with the naysayers and the growing discouragement, these two things worked to pull all the energy and joy out of my life.

During those first two years, we both prayed often and long. Matthew 16 continued to come up in my regular Bible reading and thinking, especially the verse quoted. I focused on the phrase, "I will build my church." In all our various attempts to get a church started and seeing them produce no fruit, I kept hanging on to this thought. I always knew the church is God's church, but now this knowledge seemed to become more personal, more real. I knew my efforts would yield nothing if God did not do the work only He could do. I remember sharing this verse with our friends in the Tainan Prayer Supper one night and told them that even though we were not seeing any results from our efforts, we were not discouraged. I was waiting to see how God would act to accomplish His work in building a church. In the meeting that night was a new couple, Stephen and Sara Cheng. They were Taiwanese who had returned to Tainan after living in the States for many years.

The following Sunday, two brothers, Stephen Cheng and his brother George, showed up at our church with a handful of their relatives. Both of them were Christians, Presbyterians, who had been living in the States for a good number of years. They had both been invited to return to Tainan to work in the new Presbyterian Hospital that had recently opened. They explained that they would help us get started by coming to worship with us for a time, because they said, "Chinese will not come to an empty building. You need some people in your church." Soon after they joined us, George, who was a dentist, invited me to teach a Bible class to the people in his department before they started their day's work. I added this weekly class to the other things I was doing.

A Different Conclusion

"The Spirit of the Lord is on me, because he has appointed me to preach good news to the poor. He has sent me to proclaim freedom for the prisoners and recovery of sight for the blind, to release the oppressed, to proclaim the year of the Lord's favor." Luke 4:18-19.

Our new friends brought several of their nephews and nieces with them to church every week. One of their nieces played the piano for our worship and this was a tremendous blessing for us all. I believe the sudden growth of our tiny congregation was a direct result of the prayers Phil Harris led his Sunday School class to offer for us; that by the end of 1991 we would have twelve people in our morning worship. At the end of that year, we did indeed have between twelve and fifteen people present every Sunday.

Now that there were actually people in the congregation, I had to give some thought to the format of the service. In my traditional Baptist background, every service ended with an invitation time. I started feeling uncomfortable with this format while pastoring in Bellefontaine, especially on Sunday nights. I was 99.9% positive that everyone present was either a believer or had been in the church so long that they were convinced they were. Now, in this Chinese culture, where the "members" of the church were all actually visitors from Presbyterian churches, I felt more uncomfortable than ever in offering any kind of invitation. But to just close in prayer seemed somewhat abrupt.

As I was praying about this, I read the above passage in Luke and backtracked to the original passage in Isaiah 61. I could not get them out of my mind. I was convinced that God had power to deal with any problem that any of us faced, and I earnestly, even desperately, wanted to see God do something big. As I prayed about this for a few weeks, gradually the idea came to me that I should pray for the people.

Nan and I both had a firm belief in the power of God to heal. I mentioned earlier that when we started the term, I was regularly preaching in two or three places. We often would pray for individual needs at the conclusion of the service. This prayer was not a part of the service; it was something we did when someone requested it. We would specifically ask to pray with anyone in the service that the pastor had indicated was sick or had some other big issue they were facing. I thought, "Why not do this in my own church?" So at the end of the sermon, I would pray for all those gathered.

I would start on one end of the row of seats and go to each individual, place my hands on their head or shoulder, and pray for them by name. It was a general prayer for blessing unless I knew of some specific need in their lives. After a few weeks of doing this, one or two of them would tell me during the week of some issue they faced, whether it was illness or something else. This helped my guide my prayers for them at the end of the sermon.

This simple start became the way we concluded all our services. At first it was just me, and then Nan started joining in praying for the women. Later, as other leaders joined us, both fellow missionaries and church-appointed elders, also became members of the prayer team.

When I first started doing this, there were only about twelve or so people in church on any given Sunday. That made it easy to pray for everyone in a short time. When God added more people to the congregation, we gradually shifted from praying for everyone to praying for those with specific needs. We would announce that anyone who had a need could come to the front of the church and receive prayer. In the early days, we could still finish in about fifteen minutes. But as God added even more to our church, there were times when it would take an hour or so depending on what needed prayer. Sometimes the needs were great and deep-seated. In those cases, it always took longer. Through this process we witnessed God do some amazing work. I truly believed that we were "setting the captives free" from the spiritual bondage in which they had been bound for so long.

East Asia Men's Prayer Retreat in Korea

"Come to me, all you who are weary and burdened, and I will give you rest. Take my yoke upon you and learn from me, for I am gentle and humble in heart, and you will find rest for your souls. For my yoke is easy and my burden is light." Matthew 11: 28-30

Nan and I prayed often; we each had our own private devotional time and often we prayed together. We had infrequent prayer times with our friends, Milton and Nannette. Additionally, our mission sponsored a prayer retreat for all missionaries once a year and the men of the Evangelism Department met twice a year to discuss our work. A lot of these meetings were focused on prayer. The same was true for the women in our mission and Nan also participated in the Taiwan Missionary Fellowship's Women's Prayer Retreat. So we were praying.

By spring of 1992, I was really busy. I was regularly preaching at our new church, leading two Bible studies, one in Taiwanese and one in English, and attending a couple of prayer meetings with missionaries and Chinese folks. Spiritually, I was drawing more out of the bank than I was putting in. It was at that point we received notification of a retreat being planned for the men of the East Asia and Southeast Asia regions. This included the missionaries from Japan, Korea, Hong Kong, Taiwan, Singapore, Malaysia, the Philippines and Thailand. Normally, I tend to shy away from large groups because they seldom provide the solitude I need for refreshment and renewal. But I was looking for some change, something that had the potential for "recharging" my batteries.

The retreat took place in Korea and was a joint prayer and ministry experience. The first part of the week was the prayer retreat at a resort center, followed by a ministry project. After the prayer retreat, all of us were divided into teams and sent to work in different parts of Korea. We worked with existing Baptist churches to assist in conducting weekend revivals. I was on a team sent to Pusan. It was quite enlightening to see how the Korean churches operated because they were looked on with a lot of respect by the churches in Taiwan. Korea was noted for its numerous churches and strong prayer life. It was predicted to become the first Christian nation in Asia.

I was on a team with two missionaries from Japan and one from Indonesia whose name was Ed Sanders. I forget the name of the church, but the pastor's name was Kong. The missionary from Indonesia called him King Kong because in the room designated for the deacons to meet, he had a chair – a big chair with red cushions and gold tassels – on a raised platform. From that spot, he presided over the discussions. That pattern was followed when our team was working with them. We all felt our friend aptly named him, but we were afraid to actually call him by that name. The time in Korea was interesting for several reasons that were not necessarily spiritual, but it was spiritually significant for me personally because I went seeking God. I needed some time away from the routine in Tainan to refresh my spiritual life.

(Years later, I was on an outside evaluation team for the church growth study for Central and Eastern Europe, in 1997-98, and Ed Sanders was on it too. The other

116

members were Jim West from Hong Kong, Tak Owee from Japan, and a pastor from Romania whose name I have forgotten. Ed was a fun man with a dry sense of humor and almost everything he said was funny, but he was pretty deep spiritually and I liked him a lot. He had retired the year prior to this study but came to help us. On a sad note, about a year and a half after our study, he went in for a routine physical and the doctor did a chest x-ray. He found spots on Ed's lung and diagnosed him with lung cancer. When the doctor asked him how long he had smoked, he replied, "Doc, I've never smoked a day in my life! But I did ride a moter scooter around Jakarta for decades." They figured the pollution probably got him. I grieved when I heard he had died.)

During the prayer retreat time, I read a lot of scripture and for some reason was drawn to Ezekiel. That was unusual; normally I felt drawn to the Psalms or one of the Gospels. But I spent a lot of time reading Ezekiel and two thoughts stood out to me. One was the frequent charge God brought against the shepherds. He had some hard things to say about them. I came away from those passages with the conviction that my role in the new church was to be a good shepherd. I had always tried to do that; to love the people of God and to minister to them in any way I could. But this seemed to make it more imperative than ever before.

The other point was that I noticed God often said He would bless Israel even though they had rebelled against Him, had turned their back on Him and followed other gods. He said He would bless them and use them to declare His praises to the people around Israel. The main point God made was that He would do this in spite of them and do it for His name's honor and glory. He made it plain that He would use the very people who had profaned His name to declare the glory of His name. That made a huge impression on me and underscored all over again that God will do His work. And often He does it in spite of how we mess things up.

After the ministry time with the churches, we all gathered back in Seoul before returning to our fields of service. Milton and I shared a room that last night. After entertaining ourselves wandering around in the shopping district (where I purchased a leather motorcycle jacket), we had something to eat and returned to the room. That night we had a long discussion about a book he had recently read. It was by Benny Hinn, who was just beginning his ministry. One thought from the book that really impressed Milton was that in order to live a life filled and directed by the Holy Spirit, a person had to make sacrifices. We discussed what that meant, because Hinn had not talked about sacrifice from the standpoint of physical persecution and suffering, but more from the standpoint of choosing to put God first in everything. For instance, there are times when a person has worked all day and is tired and wants to sleep. It is a sacrifice to skip sleep in order to pray and meditate on God's Word. Or there are times when a person has been working hard and wants to relax by going to a movie or something like that. At those times, it is a sacrifice to forgo entertainment in order to spend time with God. Then there are other times when a person is with family and wants to spend time with them, but must sacrifice some of that time in order to concentrate on God and worship Him. It is a sacrifice to make it a priority to spend time in prayer and time alone with God. Those sacrifices are hard, but that is the price of spiritual power and understanding. We talked a lot about that whole concept and agreed that if we wanted to see God move in power in our ministry, we would need to willingly make sacrifices. At that time, I had no idea what that meant, but was to learn when I returned to Tainan.

It was also during the prayer retreat that God placed a radical thought in my head, so radical I didn't share it with Milton. I felt quite strongly that He wanted me to carry a cross in Tainan when I returned. I tried to block it from my mind, but in His own gentle way, God would not let me ignore it.

Our flight home left late in the afternoon so it was around ten when I arrived at the airport. I assumed I would be able to catch a bus from there to Tainan, but they were all sold out. So I took a taxi to the local train station, but the last train had already departed by the time I got there. I was stuck with taking the dreaded night train, which left around midnight and stopped at every crossing between there and Tainan. It was well after sunup when I finally arrived. Nan met me at the station all excited about some wonderful meeting and speaker and said we had to go. I told her to take me home and let me sleep, so we went to the house and had breakfast together, chatted briefly about the men's conference, and then I took a nap while she went to the morning meeting. When she returned and I woke up, she brought me up to date on the unique points of these special meetings, and we went to the evening session together.

Through the work and influence of the Year 2000 Committee, various speakers would come to Taiwan from time to time, and frequently some would make their way to Tainan. The current series of meetings was held in a large municipal auditorium with over a thousand Chinese people in attendance, along with a handful of missionaries. The speaker was Mahesh Chavda, a man of Indian descent who grew up in Africa. He was led to faith in Christ by Southern Baptist missionaries, so when Nan introduced herself to him, he had an immediate connection with her, and later with me. I don't recall the sermon, but following his presentation, he invited people to come up and receive prayer.

That is when I witnessed something I could not understand. He would pray for people and they would fall down. People were standing behind those who received prayer and would catch those who fell. Mahesh invited the ones who had been prayed for in the previous meetings to come up and help him pray. Nan went forward and I continued to watch.

I was sitting by my friend Ron Lamb, a fellow missionary who was Canadian Pentecostal. I started asking him what was going on and he explained that when a person who is in desperate need of spiritual help or experiencing an intense desire for some touch from God comes to receive prayer, the Holy Spirit may come and fill them, causing them to fall down. This could produce a kind of sleep that might last anywhere from five minutes to five hours. I asked why some fell down and others did not. He said perhaps it was due to their expectations or due to their willingness to allow God to touch them. My mind was reeling.

After a short time, the stage was filled with bodies lying on the floor. The ones praying were running out of people to catch those who fell when they were prayed for. Ron said, "Let's go up and help catch the people." I figured it didn't take any kind of special whatever to do that so I followed him up on the stage.

After just a few minutes Nan came up to me and brought Mahesh. She introduced us and he said "I will pray for you." As he prayed, I felt myself growing weak and somehow knew I could stiffen myself and not fall down. But I also knew I was in need of some kind of touch from God and had been seeking something to renew my spirit. So I just let go and fell back, hoping the little Chinese women behind me could actually catch me.

Lying on the floor, I was not unconscious; I was aware of movement around me. But at the same time, I was also aware that my heart was full of praise for God. It was unlike anything I had ever experienced previously. I wanted to just stay there awhile and praise God. But I sensed movement close to me and opened one eye. There was some man holding a video camera about a foot from my face and it was focused on me. I thought,

"Okay, that is enough of that!" and got up. Immediately, Mahesh was standing by me and said, "Now you have been prayed for; pray for others." So I did. To my amazement, they also fell to the floor.

I don't know how long the evening lasted, but when we returned home my mind was still reeling. I could not match anything in my religious experience or anything in my educational experience that would explain what I had witnessed. Even so, I seemed to instinctively know I had experienced something for which I had been longing for quite a long time.

We returned to the meeting the following night and heard testimonies of people who had been healed from illnesses or had been freed from the oppression of demon activity in their lives. I knew this was the answer to the question that had plagued me for several years: "What is it going to take to make a difference in people who regularly see a demonstration of demonic power in their surroundings?" The answer was the power of God. I knew that, but now had actually seen it.

The events of that April were really the catalyst for all that happened in the following three or four years. They also started me on a different kind of search to try and understand what I was seeing and experiencing in light of my understanding of the Bible. It spurred me to look for and read books that somehow addressed this subject. All those things worked together to really reshape my theology.

Jesus often withdrew from the crowd and his ministry to spend time with His heavenly Father. I desperately wanted a new and fresh touch from God. I received it and was forever changed.

I pray for you to be open to God's Spirit and to diligently pursue Him in your life. There are blessings hard to imagine and a level of intimacy that cannot be explained in the natural world. These are the elements of the transformed life, and they equip you to face any trial or obstacle that comes your way.

Carry Your Cross

"The he said to them all: 'If anyone would come after me, he must deny himself and take up his cross daily and follow me." Luke 9:23

While I was in Korea at the prayer retreat, I read this verse again. I always interpreted it to be a kind of symbolic statement; the cross represented a person denying the natural desires he had in order to follow the principles and commands God laid out for us all through the scriptures. I never interpreted it to mean that we should literally carry a cross even though I knew some people had done that. In fact, a student we knew at Mississippi College did that very thing. He made a huge cross out of wood, put some kind of rollers on the base of it, and carried it on his shoulder around the country. He would often have an opportunity to give his testimony and would frequently be asked to preach in local churches wherever he happened to be. I thought that worked for him, but it was not me.

After I got back from Korea, the thought of carrying a cross got pushed to the background by what I had witnessed in the meetings led by Mahesh. Those meetings raised questions like, "What does it mean when a person falls down and goes into a trance? Why do some fall and some don't? Is it possible for this to be a regular part of a church's ministry to help those in need?" I struggled to find answers.

Gradually the idea of carrying a cross returned and would not go away. I argued with God that He had chosen the wrong person to do something as radical as that. Because of my size I already stood out and was probably considered a freak by many. But it is a funny thing; God does not let up when there is something special He wants you to do. I suppose that if you deny the urge long enough it will go away, but I feared that something else might be lost in the process. Ultimately, I did acquiesce and agree to do what He asked me to do. Until that time, I had not told anyone what I was feeling, not even Nan.

When I decided I would do it, I walked around the corner to the bamboo store. The Chinese used bamboo in lots of different ways, and the bamboo store sold all kinds of products from stools to brooms. They specialized in selling big, long pieces to be used as scaffolding in construction. That is what I needed.

I explained to the owner that I needed a cross about twelve feet long, and I was surprised at how easily he understood my request. He whipped one together in about five minutes, and I think it cost around $2.00. When I carried it home on my shoulder, it almost caused several traffic accidents. Imagine a white man about a foot taller than everyone else carrying a twelve foot cross and you can imagine the stares and gawks I received. That short walk prompted more talks with God about when and where I should actually carry the cross. I finally decided I would carry it early in the morning when I went out for my morning walk. I had given up jogging because that caused my hips and knees to hurt.

I mapped out a circuit that encircled the general area of our church. The route was about three miles long and passed by two significant points for prayer. I would leave the house around six in the morning and wind up back home about forty-five minutes later.

The first point of concentrated prayer was at the intersection of a crossroad which was actually a "cross path." Two narrow lanes crossed, and right on the edge of the intersection was a huge banyan tree. The Taiwanese worshipped those trees because they could grow so big, live so long, and withstand the fiercest storms. They were convinced that the strength and longevity of the tree indicated that spirits lived in the tree and protected it. I noticed that there was a simple worship place at the base of this tree. It consisted of a small idol house and a small incense pot. Every morning when I walked by the tree, incense was burning in the pot, which indicated someone had preceded me and prayed to the spirit in the tree. I would stop and pray, asking God to break the bondage Satan had placed on the Taiwanese people by opening their eyes so they would be able to see and hear the gospel of Christ (2 Cor. 4:4). Then I would go on praying as I walked.

The second point of prayer was a small Presbyterian church. When we moved into the area, we did not know it was there; it was on one of the small lanes back in one of the neighborhoods. I would stop in front of it and pray for the pastor and leaders asking God to encourage them, to give them a vision for His plans for them, and for their members to be effective witnesses for the gospel in this dark area.

After I had been doing this for about two months, one day I walked by the banyan tree and was surprised to see that it had fallen down. My first thought was, "That must have been some terrific storm last night." Then I remembered we had experienced no storm at all. I stood there staring in amazement, dumbfounded. Then a quiet voice came to me: "This is an example in the physical realm of what happens in the spiritual realm when My people pray." I stood there for a minute or so longer wondering what it all meant and finally walked on. Over the course of the next few days and weeks, I watched as the folks in the neighborhood propped up the tree, dug out the hole to make room for the roots, trimmed the limbs, and did all the usual things they did when a storm knocked over a tree. But it seemed to have little effect. I watched as the remaining leaves dropped off and wondered if the tree would ever recover. (After I stopped carrying the cross, I didn't often go by the tree and now cannot remember if it recovered or not.)

I continued to carry the cross for about four months. Then one morning in September during my devotional time, God said, "The time for carrying the cross is over. Now I will open doors of evangelism." That was really good news for me because we had not seen one single person make a decision to follow Christ since we had been in this location. It is difficult to start a new church with no members. The promise stirred hope in my heart. Even so, it was about two more months until we saw the first profession of faith and then another three months after that until the first baptism. But they did come.

Once I stopped walking in the neighborhood I had no way to watch the Presbyterian Church. But later I discovered that they moved into larger quarters on the other side of the little "stream" that separated Tainan City from Tainan County.

I learned that often God will push us out of our comfort zone to accomplish His purposes. One benefit of being pushed into unfamiliar situations is that the process helps us grow in our faith. The submission to God's direction, even when it calls one to do things he or she would not ordinarily do, always leads to blessings. I have come to believe that when we obey, we are always blessed, and often someone else is blessed as well.

I pray that you will develop such a deep relationship with your heavenly Father that if He asks you to do something that is outside of your comfort zone, you will have the courage to do it. In following His leadership, you will strengthen your faith and minister to someone who needs a touch from God.

Matt Chen and Family

"No one sews a patch of unshrunk cloth on an old garment, for the patch will pull away from the garment, making the tear worse. Neither do men pour new wine into old wineskins. If they do the skins will burst, the wine will run out and the wineskins will be ruined. No, they pour new wine into new wineskins, and both are preserved." Matthew 9:16-17

One morning, in the late summer of 1992 during my devotional time, God brought this verse to my attention. It was one of those times when I knew it was important, but didn't know what it meant or how it would apply to my situation. I thought and prayed about it for several days.

In the next Tainan Missionary Prayer Supper, once the eating was finished and we gathered to pray, each missionary related a little about what was happening in their work or something specific for which they needed prayer. That night, we had a new family, Matt and Elizabeth Chen. They were introduced to us as having recently moved to Tainan from Kansas City, Missouri, where they had been living for the past five years. We learned that Matt was a native of Tainan and the only believer in his family. His wife, Elizabeth, was from Australia and he had met her when she was in Taiwan teaching English at Trinity Baptist Church.

That night as we went around the room, I related that there was nothing new happening in our work; we were continuing with the same group of "members," and Nan and I were surprisingly at peace about where we were and what we were doing. Then I shared with the group these two verses, saying, "I am sure they are important, but I just don't know what they mean for us yet."

After the prayer time, Matt was suddenly standing at my side (he had been seated across the room; I don't know how he got there so quick) He said God had given him that same verse just about a week ago, and he wanted to come and work with me. He said he wanted to help "build a new wineskin church." I was not exactly sure what that meant, but could see how that could easily be the interpretation of those verses, so I welcomed his assistance.

At that time, we had the two Cheng brothers in the church who had come to work at the Sin Lau Hospital. Their niece played the piano and she sort of led our worship. It was not great, but it was something. Matt and family joined us the Sunday following the prayer meeting and met everyone. I thought they would become regular attenders, but strangely, in the following weeks, their attendance was irregular. When I tried to talk to him, he was withdrawn and guarded - a radical change from his initial enthusiasm. I asked him out for lunch one day to have a chat and see if I could find out what was going on. He had been so excited at first and then suddenly had turned cool towards me and the work. During lunch, we had a heart to heart talk, and I found out the root of the problem.

While in Kansas City, he had approached a Southern Baptist pastor about working with him. Initially the pastor was accepting, but when he discovered Matt had not graduated from college and seminary, he basically turned him off and refused to have anything to do with him. After that first worship service, Matt discovered I was Southern Baptist and just assumed I would have the same response to him. It took several conversations over a couple of weeks to convince him that I really wanted him to help us and would welcome him not only as a member, but also as a potential leader. I discovered that while in Kansas City he had helped lead worship in the church they attended, and felt that is what God wanted him to do in Taiwan. We finally got that sorted out, and he became a regular member and was accepted as a leader in the church. He started working with the young pianist to help lead worship. She soon left, so he became our worship leader. He played the guitar, so it was a little adjustment for us all. But it worked.

We had several discussions about the scripture that God used to draw us together. Matt and Elizabeth had been members of a Vineyard Church in Kansas City and experienced some of the manifestations of the Spirit of God that I was just beginning to catch a glimpse of, like healings, speaking in tongues, and other miraculous happenings. There were times when we tried to figure out what a "new wineskin" church would be - a topic that we worked on for the first couple of years we were together. On more than a few occasions, Matt would tell me I was holding on to too much Southern Baptist tradition to ever become a new wineskin church. In a way, I thought he might be right, but it was really hard to let go of all my previous experience and education. Privately, I was learning why Jesus said you cannot pour new wine into old wineskins. There was too much that was familiar and comfortable in all my previous educational and ministerial experiences. However, we did find much common ground, sharing many of the same hopes for the future and many of the same goals for the proclamation of the gospel in Taiwan.

I find it interesting that after all these years, I continue to see how God is doing things differently and how the traditional church either struggles with or flatly refuses to accept some of the things that are happening in today's church culture. This includes mainline Protestant denominations' refusal to accept some of the work of the Holy Spirit. Traditional Protestantism has always seemed to focus on the excesses and abuses that happen in some of the Charismatic churches. I always wondered why they could not take the approach Paul took with the Corinthian church and help them find ways to make it work without the distractions. It also includes accepting and using the growing number of leaders who have not received any seminary training, but are effectively reaching segments of the population that the traditional church has not impacted.

As you mature in your own spiritual life, I pray that you will be focused on Biblical truth and not allow the traditions of the church to stand between you and what God wants to do. God is always at work and always intends to use His own children in that work. Seek Him and follow His leading.

Living Water Church

"If anyone is thirsty, let him come to me and drink. Whoever believes in me, as the Scripture has said, streams of living water will flow from within him. By this he meant the Spirit, whom those who believed in him were later to receive." John 7:37b-39a

W hen we first started our church, we chose a name that was very generic. I can't remember now exactly what it was, but it didn't even have the word "church" in it. We had a signboard painted that we placed on the sidewalk on Sunday mornings.

The Cheng's were coming with their clan and then Matt and Elizabeth joined us. They had three children at the time so our number swelled. Nan and I felt like we were making progress and could see how the seeds had been planted for something to grow. We were happy with the results so far.

One Sunday, someone asked us about the church's name. We explained that we had chosen it when it was just Nan and me, and we always thought that when God brought members to us, then the members could help decide on an appropriate name. The response was, "Now is the time. The name you have is not good." We asked why it was not good, and they replied that it sounded like some kind of political organization that was trying to enlist people to something rather clandestine. This is another good lesson on why missionaries need input from native language speakers when naming things; we don't understand the nuances of the language and the cultural association with the characters. For example, one name we considered was the Thian-An Church. The Thian came from my Chinese name, Thian-un, which meant "heaven's grace" and An which was Nan's Chinese name which meant "peace." We reasoned that it would be translated as "Heaven's Grace and Peace Church." Not bad, right? Well, at about the same time we were thinking about a name, hundreds of thousands of students in China revolted against the government. The military rolled into Beijing with tanks and guns, resulting in a massacre that made global news. The place of the massacre? Tian An Men Square. We would have forever been associated with that cultural rebellion. Fortunately, we didn't choose that name.

The discussion took some time because a variety of names were suggested and then rejected. One big issue was whether or not the word "Baptist" would be included in the name. Matt was totally against it, the Cheng's who were Presbyterians were sort of neutral, and Nan and I kind of wanted it in there. We could see no reason for it not to be a part of our name.

In the discussion, we also looked at a couple of scripture references and encouraged the attendees to pray and think hard about what we faced and we would discuss it again the following week. The next discussion brought a few more scriptures to consider, one of which was the one listed above. We all liked the truth expressed and felt it represented what we desired to see happen. So we agreed to pray and think for another week. The next Sunday, we firmly decided on using the scripture from John 7. Then we discussed various names that could come from that reference. Several were suggested, and once again we agreed to go home to pray and think about it for another week.

When we returned, the unanimous choice was Living Water Church. It did not have the name "Baptist" included, and Nan and I were okay with that. At the time, many Baptist churches in the States were dropping the word "Baptist" and especially "Southern Baptist" from their name. In a way I could see why some churches in the Northeast, Northwest, or far West would want to do that. But I never could understand why a church in the South would go from something like Calvary Baptist Church to The Church of the Cross or Calvary Community Chapel. I guess that was my strong traditional mindset coming out.

Tradition and culture are important; they can provide a level of stability and constancy in our changing world. I pray that you will remember that God is not static; that He is always relating to us in the world and culture in which we live. You can learn from church history and tradition, but don't let tradition prevent you from seeing what God is doing.

Steve and Vicki

"Everyone was filled with awe, and many wonder and miraculous signs were done by the apostles."
Acts 2:43

T he couple of months following the time Matt joined us were rather routine. Matt planned the worship times and I planned the sermon for the day. Matt and Elizabeth had been in the Vineyard Church, where they used home groups for all their Bible study and discipleship, so it was natural that he wanted to follow that pattern. He had come back to Taiwan with the idea of working that way and had already established a home group. Nan and I attended almost every week, unless we had other commitments. He was learning about how to function as a church leader, and I was learning about the home group process. Philosophically, I could see the benefit of the home group because it was a good place to invite people who wouldn't come to a church, and introduce them to Bible reading and prayer, and it was also used as a tool to disciple new believers. But I didn't like the fact that there was no consistency in Bible study.

During this time, another speaker arranged through the Year 2000 Committee came to Tainan. This time it was a couple, Steve and Vicki Long from California. They had been members of John Wimber's Vineyard Church there for several years and had followed him around a lot. (John Wimber is the man who started the Vineyard Church movement, which has developed into a denomination. I was helped and influenced by reading two books he wrote.) I think Steve was one of their deacons or elders or somehow in leadership there. They had learned a lot about a type of ministry I had only observed from a distance. They were scheduled to speak in a Presbyterian church, which Nan and I attended. On that first night, we witnessed supernatural workings of the Holy Spirit that were very far removed from our Southern Baptist church experiences, but they fit the pattern of some of the things we witnessed when Mahesh Chavda was in town.

As we had previously seen, the session always started with a period of worship followed by a sermon, and then a time when those in need of prayer were invited to come to the front. As they were being prayed for, some people fell down, some started screaming, some started crying, some started laughing – it was all a little unnerving, to be honest.

We went back the second night and heard testimonies from some people who said they had been healed, and from others who said they had been freed from demons. I didn't know how to understand it all, but I was intrigued. For the first time, I was witnessing a power strong enough to free people who had been bound by Satan for most of their lives. I wanted to understand what was happening.

On that second night, we were approached by a woman we had met at some of these conferences. Many of them were held in different Presbyterian churches, and since we were among the very few white faces present, we kind of stood out. This woman told us that Steve and Vicki were scheduled to go to an orphanage the next night, but their ride had fallen through. She asked if we were available to drive them, and we jumped at the chance to spend more time with them and get some answers about what we were seeing.

During the drive, we got to know them and also asked many of the questions that were burning through our minds. The night in the orphanage was just like the other sessions we

126

had seen, except this time they asked us to join their prayer team. With fear and trembling, we agreed, even though all we knew to do was to follow the example we had witnessed in the other sessions we had attended.

Steve and Vicki were in town for about a month and whenever we were not otherwise engaged, we were with them. Sometimes we drove them to other churches, and at other times we just attended the churches they visited in Tainan. We ministered with them and gradually sort of moved into their ministry team. Whenever we were with them, we picked their brains on how to handle problems we witnessed; specifically how to pray for the demonized and how to pray for someone who was "slain in the Spirit" and simply lying on the floor.

We learned much from Steve and Vicki about a dimension of ministry that was unlike anything we had ever heard about. It reminded me of stories from the New Testament of when Jesus and the disciples would pray for people and God would move to meet their needs, often in dramatic ways. The first lesson we learned was to keep our eyes open when we prayed for someone so we could see what God was doing with them. Steve and Vicki taught us little things to look for that indicated God was at work or what to notice if we thought Satan was trying to interfere with the prayer session.

The other lesson was to learn to listen to God's Spirit even as we prayed for someone. At first it was difficult, and I think we often just repeated phrases we had heard other leaders use. But the more we prayed for people, the more attuned to the Spirit we became, and we were able to pinpoint specific things to ask people about. Most of the time, the topics that the Spirit revealed to us that needed prayer and confession related either to unconfessed sin or to unforgiveness. We came to believe that unforgiveness was a huge problem in the church and a significant detriment to the work God desired to do among His people.

All the while, I was searching the scriptures to try and come up with a theology that included these new workings of God while holding on to a true Biblical theology. In this process, I realized that my Southern Baptist education and experience did not include the things I was seeing, which included people healed of illnesses, set free from demonization, and being drawn into a deeper relationship with God. Finally, I arrived at the point where I accepted that even though what I was experiencing and witnessing might not be Southern Baptist, it was Biblical. I determined that I would be Biblical above all else and would try to maintain my Southern Baptist convictions and traditions as long as they did not conflict with what I saw God doing.

All of this experience and new knowledge fit right in with my desire to pray for the people in the church following the sermon. Now as I prayed for them, I was more attuned to the leadership of the Holy Spirit and more able to let Him guide those prayers.

Nan was having some of the same struggles, and we discussed the conflict between our previous experiences and the new things we were learning. We accepted the things we were experiencing and held on to them, feeling better equipped to minister to the people in our growing congregation.

I pray that when you see God doing things you cannot understand, you will search the scriptures in prayer and try to gain a mature acceptance. Remember, John said, *"As for you, the anointing you received from him remains in you, and you do not need anyone to teach you. But as his anointing teaches you about all things and as that anointing is real, not counterfeit – just as it has taught you, remain in him."* (1 John 2:27) Then later he said, *"Dear friends, do not believe every spirit, but test the spirits to see whether they are from God, because many false prophets have gone out into the world."*

(1 John 4:1) Your anointing – the Holy Spirit – will teach you as you seek Him and commit to following His leading.

First Conversion

"Preach the Word; be prepared in season and out of season; correct, rebuke and encourage – with great patience and careful instruction." 2 Timothy 4:2

I mention this verse not because it was one which seemed to be guiding me at the time, but because it describes what we were doing. We were preaching the Word at every opportunity we had. Especially in the first two years we accepted any opportunity to minister in any way possible. Once God brought some people to join us in worship, we tended to concentrate a lot on them. We helped in whatever way we could to make clear Biblical truth to young believers or to those who were trying to decide to accept Jesus. Once Matt joined us and we started going to his home group that expanded our contacts. Naturally, since they already had a relationship with him, he did most of the work with them; we were just there as backup to add our support and affirmation to what he was teaching.

Steve and Vicki left Tainan and went somewhere else for a few weeks, and when they returned, Matt invited them to the home group. Even though it was a much smaller setting than they usually were in, they generally followed the same format. Matt led a couple of songs and then Steve preached, with Matt translating. Following the preaching, Steve asked if anyone had questions. Some did and they were answered. Then he asked if anyone was there who had not accepted Jesus, and one young lady admitted that she had not. Her name was Chhui Pek-hui and her English name was Amy.

She was obviously quite interested in all that was said. Steve asked her why she was there, and she told us it was because of this man who worked in her office. His name was Ong Chhong-beng (Gary) and he was in the home group. He was a believer already. One day at the water cooler Amy asked Gary, "What is the meaning of life?" He responded, "To know Jesus," and then walked away.

She said she had been asking people that question for several years and received all kinds of answers. Suddenly, here was someone who gave her a short, direct answer and said it with such certainty that she knew it must be right. She wanted to know this Jesus. The rest of the evening was spent explaining who Jesus was and how she could believe in Him. That night she accepted Jesus. She said she wanted to be baptized immediately.

Matt wisely discussed with her the reality that her family might not agree with her decision and might react in a way that she did not like. She said they loved her and it would be all right. She was going home that night to tell them and invite them to the baptism.

The next night I was called to Matt's house. The home group met up on the third floor and I made my way up there. When I entered through the kitchen, I saw Amy sitting at a table crying, and I wondered what was wrong. Her frightened eyes were puffy, and her face bore the marks of having been slapped. Her hair was disheveled and she looked confused and distressed. The previous night when she returned home to tell her parents about her decision and to invite them to the baptism, her mother struck her several times in the face, and kicked her (literally) out of the house screaming curses at her, telling her to go to her Christian friends.

She went to the house of another home group member, a young lady named Josie, and spent the night there. After Amy left, her mother threw all her clothes and things into the street. Her brother picked them up and took them to Amy at Josie's house. So everyone was gathered to tell me what had happened and discuss what to do about the situation. She stayed with Josie several days until her mother threatened to burn Josie's mother's house down.

Gradually everyone in the church learned about Amy's situation and was very concerned about her. No one really had a good suggestion about how to help her. Nan and I discussed inviting her to move in with us since Carroll was gone to college so her room was available.

On the following Sunday after church, Stephen and Sara said that Amy could move into their house; they had room because all their daughters had married and no longer lived with them. That solved the crisis for the time being, but since Amy's parents were so against her being a Christian, it was obvious that they would not be attending her baptism. Because of their reaction and because Amy still wanted them to be present when she was baptized, she did not want to be baptized immediately. She wanted to wait a little longer to see if they would change their mind.

We saw our first conversion, but it would be a while before we had a baptism.

Our First Baptism

"Therefore go and make disciple of all nations, baptizing them in the name of the Father and of the Son and of the Holy Spirit, and teaching them to obey everything I have commanded you. And surely I am with you always, to the very end of the age." Matthew 28:19-20

I use the Scripture above not because God gave it to me at the time, but because it had been a central part of my faith for many years. If I had a life verse, this would probably be it. In our work in Taiwan, we always knew that anytime someone decided to accept Jesus, we would baptize them. Now we had a candidate.

Amy wanted to be baptized, but really wanted to invite her parents to come and be a part of this portion of her life. She hoped to use it as a testimony to them about her faith and hoped that some of us would be able to share the gospel with them so that they would find Jesus in the same way she had found Him. But finally she realized this was not going to happen and agreed to go ahead and be baptized, which took place in February 1993. We had been working there for about two and a half years and finally were able to see some fruit from our endeavors.

Of course, we had no baptistery in our little apartment, but we were only about three miles from the coast. It was an easy decision to use the China Straits as our baptistery. The beach was not the most pristine; it was used by fishermen who had a lot of oyster racks and it often was covered with a lot of debris on it from the racks and other bits and pieces of junk that had been left there or washed ashore. But we used it anyway. I do remember it was chilly that day and the water was cold.

It was soon after that baptism that Josie, another young lady who was in Matt's home group, came to the meeting one night very troubled. She had been told by her parents that it was time for her to marry. In a deviation from the normal pattern of arranged marriage, they told her she could pick out a man and if she could not choose one, then they would choose someone. It was unusual for a parent to give a daughter that kind of choice.

She shared her quandary with the group and we prayed for her. I remember Matt asking her if she knew anyone she would consider marrying. She did say that there was a young man where she worked who had caught her eye, but she was sure he was not a believer. We agreed to pray for him. His English name was Andrew. For the next couple of weeks, we prayed for Andrew, and then Josie came to home group and announced that she had invited him to attend with her. He could not come that night, but would come the following week and it was his birthday.

To understand what happened next, you have to know that the Chinese generally only celebrate two birthdays in a person's life. The first celebration is the first birthday, because they are reasonably sure by then that the baby will live. Historically, many babies died during their first year of existence. Infant mortality was very high in China and also in Taiwan at that time.

The second time to celebrate was on the 60th birthday, which was a time to celebrate a complete life. For centuries, in most parts of the world, shorter life spans were typical, and not many people were expected to survive much past fifty or fifty-five. To reach age sixty was considered a real blessing. The number sixty was also significant because it completed five cycles of the 12-year zodiac, which many Chinese depended on to guide their lives.

Traditionally, most Chinese people celebrated their birthday on Chinese New Year, along with everyone else in the country. Many did not even know the actual day they were born. Matt differed from this part of Chinese culture, maybe partly because he had married an Australian and been introduced to Western birthday customs. He was also looking for ways to make each person in the church feel valued, so he felt we should celebrate each person's special day with a cake and singing.

The night Andrew came to home group, we followed the usual format – a song or two and a Bible teaching followed by prayer time. Then we had refreshments, which was his birthday cake. We put it in front of him, lit the candles, told him to make a wish and sang Happy Birthday. He was supposed to blow out the candles and then cut the cake. But he just sat there staring at the cake. We all got silent and finally Matt asked what was wrong. He said he had never celebrated his birthday before and it was special; he didn't know how to understand his feelings. He said the cake and celebration made him feel really special. We finally cut the cake and it was a good celebration. About two weeks later, he came to the worship service for the first time, and the following week in home group, he announced that he wanted to join us in our faith.

Matt would occasionally tell me that I preached "a soft gospel" and did not talk much about the sacrifices necessary when one decided to become a Christian. He said we needed to preach "a hard gospel" and spell out the consequences of deciding to follow Jesus. I knew this came from the fact that he made a profession of faith when he was a teenager and was the only believer in his family. Then when his father died, he refused to hold the incense in front of the picture of his father. To those not acquainted with Chinese religion, to "hold the incense" was a sign of worship. So when one would hold the incense in front of a picture of a dead person and then bow before it, it was an act of worship of that person's spirit. Matt refused to do that, so his brothers ostracized him for years. So when he talked about a hard gospel, I am sure he meant that the new believer would be called on to stand firm in his faith and not participate in idol or ancestor worship. This was a real problem for any Taiwanese person who decided to become a Christian. Consequently, Matt talked pretty straight to Andrew for several minutes about what he would face, but he was firm in his decision. He said he had never been in any kind of a group where people cared for him like this group.

The following week when he came to church, we went back to the beach and I baptized him. Four weeks from the time he first heard the gospel, he was baptized. The speed with which this radical change took place both astounded me and affirmed something I had believed for quite a long time.

That whole event was very special to me for a particular reason. When we first arrived in Taiwan, I was given a copy of a book titled *Mending The Nets* written by a Lutheran missionary who had been in Taiwan for about twenty years. The premise of the book was the importance of finding ways to "close the back door of the church." Many had observed that a lot of the churches saw significant numbers of Chinese make professions of faith, but they did not last. His position was that we needed to find a way to conserve the results of those decisions. And one part of his position was that the Chinese were either pushed into making a decision before they were ready or they were allowed to decide without fully understanding what the decision meant. He believed that in order for a Chinese person to make a meaningful profession of faith, he had to hear the gospel presented three hundred times over the course of three years. It seemed that most of the missionary community had accepted his theory and were trying to develop a "friendship evangelism" type ministry; they did not expect to see any immediate results from their efforts. It was well understood that once you developed a good relationship with a Chinese person, you could discuss anything and get honest responses; no topic was off limits. But when I heard this, I thought it was the most discouraging thing I had heard in all of my preparation for missions and in the first few months on the field. I refused to believe that the God of the Bible was so limited that He had to work on that timetable. Andrew's profession of faith and baptism proved to me that I was right – God is not limited!

One of the arguments for not baptizing a new convert immediately was that the person had to have an opportunity to fully understand all it meant. Some said the new convert must "prove his faith" before being baptized. But I strongly disagreed. I had always felt that we should follow the example of Philip with the Ethiopian eunuch in Acts 8:26 and following. When the eunuch believed he said, "Look here is water. Why shouldn't I be baptized?" (v. 36) During my whole ministry, I always wanted to baptize a new convert as soon as possible following their decision. Since being in Taiwan, I had seen churches make some people wait for a year or more to be baptized, and finally those new believers just left the church. To me, that was tragic to the point of being criminal.

God gave me proof that it was right to baptize converts as soon as possible, because about two or three years later when we selected and ordained elders in the church, Andrew was one of the ones chosen. And about four or five years after that, when Living Water started another church in a village south of Tainan, Andrew was installed as pastor of the church. His decision to follow Christ was genuine and produced real change in his life.

God in His mercy allowed Nan and me to be present and witness all the wonderful things He did. We often felt like we were participating spectators watching God change lives to build His own church. We thanked Him for allowing us to be on site to watch Him work.

I pray for you that you will have eyes to see and ears to hear the things God does around and through you. Those experiences serve as proof that you are His and He is yours.

Do You Trust Me?

"Do not let your hearts be troubled. Trust in God; trust also in me." John 14:1

For the next three months we continued to worship together, meet in the home group, talk to people who expressed some interest in knowing more about Jesus and try to teach those who were new believers. In Matt's home group, there were three or four people who were already Christians. He and Elizabeth were teaching English through Trinity Baptist Church and had made some contacts there, and I think one of them may have been a friend from before he went to America.

Amy continued to live with Dr. Stephen and Sara and kept attending home group. Her parent's reaction to her conversion was strongly negative and included threats against her life. All the young believers were afraid that her parents would hurt her. Soon after they threw her out of the house, her father put an ad in the local newspaper saying that his daughter was dead to them, and included her picture. Privately they threatened to kill her if they got the chance. Of course, all the people were frightened for her safety. In spite of her situation, she was a happy person.

Then one night I got call from Matt. He said I needed to come to his house right now. I knew there was a crisis of some kind. (My association with Mrs. Gau had taught me that often the Chinese would make this kind of urgent statement and not tell you what was going on until you were with them.) Matt did say on the phone that Amy wanted to go back home and try again to show her parents that she still loved them and wanted them to accept her. I didn't think that was so bad, even though I had no idea what would happen if she did return home.

I got on my motorcycle and headed to his house. All the way over there, I was praying asking God what to say. I knew they were expecting me to provide the answer. About two thirds of the way there God asked the question, "Do you trust me?" I assured Him that I did trust Him; indeed I had no help and no hope without him. And that was the only answer I got.

When I arrived, I was surrounded by a circle of concerned faces. Everyone was troubled - everyone except Amy. She looked serene and at peace. She was smiling and looked like everything in her world was in order.

I listened to all the concerns, all the worries, all the predictions of what could happen. Dr. Stephen and Sara were there as well. Somewhere in the midst of the talk, it was mentioned that the mother had threatened to kill Amy. At one point, Dr. Stephen said, "No Chinese person would ever kill their own child." To me, his word carried a lot of weight.

Finally it was up to me. I asked Amy what she wanted to do. She said she wanted to return home and witness to her parents. She had been praying and felt this is what God wanted her to do. So I said we should let her go back home and pray for God to do the thing He wanted to do in this situation.

Matt was really outdone with me because I agreed to let her go home. The others were terrified for her safety. I kept remembering the question Jesus asked me on the way to the meeting, "Do you trust me?" I knew I had to trust Him. When the discussion had ended, we all returned home. Amy went back with Dr. Stephen and Sara to pack her things.

Just to answer your question, no I didn't think of that scripture on the way to the meeting. And I know Jesus spoke this sentence to His disciples on the night prior to his crucifixion, when He knew that He would be leaving them very soon. He knew they would be sad, worried, frightened, and lonely. But the principle is true; we must trust Jesus in all our circumstances, even those that seem dangerous and seem to have no possible human safe resolution. That is what guided me.

A couple of days later, we met at Dr. Stephen and Sara's house. By then Amy had packed up and was ready to go home. We anointed her and prayed for her, specifically asking for God's protection, and asking that God would accomplish His purpose in this situation. Dr. Stephen and Sara drove her home, and she remained there about two months. She continued to come to church and always displayed her radiant smile. She assured us all was fine at home and her parents had not threatened her in any way. She was glad to be back with her family.

Finally a big worship day was coming up, and her parents told her she would have to leave. They said it was a big worship time for their family (as well as for most of the people in Taiwan) and she no longer worshipped their gods. They were afraid that her God and their gods would get into some kind of argument or fight and it would be devastating for their lives. They said it would be best if she would go. As a result, she returned to Dr. Stephen and Sara's home.

I learned a lesson through this, and prayed that the new believers also learned that God could and would act on behalf of His own people. We never actually discussed it in church, so I will never know how they felt. But it was one more proof to both Nan and me that God was at work and directing this work. We felt honored that He was allowing us to be present and watch what He was doing.

You will face problems in your life, and some of them will seem impossible. Just remember God is in control and you can trust Him with every circumstance.

Coworkers

When the Taiwan Baptist Mission concluded the Church Growth Study and adopted the recommendations made by the committee, one of those was that every new church start would have a church planting team and that it would have a sponsoring church, or mother church. When we started what became Living Water, we had neither. It wasn't until about two years later that Matt and Elizabeth came to work with us, but we still didn't have a mother church.

In the late spring of 1993, we were reminded by our mission leadership that we didn't have a team. By then, even they knew that no church in Tainan wanted to work with us. But they encouraged us to look at some missionaries that were not assigned to a church planting team and choose one of those couples. At that time, Bill and Susan Thompson were scheduled to return from their first furlough. After their first term, it was now time for them to prayerfully consider where they would minister. Part of this process involved traveling to visit other cities and churches to see where God might lead them. We had met them and enjoyed our limited contact with them. Primarily to appease our leaders, we invited Bill and Susan to come visit us and look at what we were doing.

They had spent their first term in Kaohsiung and had good relationships with other missionaries there, as well as with the Taiwanese-speaking pastors. There was also the added factor that they knew their way around the city; always a plus for new missionaries. We were so sure they would stay in Kaohsiung that we reached out to them just to please our supervisors.

We were living near the coast a little north of Tainan and had found a beach that was only used by the local fishermen. Nan and I would go out there from time to time to walk on the beach, look for shells, and relax. (That was also the beach where we had our baptisms.) So the day the Thompson's came for their visit, we planned a picnic on the beach with them.

We talked about their furlough, their family, their joys and frustrations of the first term, the people they knew in Kaohsiung – basically anything we could think of to talk about. We never mentioned our work; our disappointments, our dreams, our goals, or anything like that. We were just doing the required thing.

After lunch, we went back to the house for coffee and pie. Pie didn't travel well to the beach and was best served at a table with coffee. While visiting over dessert, they began to ask questions about what we were doing, who we worked with, how the Chinese co-workers felt about us and things like that. We answered their questions and told them about the Tainan Missionary Prayer Supper once a month and about some of the relationships we had with other missionaries. That was about it.

We were astounded when they called us a couple of days later and said they were moving to Tainan. I never expected that to happen. But I was very glad that they did come. We developed a very deep friendship and immensely enjoyed working together. They provided a tremendous lift to our spirits and made life a lot more fun.

After they had been there about a year and we were starting preparations for our next furlough, one day Susan and I were together while we were all working on some project. Nan, Bill, and Matt were in another part of the room doing something, and I commented

136

to her that I was still surprised that they came to work with us because I knew they had so many relationships in Kaohsiung. So she told me why they moved to Tainan.

While they were on furlough, they were praying about where to live when they came back to Taiwan. Towards the time when they had to return, Susan had a dream one night. In the dream, she saw a picture of a room with curtains, a piano, chairs in a circle, and a simple pulpit. In the dream, God told her, "This is where you will serve when you return to Taiwan."

On the day they visited us, they walked into the ground floor of our apartment where we had our worship service and it was the exact room she had seen in her dream. In that instant, she knew this is where they would live and work. I had never had an experience like that and it kind of blew me away. Once again I had the confirmation that God was at work and He was going to accomplish the things He wanted to accomplish.

We helped them locate an apartment in our end of town, and they moved right in and helped with our work from the very beginning. Bill was an accomplished pianist and helped Matt with the worship quite a lot. Susan helped Nan and Elizabeth with the work they were doing in discipling the young women in the church.

The special meetings sponsored by the Year 2000 Committee continued, and we took Bill and Susan with us when we attended. I did my best to explain to them the dramatic occurrences and how they were related to the spiritual conflict between the kingdom of darkness and the kingdom of light. We had several discussions about whether or not it was Biblical and how to understand it all. They both were open to all we witnessed, and I am sure they did a lot of study and discussion on their own.

Nan and I both were extremely glad that they chose to come work with us. We considered ourselves very blessed to be able to see all that God was doing while at the same time have coworkers that developed into such good friends. They were a great encouragement to us.

As we worked together in Living Water Church, we were also seeing some of the same dramatic encounters with the Holy Spirit in our congregation. They were not as numerous or quite as dramatic as what we witnessed in the city-wide meetings. Some of our members would fall under the power of the Holy Spirit when we prayed for them, but I noticed that they would not fall every time they came and asked for prayer. Most of them would fall two or three times and that seemed to end it for them. We tried to stress that God desired an intimate relationship with each one of us and I wondered if they were growing in their faith to the point that God no longer needed that dramatic encounter to help communicate with them.

As we continued our ministry of prayer, we saw people healed of illnesses. One young man was going deaf in his left ear, but God restored his hearing. Some of the healings were not for diagnosed illnesses, like the young woman who suffered from extreme guilt and sadness. She was dramatically changed over the course of time into a joyful, fun person as she worshipped with us. But the most dramatic to me was what God did in the life of a woman in Nan's Bible class named Tan Goat-Li. One day in class, she asked Nan and the group to pray for her eyes. She said the doctors had told her that there was no cure for this eye disease. Even though Nan did not know how to translate the term, she led the group to pray for Goat-Li. After the service, we asked Matt what the term meant, and we finally got it translated. It was macular degeneration.

The following Sunday, Nan asked how her eyes were doing. She said they were fine; she could see quite clearly. So Nan asked her, "Since Jesus healed your eyes, do you think you would like to put your faith in him?"

Goat-Li responded "I did that last week when I woke from my nap and realized I could see." She was baptized soon after along with Josie's mom.

A couple of months later, she told the class that her vision was getting cloudy again. They prayed for her again, and this time Nan told her that she did not need to always come to the church for prayer. Nan explained to the class that when they believed in Jesus, God put His Holy Spirit into each one of them, so they could pray to God themselves at any time, in any place. This made an impression on Goat-Li, as it was a radical difference from the Chinese religious worldview of going to the temple and having the priest pray for every little thing.

Not long after that Sunday, she joined some of her friends on an arranged bus tour to visit Sun Moon Lake, a popular resort area in the mountains. It was quite lovely up there and because of the elevation, it was cooler than it was down on the coastal plain where we lived. On one of the stops at Sun Moon Lake, the group walked up a hill to visit a temple, but Goat-Li decided to stay near the bus. She reasoned that now she was a follower of Jesus and didn't need to go to the temple. But as she stood by the bus, she looked up at the temple admiring the bright colors. While she was looking at it, her vision got fuzzy and dim. She thought, "This cannot be happening to me again. I now belong to Jesus." Then she remembered what Nan had told them about praying to claim our victory in Jesus, so she said out loud, "Devil, leave me alone. I belong to Jesus and you have no part with me anymore. Go away and don't come back." When she came to the church the following week, she reported this to the class and said, "As soon as I prayed this out loud, my vision cleared and has not bothered me again."

For me, the greater miracle was that an illiterate woman who had spent her life in pagan worship now was a follower of Jesus and understood that she could pray and receive God's help in a time of need. Her faith was secure in Jesus and she was growing in her relationship with Him.

The Sin of Unbelief

"He replied, 'Because you have so little faith. I tell you the truth, if you have faith as small as a mustard seed, you can say to this mountain, Move from here to there and it will move. Nothing will be impossible for you.'" Matthew 17:20

As I mentioned, we had a series of speakers who came to Taiwan to encourage and motivate us to propagate the gospel there. One of the speakers we heard early in this process really stood out to both Nan and me. He was from Thailand and had a really long Thai name; or maybe an Indian name. He was of Indian descent, and had planted the Hope of Bangkok Church. From that one church start, God developed a whole network of churches throughout Thailand. He came to speak at a Presbyterian church in Tainan, and I was quite impressed and moved by his message for two reasons. First, because what he said fit so well with what I believed. He said he would not talk a lot about methods because it was the responsibility of every pastor and missionary to come before God and ask Him what he was supposed to do. He made a statement that really resonated with me. It was, "When the Holy Spirit is working, anything will produce results. But if the Holy Spirit is not working, no method will produce good results." His whole philosophy summed up the belief I had held for a long time; that God had a plan for the work and it was the responsibility of the pastor to connect with God to find out what the plan was. I was trying to do that very thing in my ministry and was trying to follow that principle. I reasoned that since it was God's church, He was the one who had the right plan and I needed to find out what that plan was and follow that.

The second reason his message meant so much to me was that he emphasized continued contact and training with the pastors of the various churches that had come out of the first church, the mother church. He called all those pastors together for a week-long conference four times a year for Bible study and to discuss the issues they faced in their various locations. In this way, all the men could share together how they had met certain obstacles and in that way encourage and train the newest pastors. That philosophy was what I had hoped to do when I went to the mission field. Unfortunately for me and my vision, in Taiwan, the Chinese Baptist Convention and our mission had followed a different philosophy; one which depended on a seminary trained pastor and had little follow-up once a man was pastoring his own church.

Another one of the visiting speakers was Jack Deere, who at the time was a New Testament professor at Dallas Baptist Seminary. In one of his sermons, he explained that the biggest hindrance to seeing God work in power today was what he called the non-believing Bible. He said we did not believe the message it contained and illustrated his position with an example from his own ministry. He developed that thought, but his message about not believing the Bible struck a chord with me.

A week or so later I was chatting about the message with one of my friends, a Canadian Pentecostal missionary named Dave Bedwell, and he was also deeply moved by it. In fact, he said he was strongly convicted, to the point that he had to go before God in prayer and repent of the sin of unbelief. I went home and thought, "Man, that is a huge statement to come from a missionary!"

Lessons from the Journey

His statement stuck in my brain for the next few days, until one morning God gently showed me that I had the same problem. I was shocked. But then I thought about our neighborhood. I pictured in my mind how we would go out the back door of our apartment and walk down little narrow lanes about two blocks to the back of a market where we bought milk, eggs, butter, bread and a few other canned things. On this route, we passed all the neighboring houses with open courtyard doors. In every yard or in the front room of the house, we saw worship tables. These were altars with ancestor tablets, a fruit offering, an incense pot, sometimes an idol and sometimes a picture of an ancestor or two. That was the center of worship for the family. One house in particular had a really large elaborate altar. It had multiple levels and shelves. There were three idols on it, along with two incense pots and offerings of various kinds. I had to confess to God that even though I was praying for Him to break through the yoke of blindness Satan had put on the Taiwanese people, I didn't really believe it could happen in my own neighborhood.

I confessed my sin of unbelief and asked God to forgive me.

I didn't see anything happen immediately, but when God started to move, He started in the house with the huge worship altar. Turns out the mother in that house had a sister who lived in Kaohsiung, a city about 45 miles from Tainan, who was a Christian and had been praying for this family for years. I was never able to find out how much she had actually witnessed to them, but one day, she called me. I still have no idea how she got ahold of my phone number. She told me to go down and "make them believe in Jesus," because the next Sunday she and her family were coming up to Tainan and they were going to chop and burn that altar table.

By then, Bill and Susan Thompson were working with us, along with Matt Chen. I called all of them and we had a meeting, and then went to see the Tan family. In the course of our conversation with them, Mr. Tan said he would be happy to destroy the alter because they had been worshiping those gods for years and never saw any benefit from it. I suspect that Mrs. Tan was sometimes demonized by the spirits they worshipped. We prayed with Mr. and Mrs. Tan and three of their children to receive Christ.

The house cleaning and idol burning was scheduled to take place on a day I was available, but the ceremony ended up being moved to a week later. I had a commitment at another church, so I missed most of the activity on the appointed day. Nan and the Thompson's told me all about it. They were there along with Matt and several people from Living Water. The sister and her family were there from Kaohsiung. The whole group went into the house and collected the altar and all the idols and carried them into the street. The altar was so large they had to break it to get it through the door. The Kaohsiung family had brought a hatchet or two and the Tan family had some hammers, and they bashed and whacked the altar until it was really broken up. They burned the smaller pieces, but some of the larger pieces were left.

Next the Christians went through the house praying for it, anointing it with oil, and commanding all the evil spirits to leave. Nan said they visited every room and also took down small altars in a couple of rooms, along with pictures of gods in the kitchen and elsewhere.

When I got home, they were putting the remnants of the altar into bags along with the idols. The family took them to the dump and dropped them there. It was quite a show. The family came to worship at the church some, maybe once every three or four weeks. I was disappointed about their irregular attendance until I talked to another missionary from the Philippines, who said that was normal considering they previously had gone to a temple only a few times a year. In fact, he thought it was pretty good that they came that often. The youngest daughter, Chhiu-Lan, was the one who came the most often and I believe she really grew in her faith while she was with our church.

That whole incident was a vivid lesson to me that the disciples were not the only ones who suffered from a lack of faith. In fact, from that point forward, I found myself praying just like the father with the demonized son in the first of the story: "Father, I believe; help my unbelief."

Through it all I discovered that, at least for me, there are times when faith is an act of my will. I must choose to believe in spite of all external circumstances telling me it cannot happen. It is hard to do, but I must do what Oswald Chambers says: "The river of the Spirit of God overcomes all obstacles. Never focus your eyes on the obstacle or the difficulty. The obstacle will be a matter of total indifference to the river that will flow steadily through you if you will simply remember to stay focused on the Source. Never allow anything to come between you and Jesus Christ – not emotion nor experience – nothing must keep you from the one great sovereign Source."

Nan's Projects

When Matt and Elizabeth started coming to the church, they were soon joined by Matt's mom. Amy and Gary continued to date and they became a couple. Also Josie and Andrew continued to see each other. Soon Josie started bringing her mom to church and she and Mrs. Chen (Matt's mom) brought another couple of women who were maybe in their early sixties. Nan started teaching a Bible class for them.

She found a little book entitled *The Life and Teachings of Jesus,* which had a fascinating history. It had been printed in 1914 in mainland China for distribution there, before Mao Tze-tung and the People's Republic of China defeated Chiang Kai-shek and the Republic of China. After Mao came to power in 1949, he was determined to stamp out religion on the mainland, including even Chinese traditional religion. His Red Guards found and destroyed all the Bibles and other religious printed matter they could find.

Sometime in the early to mid-1980's, Christians started sneaking into China and carrying Bibles. One man went into a remote village and gave a Bible to an old man. The old man was so excited that he begged the Christian man to wait on him while he ran home to get something. When he returned he gave the Christian man a package and said "This is the most precious thing I own. I want to give it to you for giving me a Bible." The Christian man took it back to Hong Kong and showed it to some missionaries.

They knew what it was - the long-lost volume of *The Life and Teachings of Jesus.* It was tattered and torn, but they were able to restore it. Then they started reproducing it and a book store in Taiwan was selling it.

It was a compilation of the four gospels and told the story of Jesus and the things he taught. The most interesting thing about it is the illustrations, all in traditional Chinese style. All the people in the pictures were Chinese and were wearing Chinese clothes. The houses and landscapes in the pictures were definitely Chinese, and the writing was in the old style characters rather than the modern simplified ones that were implemented by Mao.

For Nan's Bible class, she took the paperback book to one of the copy shops in Tainan and asked them to blow up some of the pictures. She wound up with pictures that were about twelve by eighteen inches. After carefully researching the use and significance of the use of color in Chinese culture, she used pencils to color the poster-sized pictures. As she told these women Bible stories, the pictures were a great help, especially because some of them were illiterate. It was a tremendous success. The women enjoyed the stories and enjoyed talking about the pictures.

Her other major project was the manual for teaching people how to read the Taiwanese Romanization, Lo-bat-ji. After she met Earl and Sherry Bengs and Earl encouraged her so much, she never forgot it. In the midst of all the other things we were doing, she always found time to work on it and finally had it to the point that she was ready to present it to somebody. She contacted Earl, who had moved back to Singapore after completing his language study, and he arranged a time for her to visit there to present the project to some people he and Sherry knew.

She flew to Singapore and made her presentation, and it was a smashing success. It was a small group of between ten and fifteen people, and in one evening she taught them how to read the Romanization. By the end of the first night, they were reading the little Bible story books she had found in the closet of the Salt Light Chapel several years previously. From that start, they moved on to reading in the Romanized Bible, which Earl had found in a bookstore in Singapore. She was really excited about the results of her class, for it validated all her thought and effort of the previous six or more years.

She made two trips to Singapore to teach people how to read the Taiwanese Bible, and the people there were able to learn the language they needed to communicate their faith to their parents. Everyone was excited about the possibilities for the future.

After we left Taiwan and were working in Jackson, one day we got a call from our friends, Sam and Marion Longbottom. They had retired and were living in Texas. We had not heard from them in quite a while except through an occasional email. They had been attending a reunion of the Vietnam missionaries and were passing through Jackson. They asked if they could stop for a cup of coffee and said they had a friend with them. The friend was Earl Bengs, who had served with them in Vietnam. We welcomed them into our home.

It was an exciting visit. Earl told Nan the results of her introducing Lo-bat-ji to the church members in Singapore. From that beginning, Earl had taken the little manual she produced and made a couple of modifications to it, and then introduced the method of reading the Romanization to a couple of pastors he knew. They preached in Mandarin, but were native speakers of the Fu Chien dialect. That dialect of Chinese was what we called Taiwanese. These men wanted to preach in Taiwanese, or Hokkienese as they called it in Singapore and Malaysia, but could not. Even though they spoke Hokkienese, they could only read the Bible in Mandarin characters, and they didn't know how to translate Biblical concepts into their native tongue. After Earl taught them how to read Hokkienese and gave them a Bible, they started preaching in that language.

Word spread, and in the course of time Earl and the other pastors had introduced the method of reading Hokkienese to multiple pastors in Malaysia and a couple in Thailand. He had found a place to purchase the Hokkienese Bible and bought so many that the company had to produce another printing of them.

As you can imagine, Nan was overjoyed and so overcome with that report that she walked around on clouds for several weeks. It was a tremendous validation of her dream and of all the work she had done to develop the process and then put it in print.

Be Faithful in Little

"For everyone who has will be given more, and he will have an abundance. Whoever does not have, even what he has will be taken away." Matthew 15:29

By the spring of 1994 we were seeing a slow, but steady stream of new believers in the church. The time from February 1993 until our furlough in June of 1994 we averaged one baptism a month. At that time in Taiwan, that rate was considered a flood. There were some months when we had no baptisms and other months when we would have four or six. No matter how you counted it, we were seeing new believers come into the church on a regular basis.

Matt, Bill, and I met each week for our staff meeting. (Bill and Matt met together at another time to plan the worship and discuss the music.) Then about once a quarter, we three pastors would take a morning and go to some park and spend part of the time alone in prayer and the rest of the time in discussion about the church. Usually we would spend the first hour or two in Bible study and prayer as individuals. Then we would come together and have a prayer time and talk about whatever we needed to discuss. Sometimes it would be about mundane things like whether or not to add another home group or when to schedule another outing, but from time to time we discussed more weighty matters.

We used outings as a way to fellowship together and often to provide a place for our members to go on special worship days. We were teaching them not to eat food offered to idols and this presented a conflict. On those special worship days, most families would have a family get-together and their meals included a lot of the food they had offered to their ancestors and other gods. These new believers chose not to return home so that they did not have to offend their parents by not participating in the family worship times. The outings we planned provided them an opportunity for something so that they did not have to sit at home by themselves. We usually had some kind of cookout along with the fellowship.

On one of our spring morning meetings, the topic to discuss was how to care for the new believers. We agreed on the topic before we left home and went to the park knowing this was an issue we needed to address. We all agreed that the new believers needed to be discipled, but we were unclear about how to go about it. We knew there were some discipleship materials we could obtain, but they all seemed to be quite lengthy and intense. We felt we needed something simpler; something anyone could teach.

Following our usual procedure, we arrived at the park and each found a secluded spot and prayed and read the Bible. After about an hour and a half, we came together to see what the Lord had showed us. Interestingly enough, all three of us were led to this parable recorded in Matthew 15:14-30. We were unclear why God had led us to that particular parable and how to interpret it. After much discussion and more prayer, we felt that God was telling us that if we would be faithful to take care of the ones He sent us, He would send us more. We agreed this meant that we needed to be intentional about discipling the new believers. But the question of how to do that remained.

We returned home and shared our thoughts with our wives. At least I know I did. Nan's creative mind started whirling. In no time at all, she came up with a Bible study that had eight simple lessons. Unfortunately, the work she did is lost due to many moves and many changes in computers and software. But as best I can recall, some of the lessons were things like, "How to Pray," "Who is Jesus?," "How to Study the Bible," and "Who is the Holy Spirit?" Some years later after we moved to Taipei, she met a young man named Sunny Wan who had a burden to disciple new believers and she helped him write and publish a little book titled *Discovering...* He did a lot of the research and writing, but it included many of the topics she used in that first little tool she created for Living Water Church. She found a company in the Philippines to publish it and make it available to churches.

All of us - Matt, Bill, and I, as well as our wives - agreed that the teaching should be done by the new members to other new members. Perhaps I was the primary force behind this idea, because I had done some study about how to increase the spiritual maturity in church members. I learned that this practice would not only strengthen the spiritual lives of current believers, but also give new believers a model to follow. Also, our mission board was encouraging missionaries to use believers to teach other believers, so everything did not automatically point to the missionary or pastor as the sole source of spiritual understanding and authority. Consequently, we decided to teach this material to the new believers and then when someone else was baptized, one of those who had already been through the material would be assigned to teach the newest arrival. One of the great benefits of this approach was that each new believer had someone in the church who had a basic understanding about Christian values and truths. As they built their relationship, the new believer was in constant contact with a person whom they could ask any question they had about their new life in Christ. Most of those new believers would hesitate before approaching one of us pastors, but would readily discuss their questions with people they knew. In this way, they could pray together, which was something we emphasized, and build their relationship with God and with each other. If the "trainer" could not answer a question, they could go to someone they knew who could answer it.

This whole approach led to a great spirit of unity and fellowship within the church body. Many of the members had never been a part of any group that had this level of shared beliefs and shared support.

Watching this whole process reminded me of a prayer I had often lifted up to God in the very early days of our attempt to start a new church. I would pray that God would allow me to see on this earth a small glimpse of how He intended a church to operate and function. As I watched Living Water grow and develop, I truly felt like I was witnessing what I read about the church in Acts. We were enjoying fellowship with each other, spending time in prayer and studying God's Word, and seeing God perform miracles in our midst. Even though we were few in number, we were united and had the hopeful possibility of continued growth.

On a side note, I always marveled at the continued growth. We had no outreach program, no structured evangelism program, and no visitation program. God just seemed to bring people to us. I frequently thought of the verse Acts 2:47b: *"And the Lord added to their number daily those who were being saved."* It was amazing to watch. Often we felt like we were hanging on and trying to keep up with God.

I Will Follow

"I have been crucified with Christ and I no longer live, but Christ lives in me. The life I live in the body, I live by faith in the Son of God, who loved me and gave himself for me." Galatians 2:20

"But he said to me, 'My grace is sufficient for you, for my power is made perfect in weakness." 2 Corinthians 12:9a

"God will never lead you to a place where His grace cannot keep you."

These two verses and quote seemed to come back to me on a regular basis. Often I had no idea why they would pop up in my Bible reading, or what special significance they had for me at the particular time they showed up. I knew I was trying to live like I had been crucified with Christ and was trying to do what Paul so often instructed the believers to do, which was to die to the flesh. I was not sure how to do that, but I know I wanted to do it and was trying to do so.

At the same time, I was frequently reminded of my own inadequacies and inability to do many things on the mission field. I fell into the trap of comparing myself to others, admiring their relationships with the national pastors, their understanding of the Chinese culture, and their linguistic ability, while allowing my perception of their abilities to make me feel even more inadequate. To be honest, there were times when I wondered why in the world God ever thought choosing me to be a missionary and sending me to this complicated place was a good idea.

"God will never lead you to a place where His grace cannot keep you."

Nan and I could not remember where we first heard this quote - perhaps in orientation - but regardless of where we had heard it, we quoted it often, especially when either of us had doubts. It seemed to always encourage us to continue on the path we were on; continue with the tasks we could see in front of us. We came to believe that a lot of our missionary experience was simply walking from one task to the next doing our best to make sure God had given us the task and that He was the one empowering us to continue working.

Twice a year, the mission expected me to attend the meetings of all the men who were classified as General Evangelists. Our discussions would often touch on the subject of remaining faithful to the call. I frequently heard phrases like, "We are not called to be fruitful, but to be faithful," or "We are not judged by our fruitfulness but by our faithfulness." I always felt conflicted by those and similar sayings because on the one hand, I was encouraged to learn I was not the only one struggling with the lack of visible fruit in my ministry, but on the other hand, I believed that God did want to see something from my ministry in Taiwan. I just didn't know what it was or how to define it.

I felt kind of good about my second term when I was pastor of Park Road Church. When I started working there, the congregation only had about five regular attenders. When I left, there were close to thirty-five. Of course, most of that was because some of the young people who had left Tainan for study or military service had returned home. But they seemed to be happy to be in the church. I was glad that I had seen growth, even if it was by such a superficial method.

I Will Follow

I felt pretty good about the third term when I was the Steering Committee Chairman of our Church Growth Study. It had been a very difficult task, but it did produce some good results. There were some very good insights and recommendations made by the Outside Evaluation Team, many of which our mission implemented. Those actions served to help change some of the course of our mission in a good way.

But the first two years of this fourth term were a real and constant struggle. I well remember many times when I would pray and say to God, "You made a mistake putting me here. I don't know how to handle this problem." Or "I don't have the linguistic ability to communicate what needs to be said." Or "I don't understand enough about the Chinese culture to know what to do in this situation."

In those times, I would pray about the problem and sometimes get a specific action or topic for a sermon. I would always act on whatever leading I had. Other times when I prayed, I would just get a kind of general direction that I should follow. I would then follow that direction.

Sometimes I would see God bless and do a good work. But more often, I would obey God's leading but apparently nothing would result. I would come home, go into my study, and pray, "Well, God, I thought You told me to do that. I can't see any result, positive or negative. It is in Your hands now." In those times the only thing I could say was that I had been obedient to the leading I had at the time. When I saw little result or a bad result that was small comfort.

After thinking on this periodically in various ways for many years, hindsight leads me to believe this: when we choose to be crucified with Christ, we choose to give up something of who we are. One part of who we are is the desires we have. Ideally, when I choose to follow Christ, I surrender my sinful, self-centered desires. That truth then follows in my actions as a Christian. For example, when I was in high school, I really wanted to be an Air Force pilot. I gave that up when I surrendered to be a missionary. That is simple, but it is the principle we all must follow in life.

When we want to see God bless us, we surrender the desire to prescribe how the blessing will show up.

When we want to see God answer a prayer, we surrender our own idea of how that answer will look.

When we know we need to forgive someone, we surrender our desire for that person to know how badly they hurt us.

When we choose to love others unconditionally as Jesus loves us, we surrender our desire to dictate how they should live, assuming they are not doing anything specifically prohibited by Scripture.

Oswald Chambers states it this way: "If you are faced with the decision of whether or not to surrender, make a determination to go on through the crisis, surrendering all that you have and all that you are to Him. And God will then equip you to do all that He requires of you."

If I need to forgive, He will equip me to do that.

If I need to love, He will equip me to do that.

If I have to face a difficult situation, He will equip me to do that.

This is what I have experienced in my spiritual journey. I committed to follow God wherever He chooses to lead me. On my journey, He has carried me though some difficult situations in ministry. My primary commitment is to God, which includes following His leading. When I do that, I then trust my God to do the work that only He can do. I saw

Him do things in that fourth and fifth term I had dreamed of seeing when I was a boy, but never thought I would see. God is always faithful.

If you don't learn anything else in life, learn that truth and depend on it.

The Fourth Furlough

W e prepared for this fourth furlough with happy hearts. After such a slow and agonizing start, it was concluding with a feeling of success. We had seen multiple baptisms for the first time in our missionary careers. We started with nothing and now we had an average attendance each Sunday of around 25. I calculated that we had approximately 35 actual members, most of whom were new believers. It was a joy to watch them grow in their faith. At the same time, it was a little bit scary because we knew that all they knew about God and the church was what we taught them.

Bill and Susan had jumped right in with the work and had accepted the strange and wonderful things we were learning about how the Holy Spirit works in the church today. We continued to witness His work in the special meetings in town and, to a lesser extent, in Living Water Church. As we were talking about the church one day, one of them asked how we would describe it. Nan called it a "Bapti-costal" church: we had some Baptist roots, but some Pentecostal practices. We were comfortable with that.

Matt, Bill, and I had noted that with our growth, our current location would soon be too small. We were pretty close to capacity as it was. I talked with the mission business manager, and he agreed to carry the lease on the apartment for a few months after we left to give the church time to find another location. But we knew we would be living in another area when we returned. We assumed we would return to Tainan, but were not totally sure about that. The church was to the point where if it had a pastor, we and the Thompson's would be free to go somewhere else and start over again.

Bill and I had some private discussions about the leadership in the church, specifically when to turn it over to a Chinese pastor and who that might possibly be. We both knew that the mission philosophy would not allow either of us to remain as pastor of the church; that was not our role. We were supposed to plant churches and when they were strong enough to have a pastor, the missionary should leave. In most of the church plants, the missionary worked with a mother church, which would help find the emerging pastor. We didn't have that option.

Both Bill and I felt that the pastor should be Matt, but in an initial meeting when we broached the subject, he rejected it categorically. He said God called him to come to Taiwan and be a worship leader and he was not qualified to be a pastor. He was included in the preaching rotation with Bill and me, and was doing quite a good job of it. But bringing the message once a month was a simple commitment compared to the responsibilities of the pastor's role.

One issue that came up had to do with inviting people to speak in church. I have mentioned that these special speakers were coming to Taiwan on a pretty regular basis. One of those who came to minister was a woman named Francis Thurmond. Matt had known her somewhere previously, and she had been a positive influence on him in one stage in his spiritual development. I think she spoke in a meeting in some church in Tainan, which was how he found out that she was in Taiwan. Unlike the other speakers who came and returned to the States, she stayed. I think she was invited to live with someone in Taipei, and then she was invited to various churches from time to time. Matt wanted to ask her to speak at Living Water, and I agreed that she could come one time.

Lessons from the Journey

When she came, her message was okay. But at the end of the service, it was apparent that she expected more response than she saw. Perhaps she wanted to see more people falling down under the influence of the Spirit, or someone having a demon to be cast out or whatever. In contrast, our usual prayer time at the end of our weekly service was pretty low key in terms of asking people to come forward. We issued the invitation and then waited. We prayed for those who came and if not many came, the time ended quickly. But Francis was one of those who seemed able to drag out the invitation and I got the feeling she felt we were too immature to see the need for repentance and prayer. Maybe I am being judgmental.

Following her time on Sunday, in one of our next meetings, Matt brought up asking her to come on a regular basis. I was against it and he wanted to know why. I explained that it was our responsibility to care for the sheep God sent to us. We had three pastors who knew the people and we met regularly to discuss the people's needs. We discussed the messages we would bring and how to follow up on them. I said there was no need for us to include another speaker on a regular basis and would not agree to it. Since I was the founding pastor or senior pastor or the one with white hair, for whatever reason, my position was accepted, but not without some hesitation on Matt's part. He hid it and we finished the term on a positive note.

The time finally arrived and we headed home. I was looking forward to a rest. But so much happened during that furlough, I later wondered if I got any rest or not.

Harriet concluded her term as journeyman in China and came through Taiwan to help us pack out. We knew we would not be living in that apartment when we returned, so we were packing to store our goods until we found another location. While still in Tainan, we learned that Stephen Lehnhoff (who we had only heard about) had proposed to her and she had accepted. We had six weeks to prepare for the wedding when we returned to Jackson. They married September 10.

Georgia's husband, Gene, had sold the family business started by Nan's father, Owen Gregory, to a firm outside of Chicago. They were concluding all those details when we arrived home, and Nan helped Georgia pack her goods in boxes. When moving day was near, Gene rented a U-Haul, and I helped two of the men from his business load the truck. Then I helped them move to Chicago and unpack, making it back to Jackson in time for Harriet's wedding.

That fall, we did our usual thing of speaking in lots of churches to talk about our work and encouraging the churches to contribute to the Lottie Moon Christmas offering. We both always enjoyed those assignments, especially when we were able to go into a small church that had never had a missionary speak to them. That was a very special time for us.

Nan's dad, Owen, had been suffering with angina for several years. He flatly refused to have heart surgery even though his doctor promised him that it would not only prolong his life, but improve his quality of life. He had always said, "I want to die of a heart attack and the first one." Well, he got his wish. He passed on to glory in December of that year. That was a sad time for the family.

After Christmas our speaking engagements were over. That meant we had the time from Christmas until our return in February to take it easy and be with family. We certainly enjoyed that time.

FIFTH TERM

Our Fifth Term

"They devoted themselves to the apostles' teaching and to the fellowship in the breaking of bread and to prayer. Everyone was filled with awe, and many wonders and miraculous signs were done by the apostles." Acts 2:42-43

W e returned for our fifth term in the middle of February, 1995. It had been a busy, emotional furlough, but we were excited about returning to Living Water Church to see what God was doing. We had begun that endeavor in September of 1990 with no mother church and no help. But through the term that ended in June of 1994, we witnessed God do amazing things. Many of those happenings were things I had long dreamed of seeing, but had never witnessed. To be honest, some of what I saw was difficult to understand, but as I prayed about it all, God's Spirit witnessed to my spirit that what I witnessed was from Him.

When we left for furlough, we had a membership of around thirty-five and knew we were at maximum capacity in our present facility. We had held discussions with Bill, Matt, and Herb Barrett, our mission business manager, to try and plan the next step. When we left for furlough, we had packed our goods for storage and knew we would be looking for a new apartment when we returned. The mission paid the rent on our apartment for a few extra months. This gave Matt and Bill time to look for a new location. When we arrived back in Tainan, we stayed with Bill and Susan for a little while so we could find a new place to live.

We learned that the church had continued to grow and now had around fifty members. Matt and Bill had found a place to rent for the church services that was on the third floor of a multi-storied building very close to downtown Tainan. It was a good bit larger than where they had been meeting, was more centrally located, and was more than adequate for the church's needs. The church stayed there for about another year, but then had to move again because the growth continued. The second location was on the fifth floor of a big business building just a few blocks away from the current meeting place. Nan and I always thought it was amusing that the new location was right across the street from the Confucian Temple in Tainan.

The first Sunday we were back in church, I knew things were different. There was a different feel to it all; something indefinite that I could not identify. It was natural and normal that the leadership would change in my absence. I was viewed as the founding pastor, or the senior pastor, or whatever you want to call it. Matt and Bill were seen as equals, but I seemed to hold some kind of elevated position.

We had ordained three men to be elders before I left for furlough. They were functioning and had started a monthly leadership meeting. Matt and Bill met regularly at another time to plan the worship and discuss other things about the church. The leadership meeting with the elders met at night so those who worked could attend. When I went to the leadership meeting for the first time, Matt led the discussion, but it did not take long to see that whenever he proposed something or whenever he took the final word, the young elders would all turn to me and say, "Pastor Song, what do you think?" When I went home after that meeting I told Bill, Susan, and Nan it was obvious I could not stay in the church if Matt was ever going to be accepted as the leader. That night I had clearly seen that the situation was taking authority away from Matt, and he was uncomfortable because the leaders were now turning to me instead of to him.

I think it was the second Sunday we were back that Francis Thurmond was the speaker. Bill told me that Matt had invited her to start coming each month soon after I departed. Of course I didn't like that at all. Her sermons were not bad; they were Biblically based, for sure. But with all sermons, even when they are Biblically based, one can choose which parts of a passage to emphasize and apply. It seemed to me that she was always looking to make the application in a way that instilled guilt. Then the invitation to come forward for prayer was more forceful than what I remembered our former practice was. And when not many people came, she would try and coerce the members to step out to receive prayer. She didn't seem satisfied unless we witnessed some kind of dramatic visible manifestation of the Spirit's presence. I felt that she wanted to see half the congregation fall under the Spirit or see people crying and moaning as evil spirits left them. It seemed she desired something dramatic, and unless she witnessed those kinds of manifestations, the service was incomplete and the people were not responding. I always felt like she thought we were very immature. I was uncomfortable with her presence and her direction in the service, but didn't know how to handle it. I felt that to take a stand and tell her she could not return would damage my relationship with Matt.

In the spring of the previous term, the special speakers were continuing to come to Tainan, and there was a lot of conversation in the various churches about what was happening, especially regarding the more charismatic elements of these meetings. Matt, Bill, and I discussed the situation and tried to figure out a Scriptural approach to the reality of dramatic manifestations of the Holy Spirit that we were seeing, some of which were quite disruptive and confusing. We knew it was unreasonable and naïve to assume our church members, who were new believers, would not hear about these meetings, and it was equally obvious to us that we could not forbid them from attending. There had been times when Steve and Vicki had visited Matt's home group, and they all had witnessed and experienced the work of the Holy Spirit in these meetings. After much prayer and deliberation we decided to take the following approach.

We agreed that we would tell the members that what they were witnessing was true and God was doing this in our midst today. We explained there were three things to remember when we witnessed these happenings.

First, God was doing all these things to demonstrate that He was present in our lives, and the purpose was not only to set some of us free from various spiritual conditions, but also to draw us into a deeper, more intimate relationship with Him. We chose to really emphasize God's overall purpose for a personal relationship with us. Every believer had a relationship with God and He desired for all of us to know Him better.

Secondly, we emphasized that as we witnessed God doing His work, it built up our faith. We spoke often about the importance of living a life built on and directed by our faith in God. We pointed out that God wanted us to walk by faith, and these works were gifts to help us see that God was present, which would help our faith grow.

Thirdly, we specifically said that we always had to remember that God is sovereign. He has a plan for all mankind and He is the one who implements that plan. While we did pray for healing and while we did see some people healed, it was up to God to decide how and when and to whom to distribute this healing power. Our position was that we would continue to pray for healing, but we believed that God would decide who would be healed. When we prayed and did not witness a healing, then we would do our best to encourage the ones for whom we prayed by reminding them that God still had a plan for them and that His power would equip them to face the difficulties of their illness. We assured them that the lack of a physical healing was not an indication that God was punishing them or that He did not love them.

While the three of us had agreed on this approach, it appeared to me that Francis had not been told of our position, or if she had been told, she chose to ignore it. Francis seemed to convey (to me at least) that she expected to see God heal people in every service. If there was no healing, then it was because we either had unconfessed sin or a lack of faith, which is an unbiblical position held by a number of groups that do regularly pray for healing. Fortunately for us, after about three or four months, she had to return to the States for an indefinite period. When she returned to Taiwan in the fall, we did not invite her back.

In spite of all the changes in the church that Nan and I saw, there was one constant – God through the Holy Spirit was continuing to do His work. It was not unusual to have people walk in off the street now that we were more centrally located. It was also not unusual to see them come under conviction of the Holy Spirit. We witnessed people come in and during the worship period begin to cry and continue to weep during the entire service. Others would ask when they left, "What is this place and what is happening to me?"

One day, a young lady no one knew walked into the worship service. When the invitation was given for people to come to the front to receive prayer, she joined the others who came. When asked what she would like prayer for, she responded, "I have headaches." The elder and his wife who prayed for her asked God to heal her headache, and then she left.

The following week she returned, and again came to the front for prayer. This time she was obviously excited, telling us that, "Last week after you prayed for me, I left the building and for FIFTEEN MINUTES I WAS FREE FROM PAIN!" Her name was I-Mui, which translated as Rose, and she told her story. Soon after her birth, her parents had taken her to the temple to dedicate her to their god. She started having headaches when she was very young, and her parents would take her back to the temple for more prayer. In time, they also took her to the doctor for medications to help treat the pain. Most of her life had been spent taking pain medication and returning to the temple for prayer for her headaches. On her second Sunday at the church, she received prayer again, returning the next week with the report that this time she was pain free for an hour.

She became a regular attender at the church, weekly receiving prayer and explanations of who we were and what we believed. In time, she put her faith in Jesus, and eventually her headaches went away completely.

I rejoiced because I was seeing God do amazing things on this earth through His body, the church. I thought that was the fulfillment of what Paul said in Ephesians 3:10-11 – *"His intent was that now, through the church, the manifold wisdom of God should be made known to the rulers and authorities in the heavenly realms, according to his eternal purpose which he accomplished in Christ Jesus our Lord."* Because we lived in an animistic culture where idol worship and other visible evidences of Satan's power and control were always on display, I felt God was demonstrating His power and control to those rebelling angels whom He had cast out of heaven eons previously.

There was a great spirit of love and unity among all our members. One night we had a fellowship meal at the church. (It was pizza, not Chinese food, which shocked Nan and me.) It was just fun social event which we concluded with a prayer time. At the end of the evening, Matt asked some of the men to help fold up the chairs so we could sweep the floor and be ready for the Sunday service. While the cleanup was in progress, someone put a song on the speaker system. It was a worship song in English, but the lively tune sounded Jewish. Suddenly about five or six of the young men formed a line holding each other's arms and began dancing to the music. I was awed by the spirit of joy and worship in that moment. That is what the church was like; there was great spontaneity and joy in worship, undergirded by a deep love for God and for each other.

Your Time is Up

In early summer of 1995, about six months after we returned from furlough, God spoke to me during my morning devotions. He said, "Your time is up." That was such a shock that it interrupted my devotional thoughts completely. I wondered what in the world He meant. My first thought was that my chronic high blood pressure was about to take me out. Needless to say, I was somewhat distracted for a few days. After about a week, I decided the time for my departure from this life was not right now, but still had no idea what it meant. In the following days, I did pray and ask for enlightenment or explanation, but received no clarification. I didn't tell Nan about that message, as I didn't want to upset her. I figured it would be better if I just dropped dead one day. I thought she could deal with the sudden departure better than living with the uncertainty and dread the news might produce.

A couple of weeks after that shocking message, China launched a missile towards Taiwan. It went close to the northern end of the island and landed about a hundred miles past Taiwan in the Pacific Ocean. Then about ten days later, they did it again. There was a lot of speculation about what it meant.

Ever since the end of World War II, when Taiwan had been given to the government of the Republic of China as a reward for their help in defeating Japan, the ROC had ruled the island. (This government had been in a battle for supremacy in China with the Peoples Republic of China since sometime in the early 1920"s.) In the first years, they ruled with an iron hand and under martial law. But around 1983, President Chiang Kai-shek died and his son, Chiang Cheng-gwo was appointed president. It was obvious from the beginning of his term as president that things would be different. In 1986. he lifted martial law and the island began to experience a level of freedom it had not previously enjoyed.

Before the end of WWII, the Japanese had ruled Taiwan from 1895 - 1945, and they had been granting some privileges to the Taiwanese, including the right to elect their own officials in certain cities. Some Taiwanese experienced this taste of self-rule and felt that Taiwan should be ruled by the Taiwanese. They did not like being under the governing power of the ROC. And in the meantime, China maintained that Taiwan was a "rogue province," and one day China would reunite the province with its motherland. Until the mid-80's, no one gave this philosophy much weight since the prevailing thought was that China lacked the military infrastructure and power to take control of Taiwan. But now many felt that the firing of these missiles proved that China did have the capability to settle the question of who truly governed all of China.

As that realization gained ground, many expressed the thought that if China did come in and take over Taiwan, all the expatriates would have to leave. Following the advice of some of our missionary friends who had had to leave Vietnam at a moment's notice, we packed a bag of essentials that we did not want to leave behind and kept it handy for a quick exit. In the midst of all this discussion about possibly having to leave, I thought this might be what God was talking about when he said, "Your time is up." Maybe He was telling me that all the missionaries would have to leave Taiwan like the missionaries had to do in China when the Peoples Republic of China took over there in 1949. They tried to kill all religious practices including Chinese religions. Perhaps that was to be our fate.

There were only two missiles launched and by sometime around October, emotions settled down and everyone put the threat out of our minds. But still that thought of my time being up was in the back of my mind. I tried to remain open to whatever God had to say to me, but there was no clarification.

Calvary Baptist Church's Mission Team

Oーne of the groups of special speakers that came to Taiwan was of great interest to me because they were from a Southern Baptist Church in Houston, Texas. When this team came to Tainan, we spent quite a lot of time with them. They held meetings in local churches, primarily in Trinity Baptist Church. Their ministry opened the door for us to see a dark side of life in Taiwan, and the great need for some kind of delivering prayer.

The meetings followed the usual routine: worship, preaching, and then a prayer ministry. Following one of the morning sessions, the prayer time revealed a tremendous need. There were a couple of women who were struggling greatly with guilt. It took the team a little while to uncover the source of their guilt, but finally it was revealed that these women had undergone at least one abortion at some point in their lives. They were suffering from overwhelming guilt that manifested in several different ways. One of the predominant noticeable symptoms was an inability to sleep. When they did sleep, they were troubled by nightmares.

We were not totally unaware that abortion was quite common in Taiwan. Historically, and up to the present time, it was the primary method of birth control. Susan Thompson was a nurse and had started working with a doctor, an OBGYN. She was horrified to learn that he performed abortions on his patients. He rationalized by telling her that he did not do abortions for just any woman who walked into his office off the street, but only performed them for his patients.

While the prayer team was with us, Susan and Nan were especially drawn to praying for women in this situation. And they discovered that some of those who suffered the most were Christian women, a couple of whom were pastor's wives. It was quite a shock. Susan really got motivated, doing a lot of research on the issue. She came up with some scriptures to use and a plan on how to pray for those women. It turned into quite an effective part of the ministry of the church.

I remember one woman in particular. She came to our congregation from another church, and she was already a believer. One Sunday in the prayer time following the preaching, she requested prayer. Someone prayed for her and then she went home. The next week or so, she came again for prayer. This continued until finally either Nan, Susan, or Elizabeth was praying for her. This time they recognized a visible sign that she might have had an abortion: she would wrap her arms across her belly, rocking back and forth as she cried. So they asked in a gentle way if that was possible. She confessed that it was; that as a young teenaged girl she'd had two abortions. Later, she got saved, got married, and now had two little girls. She seemed pretty happy except for the nightmares she could not get rid of. They kept her from sleeping the whole night through.

During the prayer time, she confessed the sin of what she had done. After her confession, they showed her Scriptures to prove that God had forgiven her sin and that she was greatly loved by Him. She was completely set free from the problems of the past -

159

her nightmares, guilt, and shame - and was a totally different person from that day forward. That was a joy to witness.

Another result of this team being with us affected me personally. Their pastor had studied the phenomenon of all the different manifestations of the Holy Spirit's activity that we were witnessing quite a lot. They brought some printed material that helped explain the things we were seeing happen in the various services. That was quite helpful.

They also told me about a teaching the pastor gave. He used the metaphor of a man walking. He said a healthy man needed two healthy legs on which to walk. If one leg was weak, then the man would walk with a limp. By comparison, in the spiritual life, a spiritual man needed two healthy legs on which to walk. One leg was doctrine and the other leg was experience. That is, we need the doctrine to understand the spiritual principles of God's Word, and how those principles apply in individual lives. But we also need the experience of seeing God do miraculous things; of knowing experientially that He is the God of the Bible. If either of these "legs" is weak, then we will walk with a limp. He went on to say that in most traditional churches (like Southern Baptist churches), the doctrinal leg was very strong, but the experiential leg was weak. Therefore we limped through our spiritual life. We needed to find a balance. That balance did not seem to be a problem in the early church. For example, when Paul heard about the problems with some of the experiences the believers in Corinth were having with spiritual gifts and the detrimental effects those were having on the ministry of the church, he did not forbid the practices of the gifts. Instead he gave them the doctrinal explanations that they were missing and showed them how to apply those lessons.

That explanation helped me a lot by affirming that I was not wrong in pursuing the ministry God was giving to our church. I was building up my "experiential leg."

This philosophy also affirmed our position as pastors when we did not deny the work of the Holy Spirit we witnessed but explained to the congregation what it meant and encouraged them to maintain an open heart to what God wanted to do.

I pray that in your life you will be a diligent student of God's Word while allowing His Spirit to do the work He desires to do in your life.

The Big Blowup

"Commit your way to the LORD: trust in him and he will do this: He will make your righteousness shine like the dawn, the justice of your cause like the noonday sun." Psalm 37:5-6

It was about the middle of November, 1995, and Matt, Bill, and I had gathered for our regular weekly meeting. We went to our usual small room in the church and took our seats. Before we even had a prayer, Matt suddenly verbally attacked me; there is no other way to describe it. He told me how terrible a missionary I was, and that I was totally ineffective. He said the church would be better off if I would just leave and go back to the States. He said my Taiwanese was horrible; no one could understand it. He said he had to explain what I was trying to say to the people in small groups after the service was over. He also said I didn't understand Chinese culture and was always making terrible mistakes, and he spent his time running around behind me trying to correct the mistakes I had made. He was quite angry and his rant lasted between thirty and forty five minutes. He finally wound down, but there was not a lot to discuss after that.

Bill and I walked out of the church together and stood by the car talking. He asked, "Where in the world did that come from?" I said I had no idea. I knew he and Matt had worked closely together while we were on furlough and hoped he could give me a hint as to the origin of this blowup, but he could not. We both knew that Matt had resisted our repeated probing to see if he would be willing to serve as pastor of the church, and perhaps that was putting him under some pressure. Another possible reason for Matt's attack could have been the frustration he must have felt to see the elders always turn to me for conformation of any decision or suggestion he made. But neither Bill nor I knew of anything that had happened to cause this tirade. Finally, we went to our homes.

When I got home, I went straight to the bedroom I was using as a study and fell to my knees and started praying. I poured out my frustration, my hurt, and everything else to God. That prayer time lasted a while. Finally I stopped and went to find Nan and told her what had happened. Neither of us knew how to interpret the incident.

Over the next few days, I spent quite a lot of time in prayer and reading the Bible. It was fortunate that the following Sunday I did not have to preach; one of the others had that responsibility. This meant I was not trying to prepare a sermon in my troubled state of mind.

During the time following the blowup, Nan and I prayed about it and discussed our options. We had already recognized that I would have to leave the church in order for Matt to assume his role as pastor. But now it was unclear if he would even be willing to accept that role. Our discussions centered around the topics of where could we go and what could we do and how soon could we get out of Tainan. This event made certain that I had to leave, and as soon as possible.

While I was praying about all this, I came to the Scripture listed above. I told God I was going to accept it as a promise from Him and leave the matter entirely in His hands. Once I made that decision, I was at peace.

The Sunday after the blowup was a little strange, but I tried to act normal. And when it was time for our next weekly meeting, I attended and didn't mention it at all. Neither did

Bill nor Matt. We had our meeting, discussed what was coming up, and then left. Matt seemed a little withdrawn, which was understandable.

In time, we settled into a kind of peaceful acceptance that there was something going on, but we never discussed it. I knew I didn't want to incur Matt's wrath again, and since I was not sure what brought it on, I didn't have a clue on how to defend myself. I simply trusted in God to work out His solution to this issue according to His will and purpose.

I believe it was after the first of the year that I told Matt and Bill in our weekly meeting that it was clear to me that I had to leave the church. I asked Matt if there was anything he wanted me to help him with before I left. I didn't tell him where I was going or when I was leaving and he didn't ask. (Which was a good thing, because I didn't know myself.) He said he would think about my offer.

The following week, he said he would like to have a church member's handbook that would spell out what we believed and taught in the church. Consequently, we spent the next few months working on this project. I would write a section and bring it to the meeting where Matt and Bill would edit it and make suggestions about what else to include and what to leave out. I modeled it on the Baptist Faith and Message, but did not include all the points or all the Scriptures it contained. We also added a couple of points that were especially relevant to us in our situation. One was on the issue of a Christian's response when expected to eat food offered to idols. This was a real issue in the lives of our new believers since they all came from non-Christian homes, and since most of the family gatherings were on holidays that were built on some worship day.

The other point we included was the importance of Christians not marrying non-Christians. This also was a real issue, because at that time most of the Taiwanese families still arranged the marriages for their children. We had three people I can recall whose parents arranged marriages with a non-Christian. In two of those, the husband was won to the Lord and became a strong member of the church. In the third, the young lady moved with her husband to the Eastern side of Taiwan, and we never saw her again.

When we finally agreed on the English text, Matt took the initiative to get it translated into Chinese. We planned a bi-lingual version as well as a Chinese version. He was happy with the finished product and I was glad to be finished with it. It turned into more of a task than I had envisioned.

God was true to His promise and smoothed things over for us. We worked harmoniously for the rest of the time that Nan and I lived in Tainan. There was not another blow up and Matt moved right into the role of pastor. He has provided good leadership to the church and led them to accomplish many good things.

After we left Taiwan in 1998, we worked at First Baptist Church in Jackson, MS. We planned mission trips, and one of the ones we planned in the summer of 2000 was back to Taiwan. It was specifically to provide childcare for the missionary children during the week of Mission Meeting, so a large group was needed. Several in our mission planning committees expressed the opinion that we should extend the trip to two weeks, so we could also spend some time where we had formerly served. We followed their suggestion and formed two groups; one to work in Tainan and one to work in Kaohsiung with another missionary. Nan took one group to Kaohsiung, and I took the other to Tainan to work with Bill and Susan. Matt invited me to preach the Sunday we were in town and everything was just like it always had been. It was a good experience.

We expected there to be changes in Taiwan when we returned even though we had only been gone two years. But we were shocked when we saw where Mission Meeting was held. Formerly, it was on the campus of the mission school; now it was in a brand new

162

resort hotel at the southern end of the island. We had taken many family vacations to that location and stayed in the cheapest and simplest spots available. This huge hotel had been completed after we left the island, and now the entire area was overrun by Chinese tourists, something we never had seen in all our years previously. It was quite a surprise, but it was really nice.

There has been a little contact with Matt since I left Taiwan. I have followed the church a little and found out that they are still growing and reaching a lot of young people. The ministry through home groups continues; they now have about seventy groups scattered throughout the city. They have started at least two churches and are now sending missionaries to Germany. South Africa, and China. China has cracked down again on foreigners coming to work in churches, but the Chinese from Taiwan are welcome. All of those activities are the fulfillment of the prophecy we received in the summer of 1990 when we were on our way back to Tainan. God is faithful to accomplish all He promises.

On a side note, I found it both funny and ironic that after I left Taiwan, Matt made contact with Hal Cunningham, who was on the IMB Regional Staff. He was working with churches in Taiwan and other parts of Asia, trying to interest them in a new program sponsored by the IMB. The program was built on a philosophy of training new converts to be leaders in the church and ultimately taking a role of leadership which could include serving as a pastor. Hal and Matt hit it off and Hal went to Living Water a few times to facilitate this training. The funny part was that when we first started Living Water, Matt didn't want anything to do with Southern Baptists. Now he is working with them. The ironic part was that when Nan and I were starting Living Water, the model for leadership was seminary trained pastors. Now the IMB was endorsing and implementing a program that would use men and women who had no seminary training to work in new church starts. I find that satisfying.

A Grace Gift

In January, 1996, Living Water Church began a forty day fast seeking God's blessing and direction for the coming year. This was not a new thing at all. Almost from the very first we as a church had sponsored all night prayer meetings and had held fasts praying for God's blessing and direction previously. This was the first time we had asked the member to participate in a forty day fast and we explained we were asking them to do a partial fast. That meant fasting one meal a day, or giving up one certain food for the period, or fasting from all food for one day a week during the forty day period. Matt, Bill, and I had spent several weeks in late 1995 explaining why we were fasting and how each member could plan their participation. About three or four days into the fast, Nan and I felt compelled to make our fast complete and to eat no food for the whole period. This would be our second forty day fast; we had done one in the previous term when we were seeking God's direction on the new church start. We did allow ourselves a glass of juice a couple of times a day, plus all the water we could drink. Matt was upset because we had discussed asking the church to participate in the fast and had agreed on what kind of fast it would be. He felt I should have told him if I intended to do a complete fast. I tried to explain that we had intended to follow the guidelines we agreed on for the church, but after we started, we both felt God leading us to take this step. I don't know if he understood or not, but by that time our relationship was pretty well shot as far as I could tell, so I didn't worry about it.

Sometime prior to beginning the fast, I was approached by a young man named David Moody, who was teaching English in Tainan. He had met a Chinese girl whose English name was Alicia, and had asked her to marry him. He wanted some counsel and asked if he could bring her to talk with me.

During our meeting, I discovered that she was of Hakka descent and lived in a village about two hours south of Tainan. She was a believer, as was he. But she was the only believer in her family and was a little nervous about the upcoming marriage. We talked a lot about the difficulties they would face as a mixed couple in Taiwan and about the conflicts that were inevitable since her father was a devout Buddhist. Nevertheless, they decided they would marry.

After we were about two weeks into the fast, David told me the family was holding a big engagement feast. He explained that normally the parents of the groom would attend the festivities, but he was there alone and his parents could not make the trip. So he asked if Nan and I would attend and represent his family, which we were happy to do.

A couple of days later, it hit me – this was a feast and we were fasting. I contacted a friend of mine who worked with the Hakka people, Jerry Cole, and he confirmed my suspicion: to attend this engagement feast and not eat would be a gross breach of etiquette. It would likely add one more issue this young couple would have to deal with in their marriage.

Nan and I were already fasting and praying, but this added a deeper intensity to our prayers. For two days, I really focused on this situation and asked God for His wisdom and guidance. The day before we were to attend the feast, God said, "I am going to give you a grace gift. You can go and eat what is put before you."

That was not the word I was expecting. Both Nan and I had enough experience with fasting to know that to suddenly eat a large meal after eating nothing for three weeks would be dangerous. Nevertheless, we trusted God and headed out for the festivities. All the way there, I was asking God to at least keep me from losing my meal while in the presence of the family. As I prayed, I thought, "Maybe my faith was not as strong as I would like to think it is."

We went to Pingtung County, met the Hakka family, and enjoyed the feast. What a wonderful meal! It was full of rich food that we should not have eaten. But neither of us suffered any ill effects. I even had no heartburn, which was remarkable. We spent the next few days filled with awe and wonder at the graciousness of our God. Praise was continually on our lips.

The day of the wedding came before the fast was completed. Living Water Church had started offering a Christian wedding ceremony to those of our number who were getting married. (In Taiwan when a couple got married, the only legally recognized ceremony was a generic group appointment with multiple other couples in a city government office. The presiding officer would make a few general comments about respecting each other and then hand out their signed documents. Their family members didn't attend, because the big celebration was the wedding feast.) We offered to do a wedding for this young couple since both of them were believers, and the English language church they usually attended did not have a pastor at the time.

On the day of the wedding, Alecia's family was there. For the ceremony, I briefly recounted what we Christians believed about marriage; how God ordained marriage and it was intended that a man and woman were joined together for the purpose of becoming one flesh and displaying God's glory to all around them. I even mentioned how marriage was a picture of what God intended for His bride in the age to come. Perhaps that was too much, but after the service, the bride's elder sister came to me and said, "That is the most beautiful thing I have ever heard." She was deeply touched by everything about the wedding ceremony. We could only pray that in due time the seed planted would bear fruit in her life.

There was a wedding feast and we participated in that as well.

This Grace Gift gave me a deeper insight into the purpose of fasting in a very personal way. I always knew theoretically that one major purpose of fasting was to draw close to God. But this time I discovered that even more important than the set parameters of the fast – in our case a forty day fast – was a heart attitude that allowed God the freedom to speak directly into our lives.

Additionally, it underlined that the purpose of all religious activity is not adherence to a given set of rules or practices, but the activity should lead to a truly intimate, deep relationship with a living God who desires the very best for His children in all circumstances. When whatever we do "religiously" fails to produce that result, then we are missing the most wonderful part of being a Child of the King.

One last part of the Grace Gift was that after the wedding with about five days remaining on the fast, God said, "You can stop now. You have learned what I wanted you to know." What a gift!

At the time I was walking in the neighborhood for exercise, and would pray while on my morning walk. The morning after God told me I could stop fasting, I remember telling Him I didn't want to lose the close contact with Him I had enjoyed during the fast. His response was that the closeness we shared was not dependent on the fast; it was something

I could experience whenever I was willing to make the time to totally focus on Him and spend time with Him. That should be the goal for all of us in our Christian walk.

Another Step, Another Move

"For I know the plans I have for you . . ." Jeremiah 29:11

Early in the spring of 1996 our current Mission Administrator, Hal Cunnyingham, announced it was time for his furlough and the mission needed someone to step in and serve as Interim Administrator in his absence. This was a role I had wanted to hold for some years, but God had led me on a different path. Since it was now obvious that I had to go somewhere, I called Hal and told him of my interest in serving in that position. We had a long talk about my needing to leave Living Water Church and that it would be best if I could move out of Tainan entirely to allow Matt the freedom to pastor the church without my presence serving as either a hindrance or a crutch. I was hoping I could leave later that spring and move to Taipei. He reminded me that there might be others interested in filling the position and he would take my name to the leadership in the mission for them to discuss. Ultimately, they did agree for me to fill that position and move to Taipei, the location of the mission office.

Nan and I both had known for some time that we needed to leave the church and knew it would be best if we could leave Tainan. We were agreed that this might be the best option for us. We could move to Taipei, stay a year while Hal was on furlough, and then take our furlough. Then we would have more time to decide where to go next. Guiding us in this process was the firm conviction that we were following God's leadership. We knew He had a plan for us and that He had worked to place us where He wanted us to be. We thanked him for all the ways we had seen and experienced His work in starting Living Water Church. I continued to work on the church member's handbook for Matt and do whatever I could to help the church function and get ready for the transition. Bill and Susan had another year before their furlough and they were going to stay with the church.

Nan had relationships and projects keeping her busy. Soon after our return from furlough in 1995, we had met a young Conservative Baptist couple who had moved to town and were trying to start a new church. In those initial stages, there is always a lot of trial and error and the wife, Peggy, was struggling with her role in trying to find the balance between the church work and taking care of home and their three children. After we met them, Nan could tell she was having some difficulty with her various responsibilities, and invited her to our house for coffee. Nan and Peggy hit it off and their friendship developed into a mentoring relationship. Their weekly meeting evolved into a true ministry for Nan, and she enjoyed talking and praying with Peggy. I know she was able to help this young missionary get a handle on her life and feel good about making her time with her children a priority, which is what she wanted to do. Nan could speak from experience, since before we even had children, we had made the decision to never put the ministry ahead of our children, often to the consternation of the Chinese with whom we worked and sometimes to the puzzlement of some of our own missionary colleagues.

Nan also had another task that was very important to her. Every year we attended the Taiwan Missionary Fellowship. All of the larger missions, of which Southern Baptists were one, had their own Mission Meeting in the summer. But there were several smaller missions who did not have an annual meeting and they combined for a week of spiritual refreshment. We attended because we enjoyed the fellowship with other missionaries, the worship and good preaching. Our own Mission Meeting seemed to be filled with handling a lot of business. While that was necessary, it was often tiresome.

One year at TMF we were introduced to a mission magazine, Taiwan Mission Quarterly. It was published in Taiwan, and the articles were written by missionaries stationed there. We subscribed to it and enjoyed the articles. They often gave us insights into Chinese culture and missionary methods others were using. I don't remember how or when it started, but Nan wrote an article or two for the magazine and then contacted someone on the editorial board to offer some suggestions about the layout design. Long story short, they invited her to serve on the staff, and later named her as editor of the magazine.

In college she had studied art, but her real passion was writing and editing. Perhaps due to her training as an artist, she was quite gifted in layout design and did a good job on the magazine. While she worked as editor, she even got me to write an article or two. This involvement gave her a huge sense of accomplishment and satisfaction. By this time in 1996, she had been serving as the editor for a couple of years.

The move to Taipei did not come as quickly as I had hoped. Hal was not leaving for furlough until sometime in December and they didn't want me to come up there too early since I would just be sitting there until he left. I said I would use the time there to begin Mandarin study since most of the pastors with whom I would have contact only spoke Mandarin. We finally moved sometime in November. We settled into an apartment in a building where our mission owned a couple of floors. The church next door, Grace Baptist Church, our oldest Baptist church in Taiwan, was close by so we attended an English service there. Then we learned about another English language church, Taipei International Church, and started going up there. This church was made up of business people, some Chinese who spoke English, and some missionaries. We enjoyed that church service in part because of the association with other missionaries and some of the folks from the business community. We also liked the pastor and his wife, whom Nan knew from her work on TMQ.

We settled into another "new normal." We were always looking to see where God wanted us to get involved and where He could use us.

In Taipei

"Yet I am always with you; you hold me by my right hand. You guide me with your counsel, and afterward you will take me into glory." Psalm 73:23-24

Throughout our missionary career, we maintained a daily devotional time and lived with the assurance that we were exactly where God had placed us. During our years in Taiwan, it seemed that most of the time whenever we needed to change anything in our lives, those changes were indicated by a direction the mission was taking or by the changing circumstances of our work. For example, we started working on the new church start because the mission had made the decision to pursue church planting and all missionaries would be involved in that work. After we started the church, the emphasis of our work changed from outreach to discipling to directing new believers in how to live as Christians. Throughout all of this, there was always the foundational belief that God was leading and directing everything that we did. One of the lessons we learned along the way was summarized in this little statement: "Don't doubt in the dark what God has shown you in the light." We interpreted this to mean that when we were praying though any situation and felt God directing us to a certain action, we would follow that leading. Because we had prayed through leaving Living Water, leaving Tainan and moving to Taipei, we had the assurance that God was leading us. That is the attitude we took with us in our move. We knew it would be different and we knew there was not a ministry spot ready for us. At least there was nothing for Nan; I knew that on January 1, I would fill the role of Interim Administrator. After we settled into our apartment, I started Mandarin study.

As we left Tainan, I remembered that morning when God had told me, "Your time is up." Obviously I had not died and we had not been forced away from Taiwan by invading Communists. So now I assumed that God had been telling me that I would be leaving Living Water Church and leaving Tainan. This seemed the logical interpretation of that message, but still I wondered if that was all of what God meant.

As soon as the office opened after the holidays, I went in and started my work. I was familiar with the office and its operation in a general way. I knew all the missionaries who worked there and most of the Chinese staff as well. I had been there often during my years in Taiwan to take care of business and to attend meetings. I respected all of the people in the office and was looking forward to working with them.

About two weeks into my stint as administrator, the IMB held their January board meeting at their headquarters in Richmond, VA. The news that came to us following the meeting was quite shocking and threw us all into turmoil. For starters, our Regional Leader whom we all loved and respected was replaced. Faye Pearson had come to Taiwan as a Student Worker and worked in that assignment for several terms, until she was selected to fill the position of Assistant to the Regional Leader. She served in that role until the Regional Leader, Sam James, moved to a Vice President position and he recommended that Faye replace him. The board accepted his recommendation, so she followed him as East Asia Regional Leader and did a good job. (East Asia was comprised of Taiwan,

Korea, Hong Kong, and Japan. China was also considered a part of the region even though we did not officially have missionaries there; that came later.)

That change was bad enough, but other changes the board made were extremely troubling to all of us who had served for any length of time on the field. There had been a time or two in previous years when the IMB announced some pretty big changes, and those changes led to frustration and anger among many of the missionaries. Those feelings stemmed in part from the perception that the missionary's role on the field had not been adequately understood, and in part from the fact that some of the work the IMB had traditionally done was being phased out. It would not be far wrong to say that often the missionaries felt as though the business end of the overall operation was overshadowing the ministry end of the operation. But the changes announced in 1997 went far beyond what we had seen before.

One change was so huge it was hard to comprehend. When we were appointed, the philosophy was that we would go to a country, learn the language and culture, build relationships, and be an incarnational presence. We would lead people to Christ, disciple them, and then help them find places of ministry. Often the missionary would serve as pastor of a National church or at least the Associate Pastor. That was often the case in Japan. But the missionary was often the person out front.

The new philosophy was that the missionary would conduct what was termed a "shadow ministry." They would come into a country, maybe not even develop proficiency in the language, keep a low profile, and witness to people when they could. Then when someone did decide to follow Jesus, the missionary would spend most of their time with that one person and disciple him or her. They would ask the new convert if they knew someone who might want to learn what they had learned, and would coach the new convert on how to present their testimony. Then the missionary might accompany the new convert to share his or her testimony with the person. But the new convert did all the talking. The missionary would always be in the background. If the person accepted Jesus, then the missionary would teach his own new convert the first lesson in discipleship, and that person would pass it on to the person he had led to Christ. The idea and hope was that this process would lead to a rapid expansion of the spread of the gospel that was not dependent on the missionary.

In hindsight, absent the emotions of the moment, that was in fact a better way to build disciples who would be capable of carrying on the work once the missionary was gone. The goal for any leader should always be to build an organization that would be self-perpetuating. But when missionaries who had served for between eight and thirty years using one paradigm and one methodology were suddenly told that now there is a new paradigm and a new methodology and that is how you will minister, it was a terrible shock. As we tried to understand the reasoning behind the sudden change, it was fairly easy to see why this new approach was necessary in some countries that were closed to a missionary presence because of government regulations. In those countries, the missionary had to keep a low profile and truly had no idea how long they would be allowed to stay. They were forced to find some way of doing the work which would ensure, if possible, the results of their efforts would be preserved if they had to leave in the middle of the night. In some ways, those of us in Taiwan could understand the need for the new approach in some places, but really could not understand why that approach had to be forced on us when we had freedom of religion guaranteed by the constitution of Taiwan.

Several issues seemed to drive this big change. One was the recognition that mission income was not meeting the needs of the projected work around the world. This led to a re-examination of priorities not only in expenditures for institutional work (things like schools and hospitals) but also in placement of personnel.

Perhaps the biggest influence was the acknowledgement that there are many language or people groups around the world in which there was little or no gospel influence. Recent research had identified more and more of these groups while also discovering that even in their host nation, there was very little communication between the minority people group and the majority, host people group. For example, China's population was approximately 98% Han Chinese, but within the geographical boundaries of the country, there existed more than a hundred minority people groups. Some of those had as few as ten thousand people while the largest groups had more than a million people. But there was very little communication between these groups and the host Han Chinese. That meant that the gospel, even though limited in China, had no real way to penetrate the smaller people groups.

In this mix, the IMB was examining the countries in which they had a long history of sending missionaries. They felt it might be possible to re-deploy some missionaries from one field to another. Taiwan had a population of approximately 19 million people at the time. Most missiologists estimated that Taiwan had between 3% and 5% of its population categorized as Christians. Even with that low percentage of believers in the population, the experts had deemed it was a "reached" country. Those of us who served there disagreed, believing that it was an unreached country. But since there were at least four seminaries (Southern Baptist, Methodist, Presbyterian, and Lutheran) with Christian book stores and companies publishing Christian materials, the IMB categorized Taiwan as a reached country. It was felt that in the economy of wise utilization of personnel, they should no longer send missionaries to reached countries and focus on the unreached areas of the world. That meant that some of our missionaries could be sent to other fields. In a way, it made sense if the missionaries were sent to countries with a similar language and culture. For example, missionaries from Taiwan could go to China where the language was the same and the culture was similar. But there were times when missionaries would be sent to a country where there was no similarity of language and culture. One couple I knew had served for at least twenty years in Brazil, and they went to Italy. One could argue that since both Italian and Portuguese were foundationally Romance languages, the change would not be too difficult. But still, it was a different language, a different country, and a different culture. For those of us who volunteered to serve in one country, we intended to complete our years in that host country.

At the same time in world history, some countries that had previously been totally closed to any kind of missionary presence were relaxing their restrictions just a little. This meant that now mission personnel might be able to get into those countries. But they could not go in as missionaries. They went in as teachers, travel agents, sports consultants, medical staff or anything else that seemed viable. When necessary, they would try to start their own business for support. In some cases, they would be hired by a national entity like a school or hospital.

Historically, the Foreign Mission Board (renamed the International Mission Board) sought to strictly adhere to the laws of the host country. Now they were looking for loopholes in the law to find ways to insert trained Christians (missionaries) into those countries where missionaries were prohibited. They were no longer content to send their personnel only to countries that were deemed "safe," but were now sending missionaries to places that were inherently dangerous to all Christians and especially to American Christians.

Lessons from the Journey

Given all these big changes, it is easy to see why there was a lot of negative reaction from the missionaries to the new thoughts in missions. There was widespread discontent in all the countries, and Taiwan was no exception.

This unsettled climate is what I stepped into when I moved into the role of Mission Administrator. I accepted the position assuming that the mission organization would operate as it had done in the past, allowing me to use my position to minister to the missionaries. I had noticed that we seemed to lose young missionaries unnecessarily. I was convinced (rightly or wrongly) that if they had someone in authority listen with compassion, explain some of their experiences, encourage and pray with them, we could retain most of them. In a sense, I was going to try to be a pastor to the missionaries. That all changed as a result of the sweeping, radical new direction announced by the IMB leaders. When I accepted the Mission Administrator position, there were a lot of unknowns about how to do that jobt. But now, I knew I was hopelessly overwhelmed.

The day after all the changes were announced and we were still trying to figure out what it meant for us, I met with Herb Barrett, our business manager. He was a godly man with a very even temperament. He always said one of his primary purposes was to make things as easy for the missionary as possible, and he did a good job of that. I was looking forward to working with him. Anyway, we met and discussed the situation. We decided to do all we could to present the changes in a positive light, and help the missionaries accept the decisions that had been handed down to us.

In that tumultuous situation, I turned to God. Every day at lunch, I would close my office door and spend the lunch hour praying, reading the Bible, and fasting. I continued this for most of the first year we were in Taipei. Sometimes there were specific needs in the mission I prayed about. Other times I was simply pleading for mercy and wisdom. And I prayed for all the missionaries by name every week. God brought me through that time.

Day by Day

"The LORD replied,' My Presence will go with you, and I will give you rest.'" Exodus 33:14

"You are my servant; I have chosen you and have not rejected you. So do not fear, for I am with you; do not be dismayed, for I am your God. I will strengthen you and help you; I will uphold you with my righteous right hand." Isaiah 41:9b-10

For years, I had depended on this verse from Exodus for encouragement and comfort. It was a promise to me that God was with me in whatever difficult situation I faced in ministry. I had a confidence that as I maintained my devotional time and built my relationship with my heavenly Father, His constant presence would show me the right way to go.

In much the same way, the concept in the verse in Isaiah had also been an important part of my devotional life for many years. That concept came to me from various places and always was a truth on which I depended. Now I was really depending on God to lead me through this maze of finding the right way to implement the new philosophy of the IMB while at the same time trying to encourage and minister to the missionaries who were faced with huge changes.

In order to be able to find the right way to implement this new methodology, first I had to understand it. When it was announced, we were told to dream our biggest dreams and not be bound by what we had done in the past. The only hints of what that instruction might mean was an occasional report of what some missionaries were doing in other countries. But most of those reports came from countries where missionaries were forced to try new methods because the former methods required planting churches with the approval of the host governments. Our new Regional Leader would not actually be with us until Mission Meeting that summer, so for about four months, we worked in a vacuum, trying to guess at what might be wanted or accepted in Richmond.

Early in my tenure, I started sending out a weekly report to the missionaries, passing on any information or directive I had received from Richmond. In consultation with Herb Barrett and others, I tried to suggest how to interpret the information. I also included some kind of inspiration or devotional thought in the attempt to remind us all that God is the one who called us to Taiwan and He still had something for us to do.

That summer provided some encouragement for both Nan and me. First, Carroll came to Taiwan to live for a year. She had been working as a nanny for a family in France and had been hired to teach French at Morrison for the school year of 1997-98. They needed someone short term and her availability filled that need.

Second, every year at Mission Meeting, the International Mission Board handed out service pins to missionaries on the field. The recognition of time served came in five year increments. Nan and I received our twenty year pins that summer. And the really good news to us was that they still had "Foreign Mission Board" on them; the IMB apparently had not had time to make new pins with the new name, International Mission Board. Or maybe they just wanted to use up as many of the old ones as they could before making new ones. At any rate, the pins were extra special to us because the old name had been a fixture in our lives since childhood. It was also meaningful to receive them from our "old" Regional Leader, Faye Pearson.

The daily pressure of figuring out how to interpret and apply the new guidelines from Richmond was not easy to deal with. Our new regional leader had now arrived. He had been a missionary in another country and had been sneaking into a closed country for a few years. I never knew if he'd had previous leadership positions; we all assumed he was chosen for the task since he had been doing the clandestine work that seemed to be the new focus of our Board.

We would meet with him to discuss all of the things that we missionaries were doing in Taiwan, and he would constantly tell us that our activities did not fit into the new direction. His approach gave me and some of the other leaders the idea that he wanted our mission to function as though it were in a closed country like China. We often tried to point out that it was not necessary for us to take that position, since we had freedom of religion and open opportunities to witness and train leaders; we did not have to do that in secret. But he gave us the impression that he wanted us to do that anyway. It made no sense to us.

Added to the increasing frustration was the fact that often, when we would finally come up with a firm recommendation to pass on to the missionaries, he would come back a few months later and say we could not do it that way.

My tension level was rising significantly, to the point that sometime in late October or November, Carroll and Nan told me that I needed to get away from it all and take a vacation. In a moment of candor, I said, "Fine. You plan it. I have no energy to try and make those kinds of plans." I assumed we would be making a trek to Oluanpi, the southern part of the island where we had spent many vacation days as a family. Surprise, surprise! They picked Boracay, an island in the Philippines. We went during the Christmas break and had a wonderful, relaxing week away from life in Taipei. It was delightful. (On that trip, Carroll observed that wherever you go in the world, you will find people from the United Kingdom there. She mused, "I wonder why they want to return to England?" We all wondered why someone would swap life in the tropics for life in the cold and damp of England. I guess that shows our prejudice.)

We eventually had to return to reality. But at least I was more relaxed and refreshed, and better able to roll with all the frustration that we had to deal with.

We had been attending Taipei International Church regularly and had made acquaintance with several of the people there. During Christmas, their pastor left to return to the States. After a few weeks, they asked me to preach there one Sunday, and I accepted the invitation because I enjoyed preaching, so it would give me something positive to counteract the job stress.

Then their pastor sent word that he would not be returning, and they asked me to be the interim pastor. By this time I had been in the job long enough that I gotten more comfortable with it and the stress was diminishing . The vacation had also given me fresh energy and perspective, so I agreed to fill that role for them. I assumed it would be for a couple of months until they could hire a new pastor from America. It was obvious that there were several people in the church who responded well to the sermons I brought them, so one day in early summer the deacons asked to meet with me and offered me the job of pastor of their church.

After much prayer and discussing it with Nan and for personal reasons, I declined the offer. But when the invitation first came, I remembered that phrase that had come to me in my devotional time a couple of years earlier: "Your time is up." I now wondered if God was saying that my time with the Foreign Mission Board was up. To be frank, given all the changes that were taking place, I felt that the Board was no longer what it had been when we were appointed. The thought that I could escape the turmoil within the IMB was quite appealing. But eventually I turned the offer down.

In the meantime, during my time in Taipei, our Regional Leadership had sent Nan and me, along with a few other missionaries, to a different kind of mission meeting. It was for the Southeast Asia Region and included missionaries from about four or five countries. It was usually held in Thailand; this year it was in Chiang Mai. Nan and I were very interested in how it was all handled. It was quite different from our own Mission Meetings in several ways.

For one thing, it was held at a resort facility, not on a school campus. Chiang Mai had a thriving night market that shared some similarities with the night markets in Taiwan. There were vendors selling knock-offs and faulty items from goods designed to be sold in the USA. One of the vendors was selling Warner Brothers cartoon ties and I bought a lot of them. I had fun with them back in Jackson when we returned. Nan, Jim Courson, and I also enjoyed some of the snacks in night market. Our favorite was a crepe with bananas, Nutella, and covered with sweetened condensed milk. It was so good, but if you ate the whole thing, you didn't want anything else for quite some time.

Another big difference was that very little business was conducted. It was primarily for worship and fellowship. There was a lot of down time so the missionaries could just relax with their families. It was a very refreshing, encouraging week.

During those meetings, I met their Regional Leader, Don Dent. He was a native Mississippian like me. He actually had kind of met me when I was BSU Director at Blue Mountain College. While I was there, we formed a BSU choir and every year in the spring would visit different churches to present a music program. We visited his church one Sunday night a couple of years in succession and that is how he knew me. I didn't remember meeting him; he would have been a high school student at the time. But now he was a missionary and the Regional Leader.

We had several conversations about the work in Southeast Asia, and he told me of a job that he thought I would be able to do quite well. They had a program where they would send certain missionaries on a circuit to teach new pastors how to be a pastor. They already had the curriculum developed: all the teacher had to do was go to the location, meet the pastors and lead the conference.

The beauty of it was that I would not need any language training. Since the missionary would visit several countries, like Thailand, Malaysia, India, Vietnam, and maybe one or two others, there would always be a translator to work with the missionary.

Another perk of the job was that the missionary would be based in Singapore, a city both Nan and I loved! (We loved it for its history, beauty, multi-ethnic cultures, ease of communication, and ease of travel.) He would travel from there on his circuit, so the downside was that for about six to eight months of the year, he would be living out of his suitcase in the various countries.

All in all, that was quite appealing to me. I seriously considered asking for that position.

One of my responsibilities as Mission Administrator was to appoint certain committee chairmen and make sure that the events for which they were responsible were planned and executed. One of the big ones was Mission Meeting. In 1998, we had a new Mission Meeting chairperson, an MK from Taiwan named Becky Courson. (Her husband Jim had gone with Nan and me to Chiang Mai.) Her parents, Don and Helen Jones, were on staff at Morrison. She had grown up there and was quite familiar with everything about Taiwan and Mission Meeting.

In one of our first meetings, she proposed having the mission participate in the Lord's Supper at Mission Meeting. I pointed out to her that there were several in our mission who would feel this was inappropriate since we were not a local church. They believed that the Lord's Supper was intended to be celebrated by the local church, and any other group of people should not observe it. I asked her to pray about it and we would discuss it again in our next meeting.

When she returned, she assured me she had prayed about it and felt it could help us feel more unified as a group. After all, we were all followers of Christ and had dedicated our lives to His service. Her argument was that it was entirely appropriate for this group to celebrate our Lord's life and resurrection together. I had no opposition to celebrating Jesus' life in this way and agreed that she could schedule it. I then asked her to consider who she would like to lead the ordinance. We left it at that, and her planning for Mission Meeting continued while I kept up with all my other responsibilities.

A couple of weeks before Mission Meeting, I called Becky to check on the final status of all the plans for the meeting. All was in place except for the name of the person who would lead the Lord's Supper. In discussion, I said if you don't have anyone, I would be happy to lead it. She responded that she had wanted to ask me to do it, but was a little bit afraid to do so.

That added one more item to my agenda of preparation for Mission Meeting, but it was a pleasant one. I considered several passages to read for the celebration and finally settled on Luke 22:14-20. I didn't have any particular reason for choosing that passage; it just seemed fitting to me.

The meeting week followed the usual routine of visiting with friends, tending to business matters, fellowshipping around the dining table, worshipping together, etc. Finally, the session came when we would celebrate the Lord's Supper together. As I introduced what we were going to do, I explained that I knew some would choose not to participate since we were not an organized local church. I asked those who felt so to just sit quietly and pray for the rest of us as we participated. Then I read the Scripture I had chosen.

I read verses 15-16 *"And he said to them, 'I have eagerly desired to eat this Passover with you before I suffer. For I tell you, I will not eat it again until it finds fulfillment in the kingdom of God."* As I read that verse, suddenly God spoke to me and said, "This is the last time you will be with this group." I concluded the celebration, but honestly don't remember anything else about it. You can be sure I tucked that thought in my mind to explore later.

I really had wanted to leave for furlough immediately following Mission Meeting, but there were some other matters to conclude prior to departure. Consequently, we had arranged to depart in early September.

In the final week or so prior to our departure, I met with our Regional Leader and told him I wanted to resign as Mission Administrator. When he asked why, I told him that my understanding of the new direction the Board was taking dictated that very soon certain missionaries who served at our seminary and at Morrison would be told that there was no longer a place for them in Taiwan. I also said that the way things had happened ever since the new direction, I would be the one to break the news to my friends and I was unwilling to do that.

His response was that we both knew that I was tired and that major decisions should not be made in that frame of mind. He said go home, take two months, and then let's talk.

I grudgingly agreed, knowing all the time that I would no longer serve in that position. I was too washed out to think about anything except getting home and trying to put things into perspective again.

RETURN TO JACKSON

Back in Jackson

We returned to Jackson around mid-September of 1998 to a whirlwind. Carroll left Taiwan about two months prior to our departure and spent the time traveling home via Hong Kong, Norway, Canada, and maybe other places. She arrived a little earlier than we did and had run into an old boyfriend, Burke Speed. They had broken up a couple of years earlier, but suddenly the spark from yesteryear was twinkling again. Not long after we unpacked, she left to meet him at Moody Air Force Base for the weekend and told us she fully expected to return with an engagement ring. I thought that was mighty quick, but that is what happened. She returned on Monday night and said they wanted to get married on Saturday before he left for Korea. My head was spinning. Somehow, Nan and her circle of friends pulled off the wedding in five days, a record. All of the Southern wedding traditions were either ignored or crushed.

After that, things settled down into our normal furlough routine. That meant we would accept invitations to speak in churches on the weekends and visit with family and friends in Jackson during the week.

That fall, we were invited to a mission week at Concord Baptist Church in Knoxville, TN. It was an eye-opening experience for us both because we saw elements we had never seen previously in all the other mission conferences we attended. Perhaps the biggest shock was seeing the number of missionaries present and understanding that they represented multiple mission groups, including Wycliffe Bible Translators, Campus Crusade, and Youth With a Mission. This was the first conference we had ever seen in a Baptist church that was open to mission agencies other than Southern Baptist. It was quite informative.

Another thing that really impressed us was the way the church demonstrated their love and support for the missionaries. Before we went to the conference, we were asked for a wish list of things we needed for our ministry. This was radically new to us and we were not sure how to respond. Finally we did send a request: Nan asked for a publishing program for all the work she had been doing on Taiwan Mission Quarterly. During the week, she was given the software and given a short lesson on how to use it. That was a program that would have cost several hundred dollars.

By far the most humbling and amazing facet of the conference was the invitation time on Sunday night. In the service, the speaker reminded the members that they had heard many stories of different kinds of work being done in a lot of different places. They were reminded that there was a great need for volunteers, both short term and long term. When the invitation was extended, it was for anyone who wanted to volunteer to serve in missions in some way to come to the front of the church. It was a large auditorium and the front was so packed that people could not move around. We made a quick estimate and guessed that at least five hundred people responded. We had never witnessed anything like that. We returned to Jackson with our heads spinning.

The remainder of fall followed the normal pattern of previous furloughs: many invitations to speak from early October until Christmas. Then it all stopped. We had one more invitation in February to another mission week in Tampa, Florida. That was it. Then we would have to decide what to do about our return to the mission field.

We had not discussed our situation about Taiwan at all. Nan knew of my decision to no longer serve as Mission Administrator, but that is as far as we had gone in our discussions. Even so, my intent was to return to the mission field. When we were appointed, we accepted the appointment intending to stay with the Board until we retired. Initially that was how Nan looked at our appointment as well, but she had not expressed her feelings about returning after this furlough.

So far, I had not contacted Don Dent about following up on the opportunity to transfer to Southeast Asia and headquarter in Singapore. I had not really discussed that with Nan, either. I knew we had to do something and knew I didn't want to return to Taiwan.

We had one last mission conference scheduled in Tampa, Florida, and the Sunday night before we left for it, the new mission pastor at First Baptist, Randy Von Kanel, asked us to meet with him the next day to discuss something. We said it would have to wait since we were leaving the next day and would be gone for around three weeks. So right there on the spot, he asked us to write a job description for someone to be on staff at FBCJ to plan mission trips. He was supposed to do that, but the church had kept him so busy with other things, he had been unable to fulfill that part of his job description. So during our three-week trip, we brainstormed about what that job might entail and wrote it on our computer. It was kind of fun.

When we returned, we handed Randy the job description we had worked on and he loved it. He said, "You need to stay here and do it." After a little discussion, I said we could not because we were field missionaries and we needed to be on the field. Nan didn't say anything at all.

A few weeks later, we attended the annual Women's Missionary Union Conference in Jackson. We always did that because we knew that the WMU was the greatest support the International Mission Board had. We liked to touch base with those who were so faithful to pray and provide financial support for us and all of our fellow missionaries.

On the last day of the conference, the host church provided a noon meal and it was obvious the women were anxious to hit the road home. I almost had the feeling that they were eating standing up. By the time we finished, I looked around the room and the only people present were Nan, me, and Jerry Rankin, who was the president of the IMB. We had been classmates while at Mississippi College and his wife was Nan's classmate. So we went over to have a little chat and catch up on things.

During our conversation, I said, "Here is something you will find interesting," and I told him about Randy's offer for us to stay at the church. To my great surprise, he replied, "There are three reasons I would like you to pray about accepting that offer." He then outlined why he thought it would be a good idea. I almost fell out of my chair because he was the one I was quoting when I told Randy we were field missionaries and needed to be on the field. After that conversation, I decided perhaps I should go home and pray about it and stepped into an intense time of evaluation of my understanding of God's call and how to respond to it.

When I was struggling with how to respond to God's call on my life almost forty years previously, I thought I understood what God's call meant. For me, it was a personal, specific call to serve Him in foreign missions. It had been so clear and so strong that now to consider doing anything other than foreign missions seemed like turning my back on that call. For days, I struggled in prayer trying to understand what it meant and how God wanted me to respond. I read the Scriptures looking for some guidance and didn't find anything that I could interpret as being a definite answer. Therefore, I was content to follow the axiom that had often guided us in the past when faced with a question about the future and it seemed God was not speaking. We would just continue doing the last thing He directed us to do. For me, that meant continuing to serve through the IMB.

Nan and I discussed it frequently and prayed together about it. I didn't want to mention it to anyone else since I was not sure they would understand. It was quite a battle. How could I reconcile leaving the IMB to accept a job at a big church in the States? I had heard the snide comments from the other fellows I served with in Taiwan when another one of our number would accept a position in America. To be truthful, perhaps I was considering what they would say when I told them I was leaving the Board more than I should have been. I knew what they would say about me.

After a couple of weeks, one morning as I was taking my daily walk and praying through it all one more time, God said, "You have accomplished in Taiwan what I sent you there to do." That sentence stopped me in my tracks. I stood there thinking about all that it meant.

When I returned home, I told Nan about the conversation. We discussed it and prayed together again. Then we called Randy and scheduled a time to discuss his request with him. In that discussion, he explained more completely what he had in mind when he made the initial comment and offer. We took that discussion home with us and prayed some more. Finally, we called back and told him we were willing to accept the position. But there were a lot of hoops to jump through before we actually would start working there. The process took a couple of weeks, but it was made easier because both Nan's parents and my parents were in the church, we took all our furloughs there and the church knew us well. They had been supporting us for more than twenty years, and we were always in church there when not away for some kind of speaking engagement.

Through that process, God showed me that I had not completely understood His call on my life so many years previously. I had interpreted His call as a call to foreign missions, and it was. But I missed the more important aspect: at its core, His call was to commit myself to Jesus and Jesus alone. He reminded me of all the passages in the Bible that reveal God as the potter and the man as the clay; the potter has the right to make of the clay any vessel he chooses to make and to use that vessel in any way He chooses to use it.

I also came to understand that the word He spoke to me back in 1995 – "Your time is up" – had multiple interpretations. It meant my time at Living Water Church was up; my time in Tainan was up; my time in Taiwan was up; and my time with the International Mission Board was up.

As I reflected then and in the years since, I am eternally grateful for God's call on my life and the wonderful opportunities He gave me to see Him work in Taiwan.

In June, we returned to Taiwan to pack our goods for the move to Jackson and to say some goodbyes. We were excited about the prospects of the opportunities ahead of us. We started our new job at FBCJ in June of 1999, twenty-two years after we were appointed as missionaries.

The New Job

After returning from Taiwan with our goods, we spent some time looking for a house. I was not real interested in a purchase of that size, but one of the deacons, a real estate broker, told us that if we purchased a house in Belhaven, and did return to the field, he would manage it for us while we were gone. He promised that the rent for the house would cover the mortgage note and that way when we did eventually return, we would have a home to live in. He convinced me it was a good idea and helped us find just the right house. Nan's mother had grown up in Belhaven so she had always wanted to live there. And since both my parents and her mom lived in Jackson, there was no real consideration given to living anywhere else. Therefore his proposition suited Nan just fine. The house he helped us find and purchase served us well.

We combined the house search with the new job at FBC. In fact, there was already a mission trip to Ukraine planned for that year in late July, and Randy told us it was our responsibility to lead the team. We didn't really know how to prepare the team, but he told us about a man who had led several teams and could meet with us and help in getting the team ready. We accepted his help and made a lot of notes during the process. We also made a lot of notes while on the trip, which was a big success. While we were in Ukraine, I called Dad to report that everything was going well, and he reported to me that about a day after we departed, Randy announced he was resigning from the church. That was a shock and something else to deal with.

When we returned, we were in a new job with no supervisor. In the unofficial staff chart of the church, our boss was now the Executive Pastor, Jim Baker. I got to know him pretty well during the following years and we had a good working relationship. Basically, he let me make the plans and then he would approve them. He had little input into our plans.

We learned quickly that our task at FBC fell into about five categories. First, there was the task of finding a site for a mission team to work, which would also include finding an onsite missionary or national pastor with whom to work. This person had a high degree of influence over what type of work the team would do, which would then determine the specific jobs that team members would hold. This helped us know what type of people we needed on the teams, like doctors, teachers, sports personnel, Vacation Bible School workers, or even plumbers. Two of the national pastors stand out in my memory because we worked with them over the course of many years and became good friends: Alexandru Sandeulac of Cupcini, Moldova, and Mike Stringer in Oadby, England.

The second category was the selection of the team. First Baptist had been sending out mission teams, but they were usually formed within a small portion of the congregation. The college or youth or choir would send out a team each year. No one really knew of a time when a mission trip was announced and then opened to the entire church membership. That was what we wanted to do.

The third category was what might be called logistical support. At that time, we were only concerned with teams headed to international locations. That meant the team would travel together and I would buy tickets for the whole group. These days, it's easy for individuals to purchase their own tickets on the internet, but back then, nearly all air travel was booked through travel agencies. Fortunately, a church member owned a travel agency that handled all the travel for First Baptist. I was told to get tickets through them, and the agency assigned me Kay Couch with whom to work. She became a good friend and her help was invaluable in many ways.

Another aspect of the logistical support was providing the funds for supplies and related expenses for the trip. Volunteers were already paying their own way, including airfare, food and lodging, and ground transport. I quickly recognized that it would be an added burden for them to provide these funds because it would add to the overall cost. Fortunately, the church provided me with a budget and I was able to divide it and allocate percentages of that total amount to the individual journeys. Part of those funds went to the cost of supplies needed and another part went to provide scholarships to help defray the overall cost to the individual volunteer. In this way, the cost of the trip was subsidized a little and made the journey more affordable to the team members.

The fourth category was training the teams and preparing them to effectively carry out their assignment. While we were on the field, Nan and I had experienced hosting a few mission teams. Some of them were very well prepared, while others were not prepared at all. Those few were the ones that made missionaries decide not to work with short term volunteers. We were determined our teams would not fall into that category.

To understand how to prepare a team, I searched for mission training manuals. All the ones I found seemed to deal with how to raise funds, how to pack a suitcase, what to take, how to choose a location and things like that. Almost all of them would contain a statement at the beginning of the book to the effect that spiritual preparation was really important, but this was not the purpose of that particular manual. I never did find the manual that dealt with the spiritual preparation, but Nan and I felt that it was the most important aspect of the training. Consequently, very soon after finding our office we started the task of deciding how to prepare a team spiritually for their journey.

We agreed that the foundation of the spiritual preparation should be to emphasize that these volunteers were called by God to participate on this journey. We recognized that many of the people at First Baptist were accustomed to international travel. They thought nothing of taking their family to Europe or the Bahamas for a summer vacation, and they didn't understand that a mission trip is different. We knew we had to educate them to understand that a mission journey had a different purpose than a vacation, and was a part of God's overall plan for the redemption of mankind. A lot of the volunteers told us that this was the first time in their lives that they knew God had a purpose for them like this. Quite a few of them also told us later that the training time was the most significant part of their overall experience on the journey.

A fifth category of our work was to find a way to publicize and promote what we were doing. Our first thought was to select people to give testimonies about their experience and use them in the Sunday services. We quickly found out that was not an option. The Sunday morning service was taped to be televised, and as a result was timed to the minute. It was really unusual for anything or anyone to break into the established pattern. So we had to look for other avenues. Nan's creative mind responded to the challenge.

During our first six months, fall and winter of 1999, there was only the one trip to Ukraine. But the second year, we had four or five international trips. Nan created a magazine titled *First In All The World*. I was skeptical about getting approval for the expenditure of funds to pay for it, but Jim Baker thought it was a great idea. It gradually grew year by year to be a bi-monthly publication that featured as much of the mission work of FBC as possible. International trips, North American trips, local mission activities, some of the Woman's Missionary Union activities, and college and youth trips were covered and reported to the church. It was really well done and looked very sharp. Everyone thought it was a credit to the church and she was often commended for her work on it. That, coupled with training the teams, became her primary areas of concentration in our job. My primary areas were selecting the location of the journeys, planning the logistics of the trips, securing the budget for those endeavors, and helping train the teams. We worked well together for those years and it was fun. It was quite demanding, but it was satisfying in so many ways.

Early in the job, as we worked to fill the job description we had written for Randy, we discovered that some parts of it would not work due to the internal structure of the church. Other parts were redundant because the work was being done by other departments. Of course, we had written that document in a vacuum because we didn't know much about how the church worked. Even with the parts we eventually eliminated from the job description, there was plenty to do because we discovered there were things necessary for the task we hadn't known to include. We were always working towards the goal of building a foundation on which the church could continue to do quality mission work for years to come.

One of the trips we planned for 2000 was to Taiwan. We accepted the invitation from the Taiwan Baptist Mission to provide childcare during Mission Meeting. We knew we had to enlist a large team for this and with the encouragement of our Mission Committee also decided to make the trip long enough to include a week of ministry prior to Mission Meeting. Of course, not everyone could take that long off from work, so we had some who left for Taiwan early with us, but returned to Jackson after the first week and some who came alone for the second week. I took one team to Tainan to work with Bill and Susan, and Nan took the second team to Kaohsiung to work with another missionary couple.

About a week prior to departure, I received an email from my Regional Leader informing me that my salary and benefit package would run out at the end of June. In a strange move by the IMB, Nan and I were still missionaries of the IMB, seconded to First Baptist Church. We were given the title "Missionary in Residence." This email revealed that when Jerry Rankin had suggested I pray about taking FBC's offer, he was thinking that I would be there one year, get the program up and running and then return to the mission field. (He neglected to mention that little thought.) I had thought that it would take three years to build a sustainable program so we could consider returning overseas. Jim Baker told me it would take five years.

In my subsequent conversations with Jim following that email, I also discovered that Randy had never discussed our working at FBC with the deacons, nor had he asked them to place this job on the church's staffing plan. In essence, we were in limbo with all our salary and benefits about to disappear and no way to get our goods back to wherever overseas we decided to go should we choose to do that.

We left for the trip with Jim's promise that he would put something together and have it ready to sign when we returned. He assured me that in the year we had been at FBC, everyone had seen the benefit of having us on staff doing what we were doing. Even so, it would be safe to say we left with a little cloud hanging over us.

In spite of the uncertainty about our situation, the trip was a good one. I really enjoyed being back in Tainan, visiting with Bill and Susan, and going to worship at Living Water again. It was a special treat.

The following week, Mission Meeting was not held at the Morrison campus as it had been done almost forever, but was held at a new resort in Oluanpi on the southern end of the island. I was astounded at the radical differences we saw down there. This was the village where our family and lots of other missionary families vacationed. In the early days, a few store owners made the upper floors of their houses rooms for rent. They were quite cheap. The village also had two hotels, one of which had a dining facility attached where we had taken a lot of our meals. Back then, it was just us and the fishermen, and we climbed down a goat trail to our favorite beach at a small, secluded cove.

Now there was a five star tourist hotel complete with spa, exercise facility, big swimming pool, and an underground walkway leading to our formerly secret spot at the cove. It was now a bee hive of activity, with jet skis and busloads of Chinese tourists. But the week providing childcare went well, and Nan and I were able to connect with a few of the missionaries we were close to while we had served in Tainan.

That Christmas, I experienced a "heart episode." The cardiologist told me he didn't think it was a heart attack because when he examined the heart in order to place to stents in one artery, he didn't see any damage to the heart muscle.

A year later, in January of 2001, I had a stroke. The neurologist said it was not the biggest stroke one could have, but neither was it the smallest. Due to God's grace, I suffered only very minor residual effects of that stroke. Nan and I both were glad we were not overseas when those things happened.

Then later in 2001 or early in 2002 Nan's mother, Harriet, also had a stroke. After spending a few weeks in rehabilitation, it was decided that she could no longer live alone, and we asked her to move in with us. She remained with us until her death in 2003.

All of those things combined to let us see that God really was in our move back to Jackson. It also made clear to us that we would not be returning to the mission field as career missionaries; we were in the States for good.

I was sorry about that. I really felt the most satisfaction and fulfillment in my job while on the mission field. Perhaps that was because my sense of call to be a missionary had been so strong. In fact, it was so strong that a couple of times, it was the only thing that kept me on the field. I had prayed through the decision to leave the Board and was convinced it was what God wanted me to do. But I still missed serving overseas.

Matt Chen's father-in-law was a pastor in Australia before they immigrated to America. He said that when you are involved in church planting, "You are living on the thin edge of the cutting wedge." Perhaps that is the dynamic I missed the most. My job now was a lot of routine; doing the same thing over and over. It lacked the spiritual intensity I experienced when working in Living Water Church.

The most interesting aspect of our new job was that after we had been working at FBCJ for two or three years, Nan finally told me it had been a life-long dream of hers to serve on staff there. Her grandmother, Mrs. G. A. Carothers, had been on staff many years previously, from about the late 1940's until the mid-1950's. She was the first paid WMU Director in the Southern Baptist Convention. Nan wanted to follow in her footsteps and she finally did.

As we continued with our work, we dealt with changes in the church. We got a new Mission Pastor, Ronnie Falvey, whom Nan and I both really liked. He had been the Educational Director at the church and we got along very well. He showed a great interest in our work, and I could talk with him about what we were doing, what we hoped to do, and the philosophy that drove our thinking and planning.

In early 2003, the man who had been planning the North American mission trips was asked to take the responsibility for the security of the church. As a result, the leadership asked us to take over the planning of those trips as well. That added to the need for more planning and coordination within the mission department, but it worked.

Soon after that happened, we realized we could no longer do the training we had been doing. It simply was not possible to provide six or seven training sessions for ten to twelve teams a year since the majority of those teams would be doing their work in the short summer session. That opened the door for us to consider enlisting some other people to assist in the training. In turn, that led us to compile our training notes into one volume, and we published our *Mission Training Manual*. When we did that, we knew the training would lose some of the insights our mission experience had been giving to the teams, but we rationalized by admitting we simply could not continue to do it all. And we recognized that some of the potential trainers would also be able to bring to the training some elements that needed to be strengthened where we had been a little lax. To help with this, I located a series of training tapes produced by another mission agency that provided some really good information on a few topics, and we included those in our training.

With the combination of North American and international trips, we were now sending at least ten teams a year to various places in America and around the world. That was about 150 people a year going out from our church on mission journeys.

We also designated some of the North American mission journeys as family trips and encouraged some of the young couples to take their entire family on the trip. We promoted it as a great way to instill in the children at an early age the concept of missions, and to help them understand an element of the Christian faith that was important to the church and to their parents. That was a great success and several of the parents later would share with us the wonderful experience of seeing one of their children lead another child to Christ. And a few of the young children who went on the journey made their own profession of faith while serving on mission.

God showed us multiple times through many ways that we were doing what He wanted us to do. It was good to see how He worked in the lives of so many people.

The Hard Years

Jesus said, "In this world you will have trouble. But take heart! I have overcome the world." John 16:33

We continued working at FBC, planning trips and going on some of them. We were allowed to go on four each year; Nan went on two and I went on two. On a couple of rare occasions, we were both able to go on the same trip. Generally, if there was an exploratory trip to a new field overseas, she would lead that one and then also take a different one. I nearly always took one of the North American trips just to see what we were doing and to try and see how we could be more effective in that work. We did our best to not be the team leader; we wanted to be a part of the team. Admittedly, that was difficult since everyone knew we were the ones who had helped plan the trip and had led at least part of the training. But it worked.

My parents were still alive and getting along reasonably well. At least Dad was. Mom was, in her own words, a confirmed "couch potato." She had no desire to get out very much and, understandably, gradually lost more and more of her strength and mobility. She started falling some, mostly by missing the bed when trying to get in it or by missing a chair when sitting down. I would sometimes be called to come and help get her up; Dad was not able to lift her when she fell.

My cousin, Lynda Lou and her husband David Hatchett also lived in Jackson. They had moved there about the time we left for Taiwan. Lynda's dad was mom's brother. The Hatchetts and Mom and Dad developed a very close relationship, so sometimes Dad would call David to come help lift Mom. Occasionally we would be there at the same time.

Additionally, it was clear that Mom was losing some of her memory. She would get confused and would forget things. And she seemed to have lost any kind of filter on her speech. She could sometimes get angry and say some hard things to us.

I had been talking to them for a couple of years about moving into some kind of senior living facility, but they would not hear of it. Dad said they had looked at a couple a few years ago and didn't like them. By 2007 I was getting more and more concerned about their health and ability to remain in their home.

In May of 2009 Nan went to her gynecologist for a follow up visit. In that visit, she was reminded that they were watching a spot on one of her ovaries. Now the spot had grown and was looking suspicious. That doctor told Nan, "I have made an appointment with another doctor for you tomorrow morning at 10. You will be there." She would not hear any argument from Nan about the inconvenience of it.

Nan went to the other doctor, a surgeon who was also an oncologist. This doctor told Nan that she had ovarian cancer and needed immediate surgery and scheduled it for that Friday, about two days away.

Nan tried to downplay it, but I freaked out. I always assumed the worst in any kind of medical situation. In my mind, a simple scratch if untreated could turn into gangrene and one could lose a leg. Now the diagnosis of cancer and surgery to see how advanced it was had me believing she would not live to come out of the hospital. I was a wreck.

I called the children and told them what was happening. On the appointed day, I drove her to the hospital and she got checked in. Once they took her away from me, I called a friend and he came to sit with me during the surgery. It had all happened so fast, there had not been time to tell anyone what was going on. And Nan didn't really want anyone to know anything. She could be really secretive and private.

Finally, the doctor called and gave me the report – stage three ovarian cancer. I was not sure what that meant, but knew enough to know stage three was bad. By then, I figured she would live to come out of the hospital, but didn't think she would live past the end of the year.

As God worked it out, after living six years overseas, Burke had decided he would like to be closer to family, so had requested a posting at Columbus Air Force Base. They were scheduled to leave Japan sometime in June. When I told Carroll what was happening, she arranged to come home early and was there soon after Nan got out of the hospital. Also, Harriet's school year was over, so she came as well. The three girls had fun visiting and talking.

For some strange reason, I didn't resign my job at the church and retire; I was old enough to do that, but for some reason the thought never entered my mind. So I motored on while Nan recovered.

It seemed like I spent my time running home to check on Nan, running to check on Mom and Dad, and then trying to get something done at church. It would be fair to say my heart was no longer in the job.

When Nan was first diagnosed with cancer, the next few steps happened so quick I didn't feel like I had time to pray except to call out "HELP!" When she got home, it seemed that things settled down a little and I could pray. After a couple of attempts to pray about this great need, I finally confessed to God that I didn't even know how to pray about this thing that had forced its way into our lives. In His quiet voice, He said, "I will be with you." When I heard that, I settled into a quiet calm. God's peace came over me and I was fine from then on. That is not to say I was no longer concerned or worried about how much longer she had to live. But I had God's promise that whatever came, He would be with me. I remembered again that verse in Exodus when God spoke to Moses and said, *"My Presence will go with you, and I will give you rest."*

Late that summer, I finally talked Dad into meeting with a representative from another senior living facility, Ridgeland Point. He had already checked out several of those places and ruled them out, partly because of expense. But he also said, "The thought of eating institutional food for the rest of my life gives me the shivers!" The representative came to their home and made her presentation, and Dad liked what he heard. We arranged a visit and he went and liked what he saw. He decided they would move in up there. But he made a mistake and told Mom they were going to try it out for a month or so. Even though she had lost a lot of her memory, she definitely remembered that. Not only did she remember, but she apparently was aware enough to count the days. When the month was up, she was ready to go back home. When he finally convinced her that the move was permanent, she was not happy.

"I will be with you."

Lynda and I drew real close to each other during the years from 2007-2010. We became an unofficial support group for each other as we took care of Mom and Dad. We tried to coordinate our visiting times so that one of us would be there every day, and we would not be present on the same day. It was not that we didn't want to be there together, it was just that we were both busy and that way we could cover for each other when the other one was not present. Mom was keenly cognizant of how long it had been since either of us visited her and never failed to comment on it.

The Hard Years

After Nan's surgery, she began a rigorous, radical diet in the attempt to beat the cancer into submission by eating only healthy foods. She did a lot of research, and as a result she drank a lot of freshly squeezed vegetable juice. She stopped eating any animal products, so basically I guess she went vegan. I was starving. We ate a lot of oatmeal, a lot of salads, and a lot of raw vegetables. How about "pizza" made of a slice of eggplant for the dough covered with tomato sauce, with shredded yellow squash for the cheese? Raw of course. From time to time I would meet a friend for lunch and eat some meat.

Looking back, the children and I concluded that even though this rigid diet did not cure the cancer, it most likely did help her withstand the unwanted negative side effects of the chemo treatments. Although she did lose her hair in the first round of chemo, she responded remarkably well, never experiencing the terrible nausea that so many other chemo patients complained of. Usually there would be two or three days when she was incapacitated. The first day was the treatment itself. The infusion took several hours, and they gave her a big dose of steroids to help offset the negative side effects of the drug they were administering. That made her sleepy during the infusion, but by about 10 that night, she was wide awake and full of energy. She often would just get up and work on things. Then it took a day or so to recover from that. Then she would be fine and amazingly full of energy until the next treatment. She did so well that many people thought the surgery had cured her.

I will be with you.

Late in 2009, it became obvious that Mom needed more care than Ridgeland Point could give her. Their in-house doctor recommended that she spend two weeks in a hospital for observation. Her departure from all of us was painful indeed. When I went to pick her up in the middle of December, the doctor gave me the diagnosis: stage 5 Alzheimer's.

That was a big shock to us all and it hit Dad hardest. All of us wondered why we had not seen it or recognized it for what it was. We concluded that even though the signs were there, we just didn't want to admit that something was terribly wrong; more than simple dementia.

The news was so devastating to Dad, I have always wondered if that is what put him into a health slide. He lost his energy and zest for life. It was only a week or so until Christmas, but he showed no interest even in that for the first time ever.

All the children came to our house for Christmas, and I invited Mom and Dad to come for Christmas dinner. Although they had always enjoyed that time together with their grandchildren and great-grandchildren, they declined.

On Christmas Day, some of us went out to Ridgeland Point and Dad was in bed. That was really unlike him. When we walked in, he asked for his Bible and he propped himself up on one elbow and read 1 Corinthians 15 – the entire chapter. When he finished, he lay back in bed and said, "I really like that chapter." That was the last real conversation any of us had with him. He died in his sleep sometime in the night on December 31. The morning of January 1, he was pronounced dead.

Mom died about two and a half months later.

I will be with you.

We carried on at the church until around September or October. Nan and I had several conversations about how much longer we should stay at the church. She had already lost interest in the work; I think that was partly due to her illness and partly due to the fact that she could no longer publish *First In All The World.* Due to budget constraints, she had to start publishing it online. All the church members were given a link and they could either read it online or print out their individual copy. It was still a really good publication, but it was not the same to her. So she was ready to retire as well.

I met with my supervisor, Bob Gladney and told him I was ready to retire. I said I would stay until early summer the following year. This would give the leaders time to find a replacement, and give me a little time to train that person. By delaying until the next summer, that would carry the church through the early spring when we were preparing the locations and building the teams for the next year's trips. He thanked me for the heads-up and said he would get back to me.

A couple of days later his secretary called and asked me to meet him in his office. Our pastor, Stan Buckley was present, and they asked me if I would be willing to retire at the end of the year. I assured them I would be willing, and restrained myself from kissing them both. I felt lighter than I had felt in many years. That alone was confirmation enough that it was indeed time to retire. December 31, 2010 was my last day in the office. That was about ten and a half years since we started working there.

I will be with you.

By this time, Nan had relaxed her diet a little. She still drank lots of the vegetable juice, but was now eating some animal products again, much to my relief. We tended to stay close to home with an occasional trip to Columbus to see Carroll and her family and some trips to Wartrace to see Robert and his family.

Her treatments continued and gradually I could tell she was losing ground. There were four major treatment periods, each one with a different combination of drugs. But by 2013, I knew her time was short. She, being Nan, continued to push on. But it was becoming painfully obvious to me that she could not last much longer.

Late in the spring, she consented to make the journey to Bristol, Virginia to visit Bill and Susan Thompson, our co-workers and good friends from Tainan days. She was glad to see them, as was I. We had not seen them since our visit back to Taiwan in 2000. They were now working in a church there in Bristol and were happy. On the way home, we stopped in Wartrace for a visit with Robert and family.

Soon after that, we went to Columbus for Burke's change of command ceremony. It was the last thing he had to do prior to departing. They were returning to Germany for another tour there.

When we returned home from that trip, accompanied by Harriet, Nan got so weak and ill we had to take her to the emergency room at the hospital. She rallied a little, but one of the oncologists familiar with her case, not her regular doctor, told us quite plainly that there was really nothing else to do for her. Her regular doctor was always ready to try one more thing, no matter how small the chance of success. She trusted him completely and tried one more treatment option, but in the end it was to no avail. She had gotten so weak by then that the only way for her to continue any kind of treatment was to have a feeding tube inserted. We both had always said that if it came to that, our life was over and we would just pass on out. Or in her words, graduate to the next phase of life, which was the best part.

She graduated on Saturday morning, July 20, 2013. The children and her sister, Georgia were present.

Once again we saw God's hand directing the calendar. Carroll and Burke did not leave for Germany until after the funeral. She had been able to be close to her mother for the four years she was sick.

There are some things that are not much fun about getting older. The parts don't work like they once did, and it is not as easy to get around as it once was. But on the journey you learn stuff. One of the great blessings – maybe the greatest blessing – of getting older is that you have many different experiences of seeing God at work in your own life and in the lives of those close to you. If you pay attention, you learn to see what God is doing, and you learn that He is always working, that He is always good, and that He is always with you. So when He says, *I will be with you,* your previous experiences make it easy to trust and believe that He will be with you.

He was with me – for every step, in every dark corner, in every joy, and in every victory. He was present.

EPILOGUE

Epilogue

This project is quite a bit longer than I anticipated when I started. My original intent was to identify thirty scriptures that God used to guide me and to make those into a devotional booklet, showing how God used them to direct my life. However, at the encouragement of Robert and Harriet, it expanded far beyond my original plan. I added chapters that serve as summaries of our work to fill in gaps and provide background that link together significant events. My prayer is that God will use what I wrote to help you as you make your own way on the path of life.

I know what I have written ends on a somber note. In fact, there is little levity or humor in the preceding pages; that was not my purpose. That does not mean that our life in Taiwan was dull and dreary; quite the opposite was true. There were many times when funny things happened. You might even say we started with a funny experience, even though it was not so much fun for me when it happened.

About six weeks after we arrived in Taiwan, our mission administrator, Hunter Hammett, called me to come to Taipei and be present when the customs officials opened the three crates we shipped from home, which were packed full of furniture, kitchen utensils, a piano, and a four-year supply of clothing and toiletries. This was normal procedure; the owner of the goods had to be present in order to answer any questions the customs people might have. I am sure they were also checking to make sure we were not smuggling any unlawful items into the country. The customs inspection went smoothly.

Afterwards, I met Hunter at the mission office to sign some papers. When we entered the parking lot, he pointed out a new blue car and informed me that it was ours. He then told me he could either have it shipped to us or I could drive it home myself. Since we had been dependent on everyone for six weeks, I thought it was about time for me to start pulling my weight, so I said I would drive it.

He said I could follow him in his car to the brand new freeway, which was now open to Hsin Chu, about halfway to Taichung where we lived. He told me that once I exited the freeway, to just drive through town and get on Highway 1 and drive south until I would get to this little town on the coast and then it would be a short drive into Taichung. Simple, right?

There were a couple of things he neglected to explain. For one, he failed to tell me that ALL the streets in Hsin Chu were under repair and there were multiple detours, which were only labeled with arrows. All the street signs were in Chinese characters, and everything looked the same. After many twists and turns I finally found what had to be Highway 1 and took it.

The second thing he did not explain was what a highway marker looked like. In my mind, I was thinking of the signs I was accustomed to in America. I finally figured out that the little, short white concrete post (about a foot high) was the marker and the number "1" in the middle of the black circle was the number of the highway.

The third thing he neglected to explain was the Chinese character for north and south. I did find Highway 1. But I drove north instead of south.

About the time when I should have been arriving in Taichung, I entered this huge city that was not on my map. But then I turned my map over and discovered that I was back in Taipei!

Lessons from the Journey

I finally found a pay telephone, figured out how to use it, and called the one telephone number I had. Janie Debenport, the missionary we had stayed with our first night in Taiwan, took a taxi to find me, and I let her drive me back to her house.

I called Nan to tell her I would not be home in time for supper and that she needed to repack our goods – we were going to have to move to Taipei since I couldn't get to Taichung! I was called Wrong Way Rob for quite some time after that.

I did make one interesting observation in that process. When you are lost, you see some interesting sights. And you need to look carefully at them and enjoy them. Why do you need to do that? Because when you finally do get "un-lost" you will never be able to find that spot again. You have no idea how you got there or how to go back to it!

As a family, we shared many happy hours vacationing on the extreme southern end of the island. The name of the area was Oluanpi and there was a small beach where we swam and snorkeled. When we first started going there, the population on the beach was primarily missionaries. Our children enjoyed playing with them and often met friends there.

There were also family trips to Hong Kong. Those were usually prompted by the basketball tournament at Christmas. Schools from Taipei, Taichung, Hong Kong, Singapore, Malaysia, and Japan were invited. One huge enjoyment of this trip was frequent visits to McDonalds, which had yet to make its appearance in Taiwan, as well as Watson's Drug Store. There we could purchase some toiletries and chocolate, which was unavailable where we lived.

There were many incidents related to travel; some were funny and some were not so funny. One of my favorites happened after all the children left home. Nan and I went out for a drive one afternoon and she wanted to go to the coast. Tainan was on the western side of Taiwan and there was actually an old harbor in the city. So anywhere north or south of the city, we were always close to the ocean. (You may recall that Nan was quite an adventuress.) We were south of Tainan and found a little side road leading from the main highway towards the coast. She said to take that road. So I did.

We followed the road for a few miles and then the pavement ran out. We were on a gravel road, but it was still a pretty good road. But then the gravel ran out. I wanted to turn around, but she insisted that we could find the coast.

We continued farther. The good road ran out and became not much more than a cart path. I said we should turn around. She insisted that if we continued, we would find another good road. We continued.

The cart path turned into two ruts on the top of a dike between the flooded rice paddies. I said we really should stop and get out while we still could. She insisted that on the other side of the rice paddy there would be a road. We continued.

She was right, but I was ready for a nervous breakdown when we did find it. It was a cart path, then a gravel road, and then a paved road that led into some kind of neighborhood. When we pulled up into the neighborhood, there were houses on both sides of the road, each one with their walls and open courtyards. In the courtyard on my side of the car, there were four old men sitting out in the cool of the afternoon drinking tea. I couldn't resist.

I rolled down my window and in Taiwanese, asked, "Is this the way to Taipei?" Taipei was at least 200 miles in the opposite direction. Most of the men were so dumfounded they could not even speak. One of them stood up and shouted "Taipei??!! Taipei??!! This is Kaohsiung!!! You can't get to Taipei from here!" I thanked him and drove on.

Epilogue

I often wondered what those men told around the village after we left. I also wondered if it ever dawned on them that I had been speaking to them in Taiwanese.

We never did find the coast that day.

I sometimes remember what one of my pastors, Frank Pollard, was fond of saying. He would say "Life is a journey where one beggar tells another beggar where to find bread."

I have been on this life journey a lot longer than have any of you. I hope and pray that as I share some of the bread crumbs I found along the way, those same crumbs will feed you or encourage you or challenge you. You have to find your own way as you travel your own journey. Just remember that there are markers in your own lives you can use to gauge whether or not you are sticking to the right path.

I have a friend in Taiwan, Chuck Johnston. I once heard him preach about Abraham, and he made a really good point that we all need to remember. He pointed out that Abraham made some terrible mistakes in his life. He followed Sarah's advice and took Hagar for his wife. When he went to Egypt, he asked Sarah to pretend she was his sister because he said, "Surely there is no fear of God in this place." No doubt he made some bad choices.

But Chuck pointed to Romans 4:16-23 where Paul is talking about Abraham's faith and says *"Without weakening in his faith, he faced the fact that his body was as good as dead – since he was about a hundred years old – and that Sarah's womb was also dead. Yet he did not waver through unbelief regarding the promise of God, but was strengthened in his faith and gave glory to God, being fully persuaded that God had power to do what he had promised."*

Chuck's point was that while we humans tend to look on what happens in our lives incident by incident and often let those incidents define us, God looks at the overall direction of our lives. He could see that Abraham was following the directive God had given him so many years previously. God blessed that intent to obey.

Yes, Abraham stumbled along the way. There have been times when I have stumbled as well. When I do, I remember Psalm 37:23-24 *"If the LORD delights in a man's way, he makes his steps firm; though he stumble, he will not fall, for the LORD upholds him with his hand."*

Add to that Psalm 145:13b-14 *"The LORD is faithful to all his promises and loving toward all he has made. The LORD upholds all those who fall and lifts up all who are bowed down."*

As you journey through life, no doubt you also will make some mistakes and some wrong choices; that seems to be man's nature. But as you continue to read His word, I am confident that God will give you your own precious promises to guide you as He has done with me. Hold on to those promises and depend on them.

As I look back on my life, certainly I can spot a few little things here and there I would like to go back and change. But I will always testify that I would never change the direction of my life. God allowed me to live the greatest adventure of all – a life spent following His leadership and watching Him work.

I sincerely pray the same for you.

Made in the USA
Lexington, KY
20 December 2019

58631813R00129